WILLIAM ADAMS
HIS LIFE AND LOCOMOTIVES

A LIFE IN ENGINEERING 1823–1904

Title page: O2 class 0-4-4T W20 *Shanklin* accelerates away from Smallbrook Junction with a train for Cowes on 25 April 1964, forty-one years after transfer to the Isle of Wight. (David Christie)

WILLIAM ADAMS
HIS LIFE AND LOCOMOTIVES

A LIFE IN ENGINEERING 1823–1904

JOHN WOODHAMS

AN IMPRINT OF PEN & SWORD BOOKS LTD.
YORKSHIRE – PHILADELPHIA

First published in Great Britain in 2023 by
Pen and Sword Transport
An imprint of Pen & Sword Books Ltd.
Yorkshire - Philadelphia

Copyright © John Woodhams, 2023

ISBN 978 1 39907 196 3

The right of John Woodhams to be identified as
Author of this work has been asserted by him in accordance
with the Copyright, Designs and Patents Act 1988.

A CIP catalogue record for this book is available from the British Library.

All rights reserved. No part of this book may be reproduced or transmitted in any form
or by any means, electronic or mechanical including photocopying, recording or by any
information storage and retrieval system, without permission from the Publisher in writing.

Typeset in Sabon LT Std 10/12.5 by
SJmagic DESIGN SERVICES, India.
Printed and bound in India by Replika Press Pvt. Ltd.

Pen & Sword Books Ltd incorporates the imprints of Pen & Sword Books Archaeology,
Atlas, Aviation, Battleground, Discovery, Family History, History, Maritime, Military, Naval,
Politics, Railways, Select, Transport, True Crime, Fiction, Frontline Books, Leo Cooper,
Praetorian Press, Seaforth Publishing, Wharncliffe and White Owl.

For a complete list of Pen & Sword titles please contact

PEN & SWORD BOOKS LIMITED
47 Church Street, Barnsley, South Yorkshire, S70 2AS, England
E-mail: enquiries@pen-and-sword.co.uk
Website: www.pen-and-sword.co.uk

Or
PEN AND SWORD BOOKS
1950 Lawrence Rd, Havertown, PA 19083, USA
E-mail: Uspen-and-sword@casematepublishers.com
Website: www.penandswordbooks.com

Contents

Acknowledgements 6
Introduction 7
Chapter 1   Early Years 9
Chapter 2   The Blackwall Apprentice 20
Chapter 3   A Mediterranean Odyssey 29
Chapter 4   The Origins of the North London Railway 38
Chapter 5   The Innovative Years at Bow 42
Chapter 6   A Move to Stratford 72
Chapter 7   To the South Western 87
Chapter 8   Master of his Art 115
Chapter 9   The Two Protégés, John Henry Adams and
             W.F. Pettigrew 152
Chapter 10   Legacy and Preservation 165
Appendix A   Ships Built and/or Engined by Miller and
             Ravenhill 1841–1846 175
Appendix B   Trials of an Express Locomotive 1891 177
Appendix C   Summary of Locomotive Designs and Principal
             Dimensions 191
Appendix D   Summary of Locomotives Built by William Adams 197
Bibliography 205
Index 207

Acknowledgements

This book would not have been possible without the help of many people, but I would firstly like to acknowledge the work of E.H. Wilson and the late Don Bradley for their studies of William Adams' life and work. I have drawn heavily on both. I also wish to acknowledge the work of David Turner in his thesis *Managing the Royal Road*. Particular thanks too to Dr R.J. (Bob) Adams, great-grandson of William's elder brother John Henry, who has not only patiently answered many questions, but freely provided access to documents in his care. John Adams, in Australia, and his sister Sally also kindly allowed the use of the North London Railway testimonial documents.

Jim Connor of the North London Railway Historical Society generously allowed free use of his photographs and drawings, whilst Paul Weeden and David Bousfield of the GER Society have patiently put up with queries and requests relating to the Great Eastern years. Mike Fell and Howard Sprenger provided assistance with North Staffordshire queries relating to John Henry's tenure.

Several old friends from schooldays and the final years of the O2s on the Isle of Wight have given their support: Philip Hayward for the plan of Nine Elms Works; John Faulkner for his help with photographs plus the colourised image; and Derek Gawn for his encyclopaedic knowledge of those years. Thanks also go to Terry Hastings, Andrew Summers, Iain Whitlam, Roger Silsbury, Tim Cooper and Richard Maycock.

Carol Morgan, archivist of the Institution of Civil Engineers, kindly provided the paper *Trials of an Express Locomotive*, and Lucy Bonner, her counterpart at the Institution of Mechanical Engineers, unravelled William's somewhat complex membership record of that body!

Many others have generously provided access to their photographic collections including Mike Morant and John Scott-Morgan, plus Nathan Au and other friends involved with the restoration of 563. Thanks too to John Priest for help with the maps of the London docklands. Where not otherwise credited, illustrations are either my own or from my collection, but every effort has been made to establish copyright, and credit sources correctly. In Italy, naval historian Aldo Antonicelli kindly searched through Sardinian navy archives for details of William's service and provided answers to many questions.

I am once again grateful to Roger Macdonald for proofreading the final manuscript, and to my wife, Margaret, for her sound advice and support.

Introduction

William Adams is probably best known from his locomotive designs for the London & South Western Railway. His eighteen-year tenure at Nine Elms was the culmination of a career which began formally in marine engineering, including a period at sea with the Royal Sardinian Navy, encompassed civil engineering and surveying before joining the North London Railway (NLR) as Locomotive Foreman.

He has been described as the father of the suburban train, an inventive engineer who pioneered the use of continuous train brakes, developed well-designed, free-steaming locomotive boilers for services requiring rapid acceleration and frequent stops, and his invention of a bogie with controlled side-play transformed future locomotive design. His next move was to the Great Eastern Railway (GER) where his locomotive designs met with mixed success, but included the first British Mogul 2-6-0 design, before moving south of the Thames to Nine Elms. Here, over 500 locomotives were built to his designs, with his later express locomotives for the London & South Western Railway regarded by many as his finest achievement. When asked to give outstanding

William Adams in 1894. (Dr R.J. Adams)

examples of nineteenth-century British locomotive designs, André Chapelon, the eminent French locomotive engineer, did not hesitate to name the Adams 4-4-0s. Many of these incorporated his invention of the vortex blast pipe, a patented feature largely ignored and later removed by his successor Dugald Drummond, yet employed as far afield as India and New Zealand.

Adams also proved himself a very capable designer in developing locomotive and carriage works at all three railways, improving efficiency and reducing costs.

Fortunately, two of his nephews, Thomas and Henry Adams, compiled some biographical notes about their uncle, a man they both personally knew well, so we do know something about his character, too. A big, gentle, genial, generous and cultured man, 'full of vivacity and camaraderie', with a love of music 'ready to sing at any time' he was fluent in both French and Italian, yet 'not at all studious or literary'. He was highly regarded professionally both at home and abroad, until ill health forced his retirement in 1895. He died nine years later, leaving a legacy as probably the finest of late Victorian locomotive engineers. Born two years before the Stephensons built *Locomotion No. 1*, he was brought up in his father's civil engineering environment, in the developing years of the railway industry. He would have celebrated his sixth birthday at the time of the Rainhill Trials in October 1829, yet despite becoming best known as a locomotive designer, he did not work in that discipline until he had reached the age of thirty. The years that he spent in the world of marine engineering, both in shipyards and at sea, witnessed the evolution and transition from wooden to iron-hulled vessels, the gradual displacement of sail by steam, the development of new and improved types of engine and a succession of challenges to prove the superiority of screw or paddle propulsion. Even in later life, however, he often described himself as a civil engineer. Several of his sons achieved notable engineering careers, both at home and abroad, in a range of disciplines including locomotive design and civil works, and the Adams family today can be justly proud of its engineering pedigree and heritage.

Chapter 1

Early Years

The early years of the nineteenth century were a period of rapid development of London's docklands, with new, purpose-built wet docks taking over from the riverside wharves which had been a feature of the city for centuries. The Royal Dockyards at Deptford and Woolwich had served the navy well, and a commercial shipbuilding industry had long since developed, serving the needs of the East India Company and other merchant shipowners. It was still very much the age of sail, but new developments and markets were also being cultivated by marine engineers with the advent of steam propulsion.

It was into this world that William Adams was born on 15 October 1823. His father, John Samuel Adams, by now aged twenty-seven and employed as a Clerk of Works by the West India Dock Company, had married Jane Walker at St Leonard's, Bromley-by-Bow, on 6 April 1819, and the couple took up residence at 5 Mill Place, Limehouse, very close to the Regent's Canal Dock, or Limehouse Basin, which opened for traffic the following year. Although John Samuel had been brought up in London, his own father had been born in Great Yarmouth, in an area of East Anglia with Adams family ancestry as far back as the sixteenth century. Their first child, a son, John Henry, arrived on 16 January 1820, followed by a daughter Jane in September 1821. William was baptised at the parish church of St Olave, Tooley Street, where his grandfather served as parish clerk, on 30 May 1824, but sadly a sister, Alice, born the year after, died in infancy. Younger brother Robert arrived in 1828, and all three boys would later follow their father into the engineering profession.

John Samuel Adams 1797-1855, William's father. (Dr R. J. Adams)

The development of the West India Docks had been authorised by an Act of Parliament of 1799, promoted by a group of merchants and shipowners who had become dissatisfied with the facilities – not to mention theft and delays – which were offered by existing riverside wharves. Led by Robert Milligan, who had interests in Jamaican sugar plantations as well as being a shipowner, the scheme eventually led to the building of a series of three secure wet docks situated on the Isle of Dogs. The prime minister, William Pitt the Younger, and chancellor,

An 1828 view of the entrance to the Regent's Canal Dock, close to the Mill Place home of the Adams family, by T.H. Shepherd.

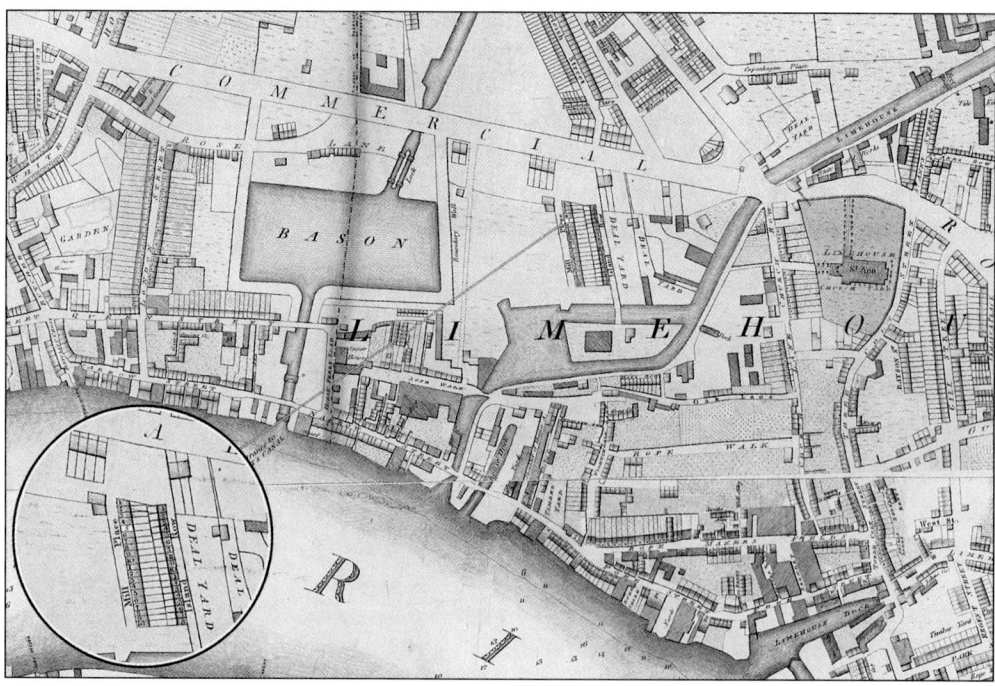

Limehouse, with the dock Basin, described here as Bason, in 1819. Mill Place, home of the Adams family, is a short distance to the east. (Boston Public Library)

The church of St Olave, Tooley Street, Southwark where William was baptised, as it was in 1820. Severely damaged by fire in 1843, the church was declared redundant in 1926 and the site is now occupied by the art deco styled St Olaf House; from *Old and New London*, 1873.

Lord Loughborough, attended the foundation stone ceremony on 12 July 1800, and the first two docks, the first commercial wet docks in London, were officially opened two years later on 27 August 1802, built to a design by William Jessop, with Ralph Walker employed as Resident Engineer.

A clause in the enabling parliamentary act – which was the first time such an act had been used for a project of this type – required all vessels engaged in the West Indian trade to use the new dock facilities. The Act also authorised the City of London Corporation to construct the City Canal, a channel across the Isle of Dogs, to the south of the first two dock basins, which would simply provide a short cut for vessels heading further up river.

The two new dock basins were known as the Import and Export Docks, and both were connected by locks to the river at each end. The combined area of the two dock basins was some 54 acres. Seagoing ships entered from the eastern side, via locks and the enclosed Blackwall Basin, whilst lighters and barges would use the western (Limehouse) passage, which should not be confused with the later, and larger, Limehouse Basin, otherwise known as the Regent's Canal Dock, at the entrance to the eponymous canal which opened in 1820.

The success of the new docks prompted other schemes, notably an Act of Parliament in 1803 authorising the construction of the East India Docks, at Blackwall, to the north east of the West India Docks. The central dock, known as the Brunswick Dock, had in

The West India Import Dock, where John Samuel Adams was employed as Clerk of Works, in an engraving from another T. H. Shepherd painting of 1828. Some years after amalgamation with the East India Docks, William's nephew, Robert, son of his older brother John Henry, became an Assistant Warehouse Keeper, eventually rising to the position of Superintendent of the entire warehouse complex.

The two basins of the West India Dock were first opened in 1802, construction having been authorised three years earlier. This elevated view looking westwards across the Isle of Dogs was painted by William Daniell in the year of opening.

fact been part of the Blackwall shipyard, which could trace its origins back to the early days of the East India Company. This became the new Export Dock, accompanied by a newly constructed Import Dock designed by Ralph Walker, who had left his West India Dock appointment following a disagreement.

Both developments were an immediate commercial success, and the West India Dock had been in operation for some sixteen years by the time that John Samuel Adams took up his position, at a salary of £150 per annum, shortly before his marriage to Jane.

Some years after this appointment, in 1829, the West India Dock company purchased the City Canal for £120,000, and incorporated it into a new third dock basin, which became known as the South Dock, a development spurred by a desire to keep the canal out of a competitor's hands. Other schemes had been promoted, including one in 1825 by the Collier Dock Company, which was intended to cater for the growing trade in coal, but although the proposal obtained parliamentary consent, it failed to raise the required capital and was abandoned.

William was sent to Margate to commence his education with his aunt, Alice Adams, who had, together with her sister Rosetta, established a Dame School for both boarding and day pupils at 34 Hawley Square, a Georgian development built around an enclosed pleasure garden, with 'an entire range of genteel houses from one end of it to the other, most of which command a fine and extensive prospect over the sea'. He later transferred to a nearby establishment at Church Field, run by Charles Lewis, before attending St John's College, an academy at Prospect Place in nearby Broadstairs, where James Cuthill MA offered 'a gentleman's classical and mathematical' education. Margate must have seemed a world away from the busy streets and docks surrounding

the family home in London, and how much knowledge of the classics was of use to him in later life is hard to judge, but mathematics would certainly have stood him in good stead.

The age at which William ended his formal schooling is uncertain, but he then commenced work with his father, as his older brother had also done at the age of fourteen. Remarkably, notes of his weight and height as a boy made by his father have survived; in the summer of 1833 (aged nine) he had attained a height of 4ft 1⅞in, with a weight of 55lb, and was 4ft 7in tall in January 1837, by then aged thirteen.

Whilst John Adams was busily measuring the height and weight of his son, Henry Daniel Martin, a figure who was to play a key role in the development of the boy's subsequent career, was appointed to take charge of the ongoing works at East India Docks in 1833. Martin was born in Greek

Overlooking a pleasant green, 34 Hawley Square, Margate, was William's first school, run by his Aunt Alice.

In the early nineteenth century, Margate was expanding as a fashionable seaside resort, with the first regular steamer service to the town introduced in 1815, the same year that the newly rebuilt stone pier was completed. Engraving by J. Newman. (Wellcome Collection)

The environment of the resort, with its Sea Bathing Infirmary, would have been very far removed from the bustle and trade of the London docklands. Hawley Square itself was a cultural centre featuring the Theatre Royal and, in this view, the Thomas Malton-Hall Library. (Anthony Lee, Margate Local History)

A building in nearby King Street, Margate, which may have intrigued a schoolboy with a mechanical interest, was a gasometer built in neoclassical style in 1824 and deemed worthy as an illustration in a contemporary guide book. (Anthony Lee, Margate Local History)

Street, Soho, in 1811, and at the age of fifteen was articled to Thomas Nicholas, an architect and surveyor. He was subsequently offered a place at the Royal Academy, intending to follow a career as an architect, but after a brief period assisting with the design of the National Gallery, his career took a different direction as he succeeded James Walker, nephew of Ralph Walker, as the dock company's engineer.

Both the West India and East India dock companies had enjoyed a monopoly of trade with the West and East Indies respectively, but as these favourable terms came to an end both suffered increasing competition from other newly built facilities. The London Docks had been built at Wapping and opened over a period of years between 1799 and 1815, whilst St Katherine's Dock, which was designed by Thomas Telford, had also opened in 1828. The East India Docks also suffered from a shortage of warehouse

The East India Docks at Blackwall, shortly after opening in 1806, viewed from the north. The Isle of Dogs and West India Dock basins can be seen to the right.

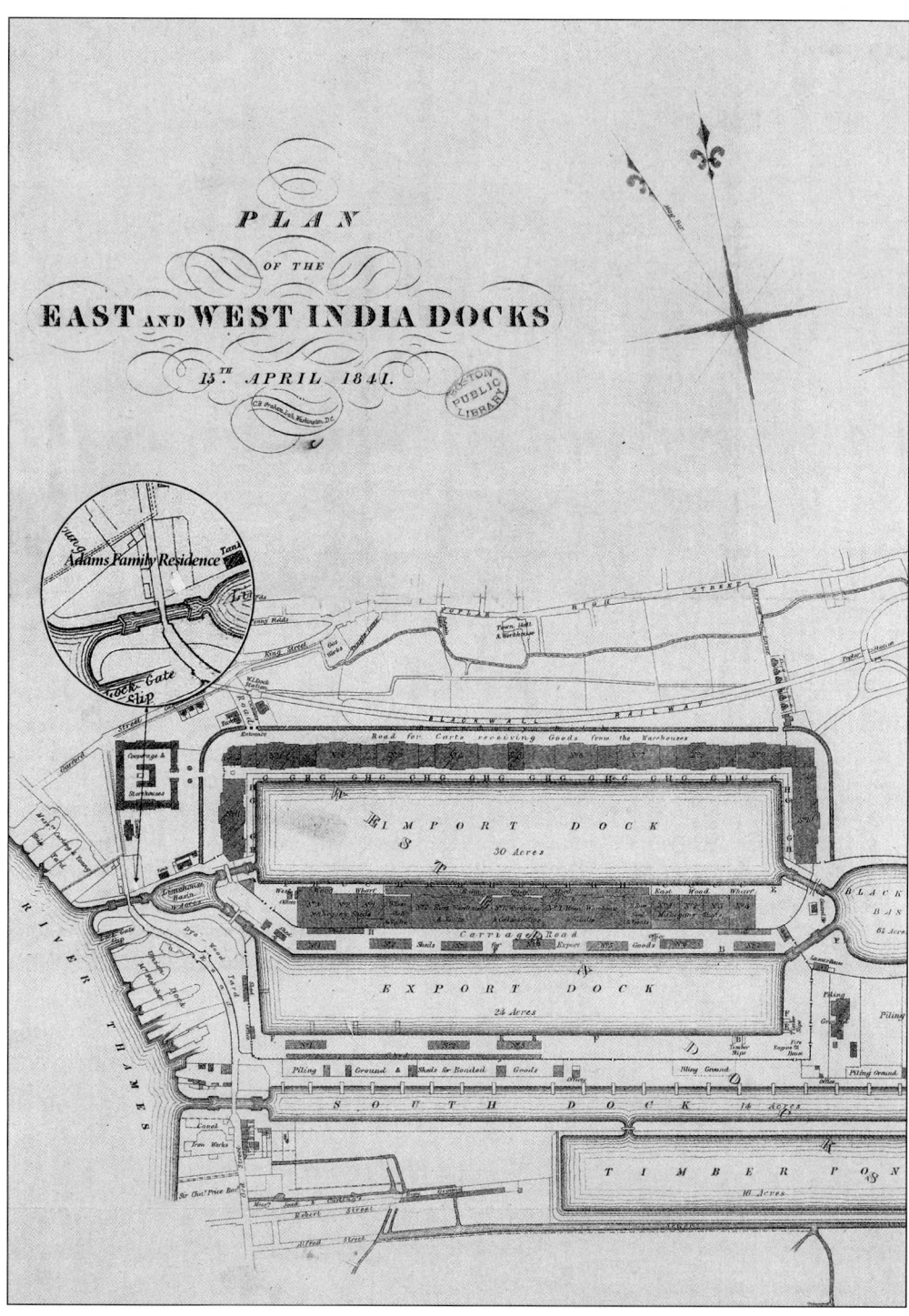

From 1838 the family lived on site at West India Docks, beside the Limehouse Basin, situated immediately west of the West Import Dock as highlighted. From a map of the West and East India Docks dated 1841. (Boston Public Library)

space, whilst its larger neighbour had spare capacity, and it became increasingly evident that a merger would make sense. Thus, the West India company made an offer for the East India's company stock, which was accepted, and a new combined operation, the East and West India Dock Company, took effect in July 1838, which began to enjoy an increase in trade, particularly with bulk cargoes, for example, grain, guano and timber. In the years of monopoly trading, the East India Docks in particular had enjoyed lucrative cargoes of tea, spices and Persian carpets, part of which had now been lost to competitors.

Henry Martin became engineer for the new company whilst John Samuel Adams was appointed Resident Engineer at the West India Docks, succeeding Thomas Shadrake, a position which provided an official residence within the site at Limehouse Basin. The two men would appear to have had a good working relationship, both treated as enjoying a similar status within the company, with John Adams essentially looking after the buildings and Martin, who was granted membership of the Institution of Civil Engineers, taking charge of dock and engineering work. Living here in his early teenage years, William would have been surrounded by the hustle and bustle of dock life, plus the activity of the nearby shipyards with, as a close neighbour, the yard of Forrestt and Sons, which had carved a niche market in lifeboat construction. He would also, no doubt, have keenly followed the development and construction of the viaduct immediately beyond the boundary of the Docks site for the London and Blackwall Railway.

Although schooled away from home in east Kent, in his early teens William would have doubtless taken an interest in the construction of the London and Blackwall Railway, which passed close to the old family home at Limehouse and the boundary of the West India Docks, which had its own station, depicted here in 1840.

This view shows the winding drums of the cable worked line, which became known as 'the fourpenny rope', at Minories station.

Today the viaduct at Limehouse is part of the Docklands Light Railway network. (Steve Keritsu Creative Commons)

William cannot have stayed in his father's engineering department at the docks for very long, as he gained a position as assistant draughtsman at the civil engineering practice of Charles Vignoles, which operated at 4 Trafalgar Square. An eminent railway civil engineer, Charles Blacker Vignoles had built an international reputation, but is probably best remembered today for the flat bottom rail section that bears his name.

Although born in 1793 in County Wexford, Ireland, he lost both parents within months, and was raised in England by his grandfather, who was a Professor of Mathematics at the Woolwich Royal Military Academy. Thus, young Charles received mathematical and legal training, followed by a commission in the army in 1814. His army career took him to America, where he was involved in surveying areas of Florida and South Carolina as an assistant to the state civil engineer, gaining experience which he would use in the developing railway industry. He returned to Britain during the 1820s, and was soon working for James Walker, who was engaged with the East India Docks development, and would no doubt have come into contact with John Adams in the course of his work.

By the time that he employed William, he had recently undertaken consultancy work for the London & Croydon Railway, plus railway projects in Ireland, and been appointed by the Midland Counties Railway. The latter engagement would end in acrimony and financial loss some two years later. His practice was also instructed to undertake surveys for Welsh schemes and, closer to home, a line between Tonbridge and Tunbridge Wells for the South Eastern Railway. A further contract related to the floating pier at Southwark Iron Bridge for Sir John Rennie.

In 1841, Vignoles was appointed to the first Professorship in civil engineering at University College, London and amongst other projects was shortly afterwards

Early Years 19

Above left: An undated photograph of civil engineer Charles Vignoles. (Wellcome collection)

Above right: William was engaged as a trainee draughtsman at the Vignoles practice when it was contracted to design a floating pier adjacent to the Southwark Iron Bridge, which had been completed by John Rennie in 1819.

engaged in the construction of the Dalkey Atmospheric Railway in Ireland and, at the invitation of King Wilhelm I, providing advice to the Royal Württemburg State Railway in Germany. He was also asked by the British government to plan a railway network for India, but terms could not be agreed.

Working for such a man must have inspired the young assistant draughtsman, showing him the possibilities that existed for a hard-working and determined civil engineer at a time of such rapid development. Particularly with his own family background, such a life could perhaps also be his. However, shortly before Vignoles accepted his Professorial chair, William decided to leave the civil engineer's drawing office, and move to a more practical apprenticeship in mechanical engineering.

The Dalkey Atmospheric Railway was one of many projects with which Charles Vignoles was involved. A train is seen arriving at Kingstown in early 1844. (Original author unknown)

Chapter 2

The Blackwall Apprentice

Messrs Miller and Ravenhill were marine engine builders at Blackwall, and it was with this firm that the young William Adams entered into a formal five-year apprenticeship as a machinery fitter, at the age of seventeen, on 21 April 1841. For a sixty-hour working week he would receive no remuneration in his first year, although eligible for a weekly wage of six shillings in the second year, rising to nine shillings in the fifth and final year.

An extensive shipbuilding and engineering industry had developed along the Thames, with a long history of construction for the Royal Navy, and more recently an increasing demand for commercial tonnage with the development of steam power. Although towards the end of the eighteenth century the Royal dockyards were no longer able to launch the largest ships into the Thames in the London area, they were still busily engaged in constructing third-rate vessels in some numbers. The commercial firms included the Blackwall Yard which had been a shipbuilding site since the Middle Ages, and had come to prominence building and repairing vessels for the East India Company in the seventeenth and eighteenth centuries. During William's childhood, the yard was operated by the firm Wigram and Green, which had built its first steamship in 1821 and also became well known for the 'Blackwall Frigates', a popular name for a class of full rigged sailing ships used on the trade routes to India and China, plus increasingly Australia and

The scale of shipbuilding activity in Bow Creek is evident in this 1854 engraving, which first appeared in the *Illustrated London News*.

The foundry of the C.J. Mare (Ditchburn and Mare until 1846) shipyard at Orchard Place in 1854, a scene which would have doubtless been familiar to the young apprentice at Miller and Ravenhill too.

New Zealand. Another firm established nearby in 1837 was the Ditchburn and Mare Shipbuilding Company, situated at the confluence of Bow Creek and the Thames, which soon became known for its iron-hulled ships, and in 1853 became Thames Ironworks and Shipbuilding Company, by which time it had also diversified into civil engineering work.

The ten-year-old William would no doubt have been aware of the Blackwall-built *Cape Breton* making a transatlantic voyage in 1833, the first such crossing against the prevailing wind by a steam assisted sailing ship, whilst at about the same time local engineer Samuel Hall introduced the condenser which allowed the development of the use of fresh water in the closed-cycle marine steam engine.

William would have become very familiar with the nearby shipyards during his childhood, and the expanding discipline of marine steam engineering doubtless offered good career prospects. Although he had been brought up with an immediate family background in civil engineering, Robert Walker, his maternal grandfather, had been a master mariner, in command of the 300 ton ship *Lady St John*, which in 1799 was engaged in regular trade with Jamaica. He probably also travelled by the recently introduced steam packet service between London and school in Margate, which would doubtless have interested him.

In 1822, John Barnes and Joseph Miller had set up an engineering business at Glasshouse Fields in Poplar, and established themselves as makers of engines for steam ships. Both men had been trained in Birmingham under William Murdoch at the Soho Foundry, and John Barnes was a godson of James Watt. Engines for river vessels soon became something of a speciality, both for clients at home and on the continent, and in 1826 the proprietors took a vessel named *Pioneer* to navigate the rivers Rhone and Saone in France.

Other engines were destined for steam packets operating in the Mediterranean from Marseilles, at Le Havre, and with the growth of steam-powered traffic on the Thames in the 1830s, the newly established Star Steam Packet Company's Gravesend-based vessels. In 1828, the company provided a 50hp engine for the 256 ton auxiliary paddle steamer *Sophia Jane*, which was built for service across the English Channel, but then, with paddle wheels dismantled, made the voyage under sail to Australia, arriving at Sydney in May 1831. With machinery refitted, she became 'the first steamer to turn a paddle wheel in Sydney Harbour' and was put to work on coastal services to Newcastle and Wollongong.

Until 1835, the firm Maudslay, Sons and Field held a monopoly for the construction of marine engines for the British Admiralty, but probably as a result of a restructuring of the firm following the earlier death of Henry Maudslay, other Thames-based builders, including John Penn of Greenwich, Seaward & Capel of Millwall as well as Barnes and Miller, were awarded approval.

In that same year, John Barnes left the partnership, with Joseph Miller purchasing the Glasshouse Fields works and forming a new firm with Richard Ravenhill. Ravenhill was a mathematician rather than an engineer, and he took responsibility for the commercial and financial aspects of the business as it was completing its first order for the Royal Navy with a 250hp engine installed in HMS *Blazer*.

In 1837, Miller & Ravenhill were invited by Francis Pettit Smith, inventor of the screw propeller, to construct the machinery for the SS *Archimedes*, the first screw-driven steamer, an offer which was declined because of the pressure of other work. The contract for the engines was subsequently awarded to G. & J. Rennie at Blackfriars; however, two years later the firm undertook repair work to the boiler and engine of the completed vessel following an accident.

Although built by the yard for cross-channel service in 1828 when William was still a small boy, *Sophia Jane* sailed to Australia in 1831, where it is pictured in Sydney Harbour in a painting by Charles Dickson Gregory. (State Library of Victoria)

The firm took on new premises at Orchard Place, Blackwall, in 1839, which enabled the construction of complete ships, and it was here that William Adams commenced his apprenticeship in marine engineering two years later. The London business was thriving, and in 1842, Miller & Ravenhill took over the Tyneside shipyard of John H.S. Coutts at Low Walker, which had failed financially following the completion of the *Prince Albert*, the first iron paddle tug for the River Tyne.

The first vessel completed at the Blackwall yard was PS *Victoria*, a paddle steamer destined for service on the Rhine, and during William's apprenticeship PS *Pink* was delivered in 1843, a passenger paddle steamer with a gross tonnage of 58, and a length of 86 feet, for the London & Westminster Steamboat Company. This little steamer with an engine rated at 28hp was sold in 1857 to Christie & Seager, also in London, but six years later passed to foreign interests.

This was followed soon afterwards by PS *Prince of Wales*, a larger paddle steamer of 246 gross tons and 180ft long for the Margate and London Steam Packet Company which registered the vessel at Ramsgate. The 120hp engine was second-hand, retrieved from a vessel named *Royal George*. In 1849, the ship was sold to General Steam Navigation, and finally broken up in 1880. A further iron-hulled paddle steamer followed in 1844 for the Star Steam Packet Company of Gravesend, a 170ft long vessel of 174 gross tons named *Meteor*.

The second vessel completed that year was a wooden-hulled screw steamer, named *Delta*, for the Peninsular & Oriental Steam Navigation Company. This vessel, 149ft long, with a 120hp engine, was built for a service between Afteh and Cairo on the River Nile, and passed to the Egyptian Government when it took over operation of the route in 1846. Another vessel followed for the same client, but this time an iron paddle steamer

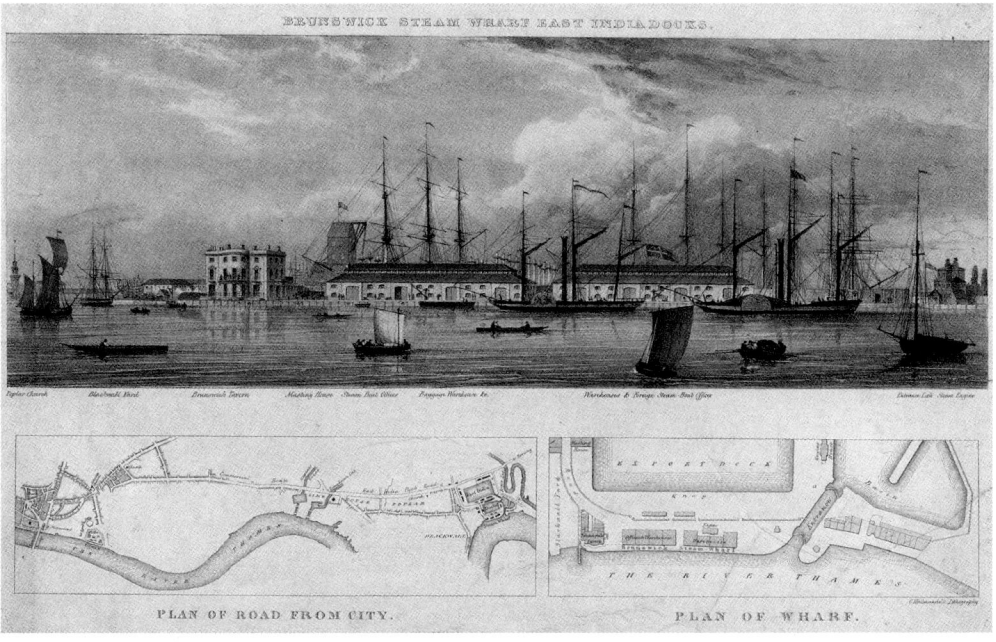

The Brunswick Wharf, part of the East India Docks, which was sold in 1835 to the developers of the London and Blackwall Railway. (Royal Museums Greenwich)

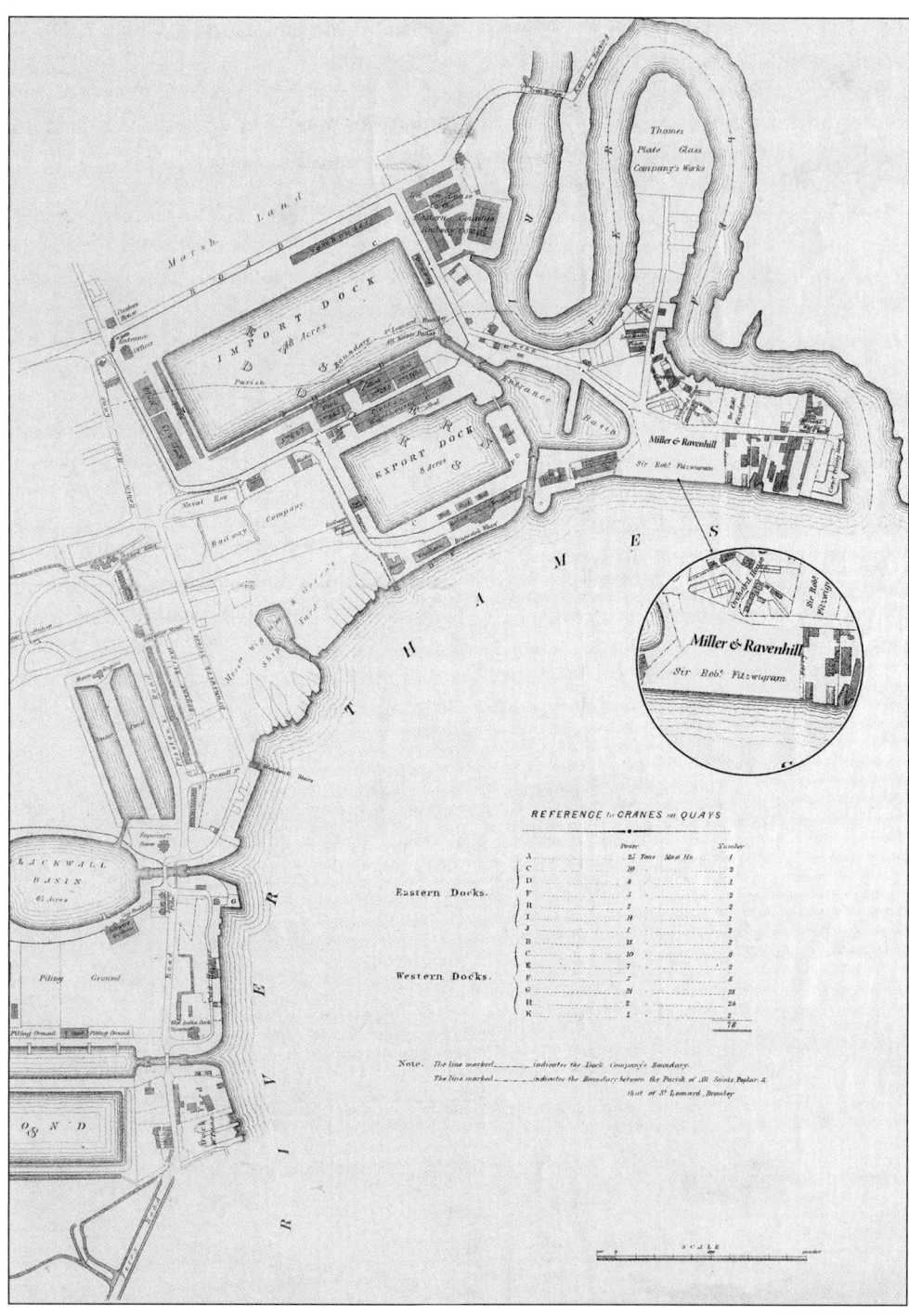

Miller and Ravenhill occupied the Thameside yard at Orchard Place, immediately eastwards of the East India Docks and Brunswick Wharf. From a map of the West and East India Docks dated 1841, which shows the name of Sir Robert Fitzwigram, the freehold owner on the site. (Boston Public Library)

of 479 gross tons, and 163ft in length, named *Madrid*, for the company's services from Southampton. Equipped with side-lever engines capable of 160ihp, the vessel was lost off Vigo in 1857. *Ondine* was a 154ft long paddle steamer built in 1845 for the Dover shipowners Messrs Bushell, who operated the Dover to Boulogne route, and were licensed to carry the Indian mail. Only five months after the maiden voyage, on 3 February 1845, the vessel was sold to the owner of the *Morning Herald*, Edward Baldwin, renamed *Undine* and refitted as a private yacht for the transport of newspapers. Two years later it passed to the Royal Navy as tender and despatch vessel HMS *Undine*. Finally, it was refitted as a mailboat for cross-channel services in 1854 but was wrecked at Ostend the following year.

The Miller & Ravenhill ships and machinery acquired a reputation for speed, with the paddle steamer *Llewellyn*, launched in 1846 for the Dublin-Holyhead service, reputed to achieve eighteen knots.

In addition to the contracts for complete ships, the firm was busy building engines and machinery for other shipyards. These included side-lever engines for two paddle steamers for the Royal Mail Steam Packet Company, *Trent* and *Isis*, both launched in late 1841 by the Northfleet yard of William & Henry Pitcher, and two two-cylinder oscillating engines supplied in 1846. The first of these was delivered to the nearby Blackwall yard of Money, Wigram & Sons for the Peninsular & Oriental company's paddle steamer *Ripon*, with the second installed in the screw steamer *Ranger* by an unknown builder for the Malcolmson Brothers of Waterford. The firm also produced the first 'direct-acting' engines for the Royal Navy, with 286hp machinery for HMS *Infernal* (later renamed *Rosamund*), and a more powerful 430hp unit for HMS *Gladiator*, supplied in 1841 and 1842 respectively. In 1844, the screw-driven HMS *Amphion* featured the first example of a horizontal engine installed below the water line, a successful innovation that led to orders from the Admiralty for similar designs for at least ten more ships over the following three years. *Amphion* had, in fact, been planned as long ago as 1828 with the name *Ambuscade*, but not laid down at Woolwich Dockyard for a further twelve years. In 1844 it was redesigned as a wooden-hulled steam frigate and only finally launched two years later. Miller & Ravenhill fitted the machinery at the East India Docks at a cost of £16,673. The machinery was designed by the Swedish-American engineer John Ericsson who, with John Braithwaite, had built the locomotive *Novelty* and entered it for the Rainhill Trials in 1829.

Tragedy struck in February 1844 when the paddle steamer *Elberfeld*, which had been built by the yard three years earlier for service on the Rhine, was returning to Blackwall for engine adjustments, very probably in an attempt to reduce reported excessive coal consumption, but was lost in the English Channel with three crew members drowned. A replacement ship with the same name was launched later the same year.

Also in 1844, the firm had appointed Edward Pascoe, the designer of the first screw steamer SS *Archimedes*, as its naval architect, which no doubt enhanced its reputation as an innovative builder of propeller-driven ships. William Adams would have thus become well aware of the innovation and development of screw propulsion, and the advances in marine steam engineering from the side-lever and grasshopper engines to the direct acting and oscillating designs which resulted in substantial savings in space and weight.

When his indentured period with Miller and Ravenhill came to an end in 1846, William Adams worked as a fitter on steamships in the West and East India Docks until an opportunity presented itself to venture away from home territory, to Marseilles

Left: In 1841 Miller and Ravenhill fitted engines to *RMS Trent*, which was constructed by William Pitcher. It is seen here in 1861 (left) being stopped by the USS *San Jacinto*, during the American civil war – an incident which became known as the Trent Affair – and nearly escalated into a war between the United Kingdom and United States.

Below: PS *Normandie* was one of two vessels built at Le Havre in 1835, and fitted with 120hp engines by Miller and Ravenhill, for service on the lower Seine, principally between Honfleur and Le Havre. In December 1840, shortly before William entered into his apprenticeship, *Normandie* was called upon to carry the coffin of Napoleon from Cherbourg to the mouth of the Seine at Val-de-la-Haye. In this view, the coffin is being unloaded from *La Belle-Poule* onto the paddler.

Fitted with two single cylinder side-lever engines by Miller and Ravenhill, the paddle corvette *Königliche Ernst Augustus* was built in 1846 by William Patterson of Bristol, but actually temporarily named *Cora* at launch. She sailed to Bremerhaven to join the navy of the German Confederation, but when the *Reichsflotte* was disbanded in 1852 was sold to the General Steam Navigation Company, and returned to sail under the British flag, renamed *Edinburgh*. However, she was lost in 1855 at Varne, Bulgaria, probably on a voyage relating to the Crimean War. From a painting by Lüder Arenhold.

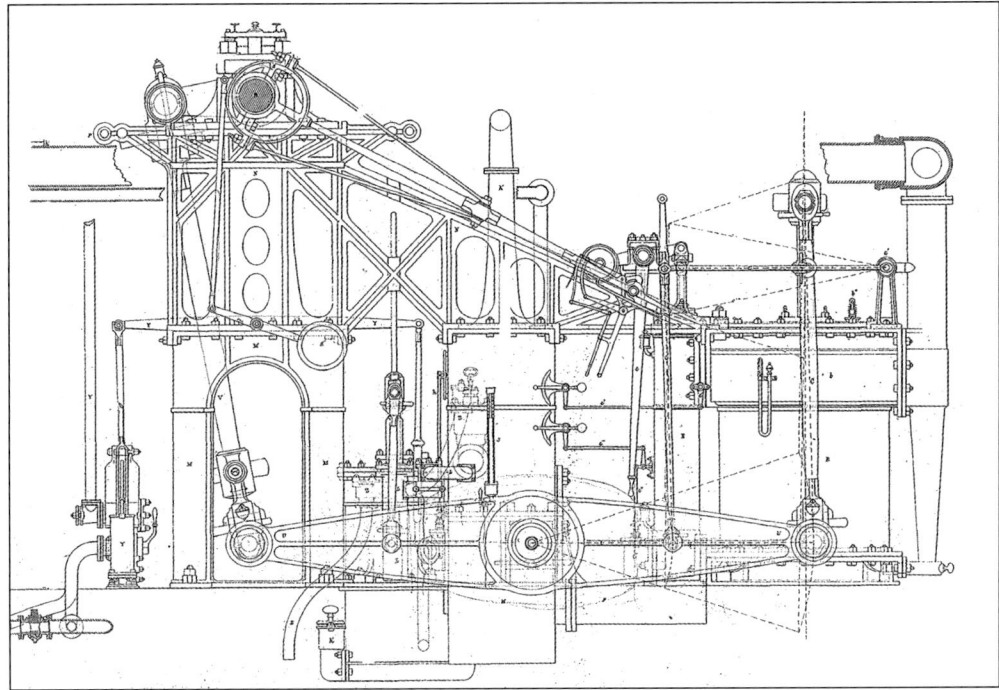

A 160hp Miller and Ravenhill side-lever engine c1840.

in southern France, taking up a position with the shipbuilder Philip Taylor in 1848. Taylor had bought the shipyard in 1845, following a somewhat varied earlier career.

Born in 1786 and brought up in Norwich, Philip Taylor studied surgery from 1801 to 1805 at Tavistock, Devon, where his older brother John worked at a nearby copper mine. He then returned to Norwich and worked in a pharmaceutical business until 1812, when he joined his brother John, who had established a chemical works at Stratford in east London. Before very long he had entered into business with John Martineau in an engineering works and foundry venture, building steam engines, pumps and gas generators. The partnership was terminated in 1827, by which time Philip Taylor had several innovations and patents in oil-gas lighting, brewing, ironmaking and high-pressure steam engines to his name. He was also an associate of Marc Brunel, and for a time was a director of the Thames Tunnel at Wapping.

In 1828 he founded a new engineering works in Paris and took on a contract to equip a flour mill at Marseilles with machinery in 1834, which in turn led to the establishment of a new engineering venture in that city with his sons in the following year. An opportunity arose to acquire a shipyard at La Seyne, near Toulon, in 1845, for which Taylor actively sought British engineers and foremen. The following year he entered into a partnership agreement with a local ironmaster, Amédée Armand. The shipyard was capable of building modern steam-powered iron ships, and eventually employed some 2,000 workers.

Taylor not only recruited a future innovative and eminent designer of steam locomotives, but another whose legacy was rather less benign – Robert Whitehead, a young man of similar age to Adams, whose subsequent career largely involved the development of the torpedo.

By the time that Adams arrived in southern France, Philip Taylor was actually living in San Pier d' Arena, near Genoa, where he had been invited by the government of Sardinia – which was a separate state until 1861 and ruled a region adjoining the French border in addition to the island of Sardinia itself – to establish an engineering facility in partnership with Turin businessman Fortunato Prandi, with financial backing from the state.

Soon after his arrival in Marseilles, the former Blackwall apprentice was sent to join the new venture at Genoa as an assistant works manager.

A notable visitor to the Thames was Brunel's SS *Great Britain*, which, as the first iron-hulled screw steam passenger liner, and the largest ship afloat at the time, would have been of great interest to William. Launched at Bristol, this view at Blackwall, by Richard Ball Spencer, almost certainly predates her maiden voyage from Liverpool to New York in July 1845. Note the Royal Standard, plus French and American flags. (Royal Museums Greenwich)

Chapter 3

A Mediterranean Odyssey

The nineteenth-century kingdom of Sardinia, ruled by the Savoy family, included not only the island of Sardinia, but the mainland regions of Piedmont and Liguria adjoining the French border. With the acquisition of northern Liguria, the state had acquired the port and infrastructure of Genoa in 1814, which led almost immediately to the establishment of the Royal Sardinian Navy, initially to guard the coastal interests of the kingdom, and protect merchant traffic from Barbary pirate raids.

The mainland acquisitions were confirmed by the Congress of Vienna, a meeting of European ambassadors which was hosted and chaired by the Austrian statesman Klemens von Metternich between November 1814 and June 1815 in an attempt to stabilise and remake the continent following the downfall of the emperor Napoleon. The kingdom of Sardinia was ruled at the time by Victor Emmanuel I, who was succeeded in 1821 by Charles Felix, who held the throne for ten years until it passed to a distant cousin, Charles Albert. The Victor Emmanuel era was a reactionary period of rule, with land and power returned to the church and aristocracy, and it was only at the start of Charles Albert's reign that the state began to slowly reform and industrialise its economy. In March 1848, he signed a constitution in the form of the Statuto Albertino, as a result of which the island of Sardinia lost its remaining autonomy to mainland rule.

From the mid-sixteenth to mid-seventeenth centuries, Genoa had not only been a prominent maritime and trading city, but the banking centre of Europe. The Renaissance period left an architectural legacy which made it an essential stop on the Grand Tour, but with the growth of industry, the area of San Pier d'Arena became known as the Manchester of Italy. Soap and dye manufacture which had begun on a small scale in the seventeenth and eighteenth centuries adopted new industrialised processes, followed by sugar refining and chemical industries, but the first major engineering works and iron foundry was established by the Ballydier brothers in 1832. Philip Taylor first visited the area around 1840, but it was not until 1846 that he and Turin businessman Fortunato Prandi formed their new venture, with the backing of the government, which provided an interest free loan of 500,000 lire. The government was keen to establish a suitable engineering works capable not only of providing locomotives and other equipment for the proposed Turin-Genoa and Genoa-Voltri railways, but also iron steamships with locally built machinery. Taylor purchased the site for the venture, and contracted Nicolo Scaniglia in July 1847 for the building works. However, despite the initial optimism, the venture never lived up to its expectations, and before long the company was struggling to survive with just naval repair contracts. The new steamships for the Royal Sardinian Navy were either ordered from British firms, or the Genoese shipyard at La Foce – Cantiere della Foce – whilst the anticipated orders for railway locomotives often went abroad too; despite the government's investment, the promised work did not follow, Taylor found himself in some financial difficulty, and Adams, along with several other expatriate colleagues, decided to join the Royal Sardinian Navy as an engineer. We cannot know if he had earlier ambitions as a seagoing engineer, but the opportunity which presented itself was not only convenient, but probably quite an exciting prospect for a young man.

The navy did not consider its engineers as enlisted officers or crew, but simply hired them on a contract basis. Guglielmo Adams was duly appointed as a *'machinista di 2 classe'*, i.e., a second class engineer, for a three-month period on 1 July 1848. Evidently satisfied with him, his contract was then extended on a rolling monthly basis. This may indicate that he did not initially intend to stay for long, as most of his contemporaries were hired for a fixed term of between one and three years. Virtually all the naval engineers were British, with the exception of one or two of French origin, and the first local engineer was not appointed until 1854.

However, this was also a politically unstable period for many of the small states which were part of the Austrian Empire but would eventually form the unified nation of Italy in 1861. Although 1848 would prove to be particularly turbulent throughout Europe, it was also the year in which Charles Albert, encouraged by revolts in Tuscany, Venice and Milan, decided that the time was ripe to attempt to unify Italy, and declared war on the House of Hapsburg on 23 March, opening a conflict which would become known as the First Italian War of Independence.

The revolt in Venice had led to many of the officers and men of the Venetian-based Hapsburg navy siding with the insurgents, whilst the ships themselves remained in Austrian hands. As soon as the ships could be manned, Austria attempted to blockade the city from the end of April to late May 1848, but with the arrival of most of the fleets of the Sardinian and Neapolitan navies in the Adriatic, retreated to the port of Trieste. Here, they were themselves blockaded, until an armistice was agreed with Sardinia

Although dating from 1871, some two decades after William returned to England, this view of the La Foce shipyard would doubtless have been quite recognisable to him.

in August. Following a further blockade of Venice by Austria over the following winter, Sardinia abandoned the armistice agreement and launched further ultimately unsuccessful land operations. Thus, despite some initial military success, Charles Albert was eventually defeated, and abdicated on 23 March 1849 in favour of his eldest son, Victor Emmanuel II, fleeing to exile in Portugal, where he died only four months later.

Although it remained comparatively small in size, the development of the navy was largely through the initiative of Baron Giorgio Andrea Agnes des Geneys, who was in command from its inception until his death in 1839, by which time the fleet had been deployed in the Aegean and eastern Mediterranean to protect merchant shipping during the Greek war of independence, and some vessels had even made transatlantic crossings to South America. The service had also begun to embrace steam power.

The navy took delivery of its first steamship, named *Gulnara*, in 1834, a wooden paddle steamer built by Thomas Pitcher at his Northfleet shipyard on the Thames. With a two-cylinder oscillating engine rated at 90hp built by the Liverpool firm Fawcett, Preston & Company Ltd, the vessel was capable of a speed under steam of 7 knots. With a length of 114ft, the vessel had a displacement tonnage of 450, was armed with four 200mm muzzle-loading guns, and manned by a crew of fifty-seven officers and men.

Next came the *Ichnusa*, taking the Greek name for Sardinia, in 1837, more or less a sister vessel, but in fact the first steamship to be built at La Foce shipyard in Genoa, under licence from the Thames shipyard, although with machinery once again by Fawcett, Preston & Co. The two ships were employed on a regular postal and passenger service between Genoa and the island of Sardinia, taking over from sail-only vessels, rapidly gaining widespread approval.

Then followed two more steamers from La Foce shipyard, *Tripoli*, with a length of 140ft, launched on 25 May 1840 and *Malfatano*, which entered the water on 18 June 1844. The next order was for the 142ft long *Authion*, built in Blackwall and launched in 1847.

By the time Adams arrived in Genoa in 1848, the navy had five steamships in service, whilst in the same year it acquired a former passenger paddle steamer, *Mongibello*,

Malfatano was launched at the La Foce shipyard in June 1844, and in its first few years of service was used on the regular service between Genoa and Sardinia.

which had been built at the Pitcher yard in 1840 for the Two Sicilies Steam Navigation Company of Naples. The vessel was luxuriously fitted out with marble, bronze and mirrored finishings, with well-furnished cabins for 140 passengers. It had endured a difficult, stormy delivery voyage from the Thames, but entered service from Naples on 7 June 1841, with its first commercial sailing to Genoa and Marseilles. On the return leg, however, the ship was involved in a collision which sank the other vessel, the Genoese flagged *Pollux*. It was acquired by the Sardinian Navy in May 1848, promptly renamed *Monzambo* after a battle victory of the previous month, and despatched to the Adriatic as part of the naval blockade of Trieste.

The ship was equipped with oscillating engines, with cylinders of 40in diameter and 60in stroke supplied by Maudslay, Sons & Field, described by conflicting sources as either a four-cylinder engine or two two-cylinder machines. Whichever is correct, the boiler required replacement in 1848, but the new installation was unable to deliver sufficient steam and itself required replacement only three years later with yet another from Maudslay, Sons & Field.

Two more steamships were acquired from the Pitcher shipyard, with *Constituzione* and *Governolo* launched on the Thames in January and October 1849 respectively. However, whilst *Governolo* was actually ordered by the Royal Sardinian Navy, *Constituzione* was originally laid down for the Peninsular & Oriental Steam Navigation Company, with the intended name of *Ganges*, but was sold shortly after completion in June 1849 and P&O subsequently applied the name to another new build the following year. Adams would certainly have been familiar with the engine of this ship, a two-cylinder oscillating machine built by his former employer Miller & Ravenhill.

Constituzione was 250ft 4in long, with a displacement tonnage of 1,600, and with her twin boilers was capable of 11.5 knots. In naval service she carried a crew of 260 officers and men.

Above left: The navy once again turned to a Blackwall shipyard to build its *Authion*, which entered service in 1847, just prior to the conflict of 1848. (Aldo Antonicelli)

Above right: A model of a contemporary paddle steamer oscillating engine by Maudslay and Field, machinery with which William would have become very familiar.

Governolo was of similar length, but with a slightly larger displacement tonnage of 1,700, and her four boilers provided steam for an oscillating engine by Maudslay, Sons & Field. Armed with twelve 200mm guns, she carried a complement of 331 officers and men. In a letter to his family written in February 1850, Adams told how he had been expecting a voyage to England to take the crew for the new ship, which would have allowed him to surprise his family with a visit, but disappointing news had been received that the new crew was to travel aboard the Miller & Ravenhill built P&O steamer *Madrid* instead. *Governolo* was duly delivered and entered service in May 1850 under the command of Emilio Faa di Bruno, initially employed in combating pirate raids off the Barbary coast, and was soon highly regarded as one of the finest steamships of the era. However, the following year she returned to British waters, under the command of Captain Persano, who was arrested and detained for eleven months at Sheerness for sailing up the Thames without a pilot.

Adams' letter also reported that he was undertaking six voyages a month on the regular service between Genoa and Porto Torres on the island of Sardinia, which he found to be 'jolly hard work [as] we have scarcely time to do the regular work to the engines'. In spare time at Genoa, he was learning Italian, with a tutor charging two francs each lesson, and was evidently quite pleased at his progress with grammar.

During a recent but fairly lengthy period of bad weather, they had put into the port of Spezia, about forty miles to the south east of Genoa, for shelter. The following morning, they were called upon by the port authorities to go to the assistance of a merchant ship in distress, but the captain had ordered the fires to be dropped, and no wood could be found to relight them. The unfortunate consequence was that the merchantman was lost with all hands, resulting in a court martial for the captain, and transfer to a lower grade. Furthermore, he had apparently been advised by the chief engineer, William Meriton, that as no wood was available, the fires should have been

Governolo was a larger vessel of 1,700 tons, once again a product of the Pitcher yard, with Maudslay and Field engines. (Aldo Antonicelli)

Two steamships of the Sardinian fleet, *Constituzione*, fitted with Miller and Ravenhill engines, and *Governolo* beyond, dressed overall for review in 1861. (Aldo Antonicelli)

William would have doubtless been interested to learn that in June 1849, whilst he was away, HMS *Basilisk* took part in a tug of war with HMS *Niger* in the English Channel, in an attempt to evaluate the superiority of screw versus paddle propulsion, The paddle sloop *Basilisk*, fitted with 400hp Miller and Ravenhill engines, lost against the screw driven *Niger*, with the result that the paddlers *Baracouta* and *Valorous*, at the time under construction at Pembroke Dockyard, and both engined by his former employer, were the last to enter the Royal Navy fleet in 1850.

retained. Adams concluded that wood should have been found, even it meant burning the cabin furniture, adding 'as I am sure an English captain would'. However, along with the rest of the crew he gave evidence in his master's defence.

Although employed on a contract basis, Adams apparently enjoyed the status of a government officer and associated perks, one being the right to shoot without obtaining a licence, for which purpose he 'bought a beautiful double barrel gun which formerly belonged to our present admiral'. The island of Sardinia provided good territory for shooting with 'hares and partridges in most extraordinary abundance', and he was 'beginning to knock down the birds tolerably well'. Despite the pleasures afforded by shooting on the island, Adams did not think much of Porto Torres, which he considered:

> ... in the summertime ... a most unhealthy place, it is low and swampy, they are scarcely ever free from fever and agues and in some months have been known to die twenty and thirty per day. The convicts that are transported there from Genoa seldom come back, or if they do their constitutions are completely destroyed – just now it is not so bad – but the night air is always injurious, we are obliged to take care of ourselves and not remain out at night time. In summer time the steamers only touch there, land and disembark passengers, and go off to a little island a few miles off.

Neither was he overly impressed by the Sardinians themselves, whom he regarded as:

> a most revengeful set much worse than the Corsicans for they are more treacherous – If one man kills another, one of the family of the murdered man is sure to take revenge, not only by killing the murderer, but often the whole of the family - and all this is caused by the bad laws of the country.

On the following Monday his ship was due to depart for Sardinia, with a call en route at the island of Maddelina where, he reported:

> there has been an unpleasant occurrence – the captain of a band of brigands wrote to the commander of the port for permission to live there unmolested as he

An early photographic image of the harbour at Porto Torres, thought to be by Eduardo Delessert.

was tired of his unlawful life - he returned him and a few days after the brigand came to thank him for his kindness – he told him it would be better to go to the prefet de police and get proper papers of security and in going out together to the police office the commander of the port seeing four soldiers ordered them to seize him. Unfortunately the soldiers had nothing but their side arms and the brigand was armed to the teeth – he threw the soldiers off and wounded one of them severely and made his escape previously telling the commander that he should pay him for it and no doubt he will if he remains there – for these men generally keep such promises; the best thing for the commander to do is to leave the island at once or they will be sure to take his life.

The letter also tells us that he was lodging with an English family based in Genoa, and that the house was the highest in the town, with his own room in the highest part of it.

The host family was that of Charles Park and his wife Catherine, who had moved to Genoa in 1848. Charles had been born in Aberdeen in 1807, where he grew up and married Catherine Milne in 1829, at which time his occupation was given as a blacksmith. In 1842, he took his family to live in Leghorn, or Livorno, on the western coast of Tuscany, where he established an engineering business. However, the turbulent times of 1848 forced him to move again, this time to Genoa.

By the time that Adams joined the household, Charles and Catherine Park already had seven children, with another born in 1852. Eldest was Isabella, who had been born in 1830, followed by John Carter arriving two years later.

John Carter Park had just commenced an apprenticeship in Livorno before the upheaval of the move to Genoa, but was able to complete it under Philip Taylor, at which point he too followed Adams as a seagoing engineer.

Clearly, Isabella had caught William's eye, and in his letter of February 1850 he described her as 'a very fine girl' with whom he was on good terms. On 13 September

A general view of Genoa from above the lighthouse circa 1850. La Foce shipyard is just beyond the headland to the right. (A.H. Payne)

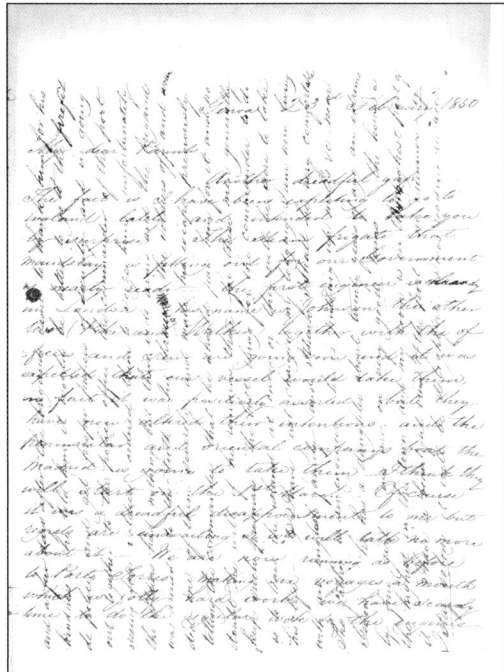 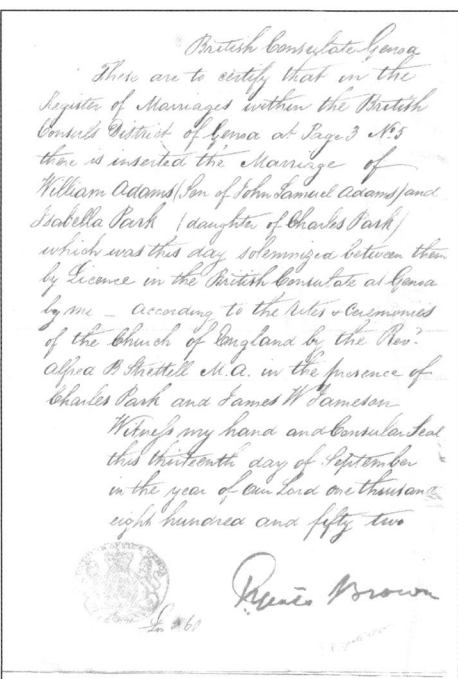

Above left: An extract from William's letter to his parents dated 23 February 1850. Not an easy read as he used each page twice, with a second script superimposed. (Dr R.J. Adams)

Above right: William and Isabella's marriage licence, issued at the British Consulate in Genoa on 13 September 1852. (Dr R.J. Adams)

1852 William and Isabella were married by licence at the British Consulate in Genoa, with Isabella's father Charles and James Jameson as witnesses. James Wardrop Jameson was another expatriate recruit for Philip Taylor, having been apprenticed to James Stirling at the East Foundry in Dundee, following which he found employment first with Sturrock at the Great Western Railway in Swindon, and then with John Gooch at the London & South Western Railway (LSWR). In 1845, he was appointed Chief Superintendent of the Locomotive Department of Rothwell and Company, at Union Foundry, Bolton, which was largely engaged in the construction of motive power for his previous employer, the LSWR. He too had moved to Genoa in 1848.

During the month before their marriage, the former employer Taylor and Prandi was forced into liquidation, with the debt to the government now standing at 810,000 lire. Adams was clearly aware two years earlier that the business was not faring well, and he was hoping to find time to visit Mr Taylor. The assets were quickly sold by the state to Giovanni Ansoldo and his partners, who developed the San Pier d'Arena works into a major shipyard, locomotive builder and general heavy engineering works, which commenced building locomotives for the Genoa-Turin Railway almost immediately.

Adams left his employment with the navy on 13 October 1852, and the newlywed couple returned to England shortly thereafter, whilst the groom's new brother-in-law, John Carter Park, his apprenticeship completed, remained at sea.

Chapter 4

The Origins of the North London Railway

Adams' railway career properly commenced with an appointment by the North London Railway, the formation of which is closely linked with the continuing development of both the West and East India Docks companies, and the influence of Henry Martin. A more detailed explanation of the origins of the NLR is therefore perhaps appropriate.

The London and Birmingham Railway opened in 1838, with its city terminus at Euston, but within a few years sought to provide a link to the developing commercial docklands in the East End. The first proposal to link the City with the London and Birmingham was a proposal as early as 1836 by the London Grand Junction Railway for a line of 3½ miles from a new terminus at Skinner Street to link with the main line at Camden Town. Although the line was authorised, the scheme was abandoned shortly after construction work actually started.

At the height of the 'railway mania' in 1845, three schemes were promoted, each with a similar objective. The North London Junction Railway, North Metropolitan Junction Railway plus the East and West India Docks and Birmingham Junction Railway (E&WID&BJR) all sought approval, but the last, with the backing of the London and Birmingham Railway, was authorised by Act of Parliament which gained Royal Assent on 26 August 1846. The scheme proposed to build a railway of some eight miles in length from a junction at Camden Town to the West India Docks, and was essentially designed for freight traffic only, to provide rail access for manufactured goods from the Midlands and North directly to the docks.

One of the recommendations of the railway gauge commission, also convened in 1845, was that schemes which would lead to a circular link around London should be favoured rather than proposals for new London termini, and another advantage of the E&WID&BJR scheme was that it could link to another existing railway, the London and Blackwall, at its eastern end.

The London and Blackwall Railway, originally promoted as the Commercial Railway and opened in July 1840, followed a route from Minories, in the city, via Stepney to Blackwall, passing to the north of both the West and East India Docks, although it did not provide direct access for freight traffic. An extension from Minories to a new terminus at Fenchurch Street opened the following year. The enabling Act of Parliament of 1836 stipulated a gauge of 5ft ½in, which was proposed by the original engineer, John Rennie, but he was replaced by Robert Stephenson, who found himself inconveniently bound to the odd gauge. He also proposed that the line be worked by cable haulage rather than locomotives.

Henry Martin was appointed to survey the route of the E&WID&BJR, under the supervision of Robert Stephenson, from a junction with the former London and Birmingham Railway, by now one of the constituents of the recently formed London

The Origins of the North London Railway

The dock companies were anxious to establish a railway link with the London and Birmingham Railway which opened in 1838. An Edward Bury 2-2-0 leaves the eastern portal of Primrose Hill tunnel, London's first railway tunnel, and close to the site of the junction with the East & West India Docks & Birmingham Junction Railway at Chalk Farm, circa 1840.

and North Western Railway, via Kingsland, Hackney and Bow to the West India Docks. William Adams' elder brother John Henry was also appointed as a Resident Engineer in June 1848 and was provided with a house at Kingsland.

However, 1846 was also the year that a total of 272 railway parliamentary acts were passed and the 'railway mania' bubble finally burst. The Bank of England had increased interest rates late in the previous year, making alternative forms of investment more attractive, and the new company found it difficult to find subscribers for its £600,000 authorised share capital.

The London and Birmingham Railway merged with the Grand Junction and Manchester & Birmingham Railway companies to form the London and North Western Railway (LNWR) in July 1846, and although the E&WID&BJR remained independent – and retained its lengthy title – two thirds of the latter's board was appointed by the LNWR, which reflected the financial stake it held, with £50,000 subscribed by the dock company.

The first section of the line between Islington and Bow Junction opened on 26 September 1850. An Act of that year authorised an extension to link with the London and Blackwall Railway, which was consequently rebuilt to standard gauge with locomotive operation. A further link to the Eastern Counties, which had earlier opened a route into London from Colchester, was also built.

The route between Islington and Camden Town was delayed by the collapse of works at Maiden Lane, but was finally opened on 7 December 1850, with an extension to Hampstead Road and a junction with the LNWR on 9 June 1851. The continuation of the line from Bow to Poplar and the West India Docks was officially declared open on 1 January 1852.

From its inception, the line was intended purely for freight traffic, but a passenger service was provided from its opening, between Islington, Bow Junction and thence over the Blackwall company's line to Fenchurch Street. Trains ran every 15 minutes during the day, and such was its success that 97,000 passengers were carried in the first month of operation, with a total approaching 1.5 million in the ensuing six months. The route between Bow Junction and West India Dock, however, remained freight only.

The North and South West Junction Railway (N&SWJR) was a scheme proposed in 1852 to link the LNWR, from a new junction near Kensal Green, to the London and South Western Railway at Kew Junction, which would thus provide a link across the northern perimeter of the city between the docklands and routes to the south and west. The new line was opened to passenger traffic on 1 August 1853, and although it was originally agreed that train services would be operated jointly by the North Western and South Western companies, it was, from the outset, worked by the NLR, the less cumbrous and far more appropriate name adopted on 1 January that year by the E&WID&BJR.

The N&SWJR then gained approval for, and constructed, a short branch from Acton Gatehouse Junction to Hammersmith. Shareholders complained that the directors had acted unlawfully with its construction, and it was soon evident that neither would it be the anticipated commercial success.

However, the NLR, with services from Fenchurch Street looping around the northern side of the city to the junction at Kew, was proving to be a valuable asset, although as yet lacking its own direct route into the city.

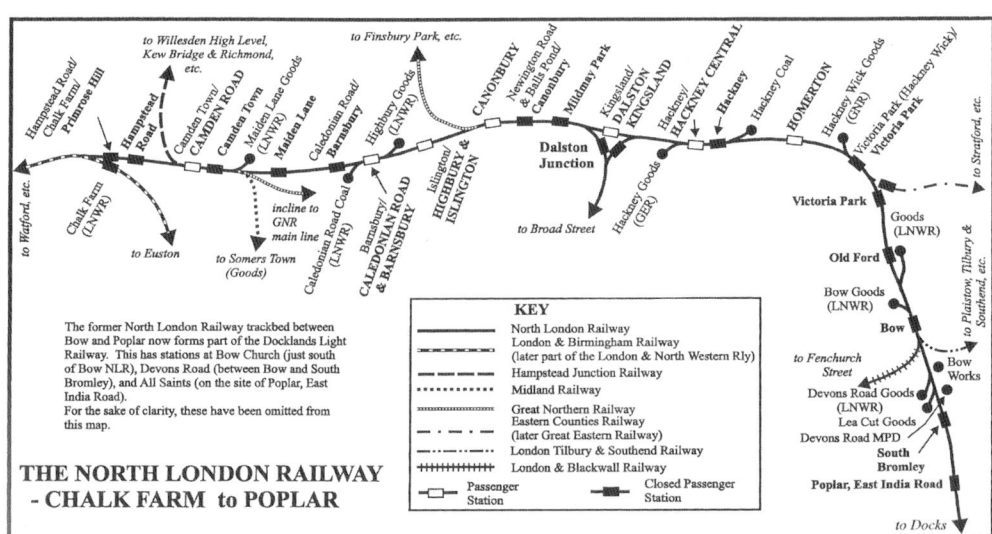

Map *Jim Connor*

The Origins of the North London Railway

Right: The coat of arms of the North London Railway demonstrates its origins as the East & West India Docks & Birmingham Junction Railway. The East India Dock is represented to the top left with the lion and anchor, with the West India Dock entrance depicted to the bottom right. The shields of the cities of London and Birmingham occupy the bottom left and top right quarters respectively.

Below: In this 1860 view, locomotive operation has superseded cable haulage on the London and Blackwall Railway, providing a link from the NLR at Bow Junction to the city at Fenchurch Street. The adjacent Forrestt's lifeboat building yard was situated close to the Adams family home at Limehouse. (Original author unknown)

CHAPTER 5

The Innovative Years at Bow

For the first few years of operation the NLR was worked by locomotives provided by the LNWR, but by 1853 the NLR was experiencing difficulties with the reliability of the motive power provided and decided that it should provide its own locomotives. However, the Marquess of Londonderry's Northumberland and Durham Coal Company (N&DCC), which brought coal to London by sea, procured an arrangement to work coal trains over the line, from a new rail-linked dock facility at Poplar, using its own locomotives and wagons for an annual access fee of £10,000. In March 1851, William Adams' older brother John transferred to the coal company as its Coal Traffic Superintendent at Poplar, and five years later also became Goods Station Master for the NLR, retaining both positions until the N&DCC gave up working its own trains in 1858.

Apart from his NLR appointment, Henry Martin was still practising as a consulting engineer on his own account from his office in Leadenhall Street, and was quick to engage the assistance of William Adams shortly after his return to England. One of his first tasks was to undertake a survey for a proposed new railway in the Isle of Wight intended to link Cowes, Newport and Ryde, with a line via Godshill to Ventnor. This proposal was one of three put forward in 1852, and a re-run of an 1845 scheme, for which Charles Vignoles had undertaken a preliminary survey. In the event, it failed at the parliamentary hurdle, but Henry Martin would in the coming years become very heavily involved in the subsequent development of the island's railways, eventually taking up permanent residence there, and could in many respects be described as the father of the Isle of Wight railway network. Another project then awaited Adams – this time at Cardiff.

The West Bute Docks, the first proper facility for the city, had been designed by Admiral William Henry Smyth, and opened in 1839, promoted by John Crichton-Stuart, the second Marquis of Bute, who was not only the most prominent land owner in the area at the time, but an industrialist involved with the development of Dowlais Ironworks in addition to extensive mining interests which had led to a rapid growth in coal traffic.

John Batchelor, together with his brother Sidney, had established themselves as timber merchants in the city before developing interests in ship repair, initially by taking over an existing yard on the banks of the River Taff in 1843. They subsequently built a new facility, equipped with a graving dock, adjacent to the West Bute Docks in the early 1850s, advertising the firm, Batchelor Brothers, as an 'Iron and Wood Shipbuilder, Boiler Maker, and Bridge Builder'. William Adams was employed to manage the machinery contracts for the new graving dock and then returned to London, where he was able to use the experience gained at Cardiff in the installation of hydraulic machinery at Poplar Docks.

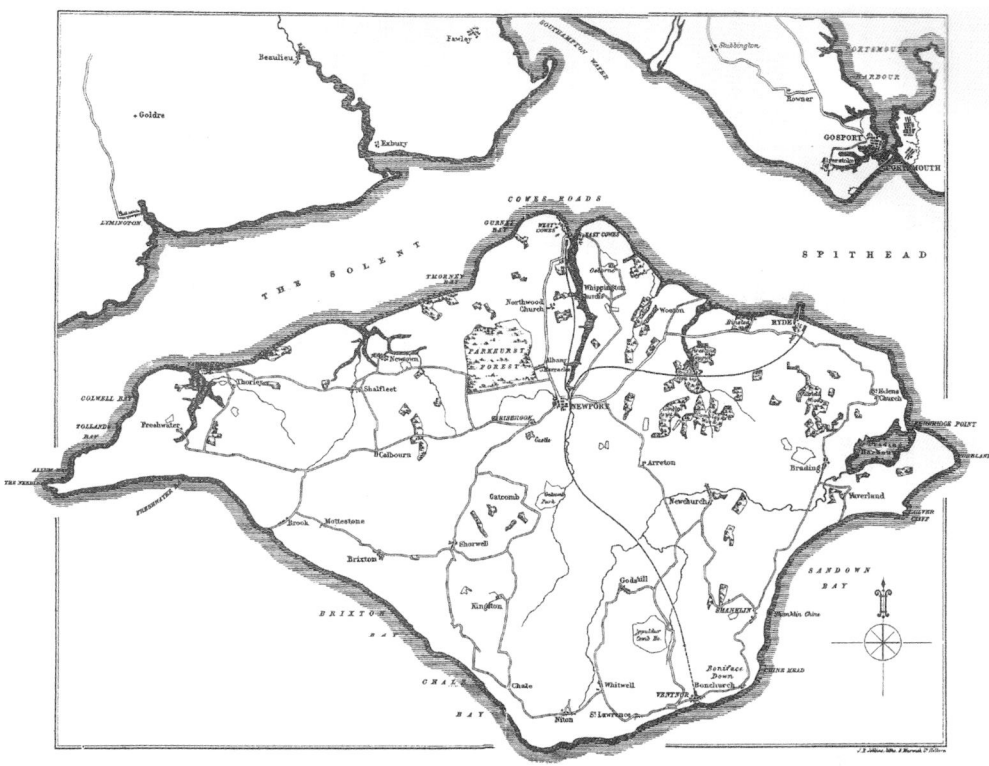

Map of the Isle of Wight Railway scheme first proposed in 1845 and resurrected in 1852 when William Adams was sent to survey the route. (Richard Maycock)

On 9 August 1853 Isabella gave birth to their first child, William John, who was baptised two months later at St Olave's Church, Bermondsey. He was joined two years later by a sister, Catherine Alice, but unfortunately William's father, John Samuel, 'civil engineer, late of East and West India Docks', passed away on 26 May 1855.

Prior to his appointment with the NLR, Henry Martin sent William to Cardiff to oversee machinery installation for the new graving dock at the Batchelor shipyard, adjacent to Bute West Docks, depicted here in 1859.

Younger brother Robert was engaged in the design of the tubular iron Saltwater Bridge shortly after emigrating to Victoria, Australia.

Robert was also involved with the design of Taradale Viaduct which carries the Bendigo railway line over Back Creek in the state of Victoria.

Just as William and Isabella returned to England in 1852, his younger brother Robert departed for a new life in Australia to try his hand at digging for gold. This venture met with little success, and he found employment as a civil engineer on the construction of the Melbourne, Mount Alexander and Murray River Railway in Victoria, where he was partly responsible for the design of two notable structures, the Taradale Viaduct and the tubular iron Saltwater Bridge, which featured a single span of 200 feet. Although described as 'the ablest engineer in Victoria', he was laid off on

The Innovative Years at Bow

completion of the line to Echuca, but by 1861 he was Resident Engineer of the Victoria Railways Board, which had been established in 1859 to take over most of the region's hitherto privately promoted and owned lines. However, he left the railway industry and became openly critical of his successors, in particular relating to the design of a viaduct at Campaspe. He died in 1873 from injuries sustained in a domestic fire, at the young age of forty-four, whilst holding the post of city surveyor in St Kilda.

Martin's wide-ranging responsibilities as Engineer to the NLR included infrastructure and building work, plus supervision of contracts to obtain locomotives and rolling stock to the extent that in addition to his salary, he was entitled to a commission of 1¼ per cent on all such contracts.

Back in London, Martin was instructed by the NLR board to prepare drawings and documentation for the construction of ten new locomotives, plus design a new engine shed and works at Bow, for which he sought Adams' assistance. The contract for the new locomotives was confirmed with the Bristol firm of Stothert and Slaughter in July 1853.

Bow Junction, with the locomotive works beyond the signal box. The route alongside the works continued southwards to Poplar, with the link to the Great Eastern Railway curving away to the right. (North London Railway Historical Society, Jim Connor collection)

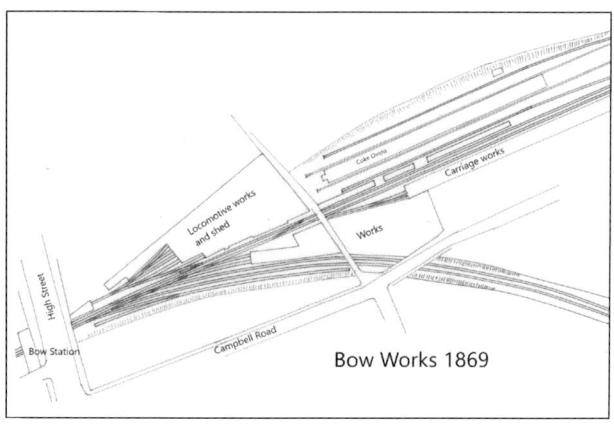

A plan of Bow Junction c1869 which gives an indication of the cramped nature of the original locomotive works, and later running shed. The subsequent additions and carriage works are also shown.

William Adams was formally appointed Locomotive Foreman by the NLR in March 1854, following the unexpected resignation of the previous post holder, a Mr Miller, at an annual salary of £200, with the contract for the new buildings let the following month. The position would soon allow him to demonstrate both his organisational skills with respect to the new works, and his innovative thinking in regard to the motive power and rolling stock requirements of the company.

The new locomotives, numbered 1-10, were 2-4-0 rigid frame well tanks, with outside cylinders 15in x 18in and 5ft 3in diameter driving wheels. Four-coupled engines were in themselves still comparatively rare at this time, with many locomotive designs still employing a single driving axle. Delivered in 1853/4, they were clearly soon regarded by the board as successful, and five further locomotives were ordered from Robert Stephenson for delivery in 1855, to be numbered 21-25. However, this time four-coupled inside cylinder side tanks were specified, together with a four-wheel leading bogie. Principal dimensions were 15in x 18in cylinders, and once again 5ft 3in diameter coupled wheels. The bogie was pivoted by means of a spherical bearing, originally introduced by Gooch in 1849, but, because of a lack of side-play, the wheelsets of the leading coupled axle were flangeless, with the springs of both coupled axles linked by a compensating beam – an arrangement which would feature in many Adams designs over the years. Eight further similar locomotives were ordered from Slaughter Grüning & Co (which Stothert & Slaughter had become) in 1861.

The NLR also acquired an assortment of other locomotives, the oldest being a former London and Birmingham Railway 2-2-2 well tank by Rothwell dating from 1837, and in 1859 took over those hitherto operated by the N&DCC. The following year, five 0-4-2 saddle tanks were ordered from Beyer, Peacock for use as dock shunters.

One of Adams' early experiments in 1857 was a trial of the air-induction steam jet in a locomotive firebox, by means of which air was introduced into the firebox when the regulator was shut. It was a measure intended to aid combustion and reduce smoke

No. 24 was one of five locomotives ordered from Robert Stephenson in 1855, the first class of 4-4-0 tanks for the NLR. Note the short wheelbase of the bogie, which featured a central ball type pivot, with no lateral side play. (NLRHS, Jim Connor collection)

Messrs Slaughter Grüning won the contract to supply eight further locomotives in 1861. NLR No.35 was sold to Henry Martin in 1880, and is seen here in later life as Isle of Wight Central Railway No. 7. (John Scott-Morgan collection)

and followed a concept which had recently been introduced by Daniel Kinnear Clark on ten locomotives of the Great North of Scotland Railway.

The Adams household continued to grow with five children by 1861, the family, plus two servants, now living at 21 Carlisle Terrace, Fairfield Road, Bow. The eldest children, William and Katherine, had now been joined by Isabella, Charles, and baby John, who would only remain the youngest until the following year when another brother, Alfred, arrived.

1861 was also the year in which Henry Martin found himself obliged to resign from both the NLR and the dock company. Financial irregularities, to the tune of £12,000, were uncovered relating to dock contracts with Messrs Hack, a firm which was also a contractor to the NLR, and it was shortly after the exposure of this scandal that he moved across the Solent to further develop his interests in the Isle of Wight.

Adams continued to refine the basic 4-4-0T design, and in 1863 the first locomotives were built at the new Bow works. The NLR must have been well satisfied with their choice of superintendent, as his annual salary had increased to £350, and his duties were now defined as 'in charge of Locomotives and Rolling Stock, Workshops & Machinery, and Gas & Water'.

Within six months of his appointment in 1854, the board was able to report that the new sheds and workshops at Bow were nearing completion, and by the end of the year the development had cost a little over £31,500. A six-road building was initially provided at Bow which housed both the works and locomotive running shed, occupying a site south of Bow station, but in 1857 tenders were sought for a separate paint shop. In that same year, Adams was authorised to spend £236 on further machinery and equipment, to be obtained from Messrs Hack & Co. – the firm later implicated in the financial scandal with Henry Martin. Initially engaged in the repair of locomotives and rolling stock, by the early 1860s the facilities were now such that the company was not only able to construct new carriages and wagons, but locomotives too – a very high degree of self-sufficiency for a relatively small railway. However, before this was achieved, the original carriage shed was destroyed by fire in 1858, and the report following the incident demonstrated that the facilities already suffered from insufficient capacity, with wagon repairs having to be undertaken at a separate workshop at Poplar, and some locomotives were being based at a temporary shed provided by the N&DCC. The contract for the replacement carriage shed and other works was let to Hack & Co. In the early 1860s, the board explored the possibility of building a new carriage works at Old Ford, and sought to purchase the required land, but the scheme was not pursued, and in late 1863 the NLR acquired 7½ acres of land at Devons Road, where a new carriage shed was authorised, with the contract for construction let the following year. Devons Road would, long after Adams' departure, and the acquisition of more land, eventually be the site of a new locomotive running shed, which further eased pressure at the Bow site. In the meantime, he sought approval for an extension to the boiler shop, and additional equipment, doubtless urgently required as the railway was now building its own locomotives. Further land was acquired in 1866 for future development and Bow works would gradually expand to occupy an area of some 31 acres.

All carriages built at Bow were of the four-wheel type, and were marshalled into close-coupled sets, with single-link couplings and buffers at one end only, which maximised train length on available platforms. Thus, relatively lightweight, high-capacity trains could be provided, in rakes ranging from eight to twelve coaches, with a brake van at each end. Passenger stock was finished in a varnished teak livery.

In 1862, Adams also pioneered the regular use of coal gas lighting in carriages, with the result that guards' vans were predominantly occupied by large gas bags to store the fuel on board. These were later replaced with steel cylinders below the underframes. The idea had previously been trialled in Ireland, but the NLR was the first to make widespread use of coal gas lighting.

Adams very quickly recognised the need for improvement in train braking, with continuous brakes fitted to all carriages in the train formation. This would be a key feature in speeding up timetables for services with frequent stops, as found on the North London.

John Clark had started experimenting with chain brakes in the 1840s, with chains slung under each vehicle, linked together and operated manually from the locomotive. One of the inherent difficulties was ensuring a constant tension throughout the train during a brake application, as efficiency would reduce towards the rearmost vehicles of a longer train, and further it was not always straightforward to ensure correct adjustment. The NLR was using the system as early as 1855, but it was not until 1873 that the system as modified by Francis Webb of the LNWR was adopted. The early continuous chain brake was operated by the guard, rather than the driver, which relied on whistles as a means of signalling instructions – a system which was by no means automatic, let alone failsafe, yet was surprisingly effective. On longer train formations, an additional brakesman could be required in a second brake van. Adams also explored the use of electric and Barker's hydraulic systems but found favour with Clark's developments. He was also, perhaps surprisingly to later engineers, at that time broadly in favour of brakes being applied by the guard rather than the locomotive driver. The Westinghouse air brake had also been considered, but in an 1873 discussion on the topic he expressed reservations about that option relating to costs, and the fact that the brake would continually require power from the locomotive, rather than just at the time of its application.

In February 1863, the board authorised Adams 'to make arrangements for the construction in the Company's shops of six additional goods engines, similar in character to those last laid down, as the opportunity may arise, without undue increase in staff'. The new Bow-built locomotives became known as class 43, being numbered 43-50, with the first of the eight outshopped in December that year. Four more followed in 1864, with the last one turned out in May 1865. Whilst the board minute notes the need for goods engines, the new locomotives were also required and used for passenger work, although shown as goods engines in subsequent Board of Trade Returns. The design was very similar to the last order supplied by Slaughter Grüning, but with a variety of detail modifications and improvements. Adams realised that he needed to provide stable, free-steaming locomotives, capable of rapid acceleration in order to meet the demands of the service. With class 43 he broke new ground by raising boiler pressure to 160lb per square inch – the first in Britain to do so, with 120lb a more normal figure for the time. This was, perhaps, all the more remarkable because he had spent his earlier years in marine engineering working with low boiler pressures in the 5-16lb per square inch range. He was thus able to retain a comparatively small boiler, but with an ample size grate, to provide sufficient steam. Unlike the Slaughter Grüning engines, which featured a dome with safety valves over the firebox, class 43 had a separate closed-top dome located midway along the boiler barrel with a Ramsbottom-type safety valve over the firebox. He also located large sandboxes atop the boilers to aid gravity sanding – a constant requirement on the steeply graded route. Cylinder sizes were amended to 16in bore with a slightly longer 24in stroke, but driving wheel diameter remained as before at 5ft 3in. As originally

No. 43, the first locomotive to be built at Bow in 1863, standing outside the works in near original condition. (NLRHS, Jim Connor collection)

built, the engines featured only a wheel operated handbrake with wooden brake blocks. They were outshopped in a mid-green livery, ornately finished with black bands lined in red and white with a copper capped chimney, to the front of which was also fixed the locomotive's number, similar in style to those carried to this day by the Isle of Man Railway's Beyer, Peacocks, and a polished rather than painted dome. To aid maintenance, the side tanks were fabricated with a cut away section around the leading driving wheels, and as built the engines were cabless, with just a small weatherboard above the firebox backhead. Cast oval plates bearing the number surrounded by the company name were fixed to tank sides.

The first Adams design built at Bow works was a development of the Slaughter Grüning order, and became known as Class 43, completed between 1863 and 1865. No. 49 was later rebuilt with a new boiler and enclosed cab for working Plaistow and Hammersmith branch trains, renumbered 107. (ETH Archive)

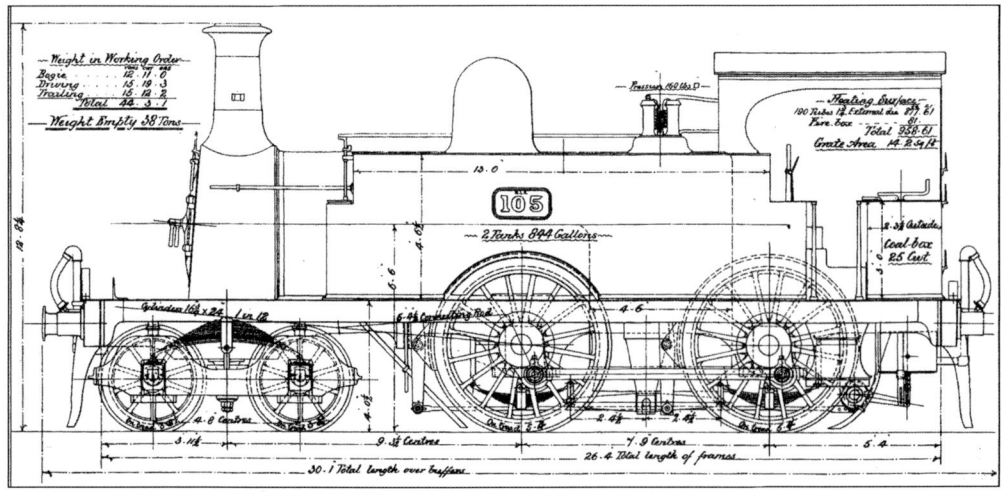

An NLR drawing of class 43 No. 47 rebuilt with cab and renumbered 105. (NLRHS, Jim Connor collection)

As passenger traffic developed, the NLR sought to build its own route into a city terminus, which would provide a more direct route from the north west than the longer journey around to Fenchurch Street. An Act was sought, and granted in 1861, to build a new line from a junction at Kingsland to Liverpool Street. The new link and terminus, known as Broad Street, was opened on 31 October 1865, largely financed by the L&NWR. Traffic soon doubled, resulting in increased demands on the locomotive department, which was now required to provide sufficient motive power for additional trains over the N&SWJR line. The new terminus also provided facilities to recharge the carriage gas lighting systems.

With the first two class 43 locomotives delivered by the company's own workshops, in April 1864 the board was engaged in calculating the likely additional motive power and rolling stock requirements for working the new extension into the city at Broad Street, although it would not reach a final decision for another six months, when it was minuted:

> In lieu of the proposed purchase of ten new engines, six engines of the same class as recently built, but fitted with radial axleboxes for the leading wheels, be constructed in the Company's works at Bow, the construction of four additional engines which it is estimated will be ultimately required, to be deferred for the present.

Above left: William Adams photographed in 1863, at around the time that he first grew a beard. (Dr R.J. Adams)

Above right: Isabella circa 1863. (Dr R.J. Adams)

However, to confuse the story at this point, an engineer named William Bridges Adams, who was no relation, but coincidentally also owned an engineering business at Bow, entered the scene. He developed, and in July 1861 patented, a radial axlebox, and it is to this innovation that the board minute refers.

He was born in Shropshire in 1797 and commenced his career as an apprentice coachmaker with Baxter and Pierce, of Long Acre, in London. After a period employed as an estate manager at Valparaíso in Chile, and a spell in the United States, he returned to London and the coachbuilding trade.

He also patented an improved carriage spring, which could be transferred to railway practice, and invented the fishplate in collaboration with Robert Richardson of the Eastern Counties Railway. In 1843 he set up the Fairfield Locomotive Works at Bow, where he developed and built small numbers of steam rail carriages and railmotors. He was also involved in William Henson's unsuccessful experiments with a flying machine, promoted as The Aerial Steam Carriage. A small vertical boilered inspection carriage was built in 1847, followed by the Fairfield steam carriage for the Bristol and Exeter Railway the following year (although not finally accepted until 1850). The Eastern Counties bought the Enfield design, which had a 2-2-0 power unit with conventional locomotive boiler, built specifically for its Enfield branch in 1849. He also built two small 2-2-0 well tank locomotives, one for the Eastern Counties – named *The Cambridge* – and the other for an Italian railway. Two more, works numbers 9 and 10, were under construction when he became bankrupt in August 1850. One, delightfully named *Wee Scotland*, was destined for the Caledonian & Dumbarton Railway, whilst the other was intended for the Edinburgh & Glasgow, which later took over the C & DR. The name *Wee Scotland* was apparently a play on George England's Little England designs.

William Bridges Adams was also a writer. *English Pleasure Carriages* appeared in 1837, followed by *Roads and Rails* in 1862, but in later life he used the pseudonym Junius Redivivus for works on political reform.

As well as his radial axle, he also invented and patented a 'spring tyre', which involved fitting a spring hoop between tyre and wheel, with the intention of absorbing shock, and apparently improving adhesion between tyre and rail.

In November 1863, the St Helens Railway completed a 2-4-2T locomotive, designed by James Cross, its locomotive engineer, who at around that time left the company to commence his own business, the Sutton Engine Works. Named *White Raven*, the engine not only featured the W.B. Adams radial axleboxes on leading and trailing axles, but also his patent 'spring tyres'.

Although built in the north west, William Adams agreed to trials on the NLR, presumably because it offered similar steep gradients and sharp curves to the Lancashire line and it was close to W. B. Adams' own Fairfield Locomotive Works. The principal dimensions of the locomotive were 15in x 20in cylinders, with 5ft 1in diameter driving wheels, 3ft 3in diameter wheels on the leading axle and 3ft 1in at the rear. The wheelbase between driving axles was 7ft 9in, with 7ft 10in between leading and trailing axles and their respective drivers, giving an overall wheelbase of 23ft 5in. Each radial axlebox had a lateral side-play of some 4½in, and the overall effect was a locomotive with too much flexibility, and a tendency to derail. The LNWR took over the St Helens Railway, and with it *White Raven*, in August 1864. Subsequently it was converted into a 2-4-0 tender engine with conventional wheels and axleboxes.

The Innovative Years at Bow 53

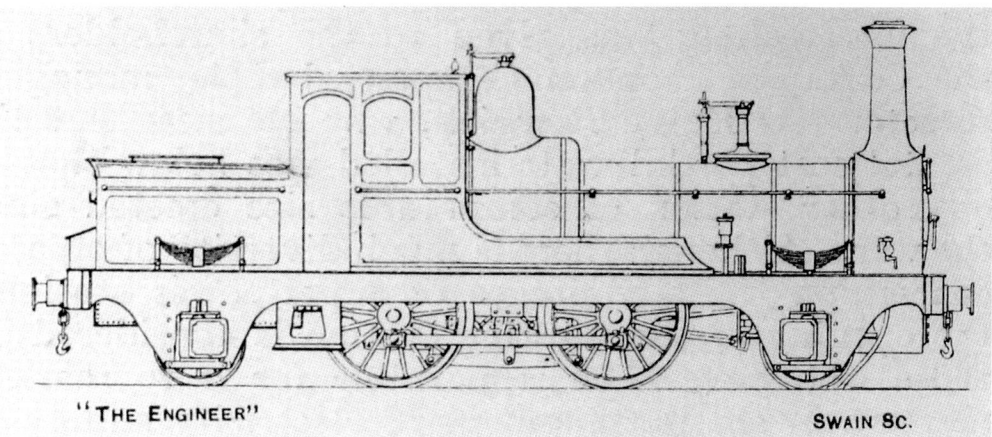

White Raven was built by Cross & Co. for the St Helens Railway in 1863, incorporating William Bridges Adams radial axleboxes and spring tyres. William Adams agreed to trials with the locomotive on the NLR, but although he was impressed by the idea of the radial axlebox, he was concerned that too much flexibility was evident.

The LNWR absorbed the St Helens Railway and *White Raven* was converted into a 2-4-0 tender engine, with a rigid leading axle.

William Adams reported on the trials to the NLR board in May 1864, in the course of which he recommended adopting the W. B. Adams radial axlebox for future new locomotives. Apart from assessment of the locomotive itself, *White Raven* was also used to trial the Clark Continuous Break, during which speeds of 60mph were recorded near Edgware Road. The board accepted William's proposal to adopt the axlebox and drawings were prepared, but as a further trial the trailing axle of engine No. 38, one of the five Beyer, Peacock 0-4-2 saddle tanks, was thus fitted. Following William Adams' subsequent reports of August and October that year, the board authorised the expenditure of £250 for the purchase of Mr Bridges Adams' patent. In the event, this did not happen, and William Adams shortly thereafter designed his own radial bogie – an innovation which should not therefore be confused with the W.B. Adams radial axlebox. With the radial bogie, the NLR had no further use for the W.B. Adams axlebox, which in a further twist was adopted by William Adams later in his career.

The concept of a leading bogie was still a relatively novel feature in the early 1860s, but with a fixed central pivot it was not entirely satisfactory in guiding a locomotive around a curve. William Adams sought to correct this difficulty with his own design of a bogie permitting controlled lateral side-play, rather than rely on the Bridges Adams radial axlebox as he had earlier recommended to the board. Essentially, the new bogie allowed a lateral movement of about 4in either side of the centre line, with a lateral spring each side and the use of a centrally located india-rubber block to absorb shock. For this he was granted a patent on 13 February 1865, and the design was incorporated in the next batch of locomotives, known as class 51, to be constructed at Bow. William Adams himself described the primary purpose of the 4½inch thick india-rubber 'washer' or block as a device to minimise any twisting movement of the locomotive frames and consequent strain on main springs on an uneven road. The rubber rested on a block of cast iron which was able to slide laterally on the bogie frame as the engine traversed a curve, with that motion controlled by springs at each side of the bogie frame. Further, the rubber reduced friction with the bogie pin. The initial designs also incorporated a cast iron cup between the rubber and sliding block, lubricated and intended to swivel as the locomotive adjusted to a curve, but this was found to be unnecessary and was subsequently dispensed with.

Adams had no doubt become acquainted with, or at least the work of, George Spencer, who trained and worked as an engineer and surveyor, being employed for a number of years by Fox, Henderson and Company, a firm whose expertise ranged from the design of railway bridges and rolling stock, to the manufacture of the ironwork structure for the 1851 Great Exhibition in the Crystal Palace. Whilst there, he had

A proud moment for William, wearing stove pipe hat, as he stands with some of his staff alongside No. 51, the first locomotive to be built with his patented bogie, outside Bow works, almost certainly when new in October 1865, and still in works grey livery. (NLRHS, Jim Connor collection)

The Innovative Years at Bow 55

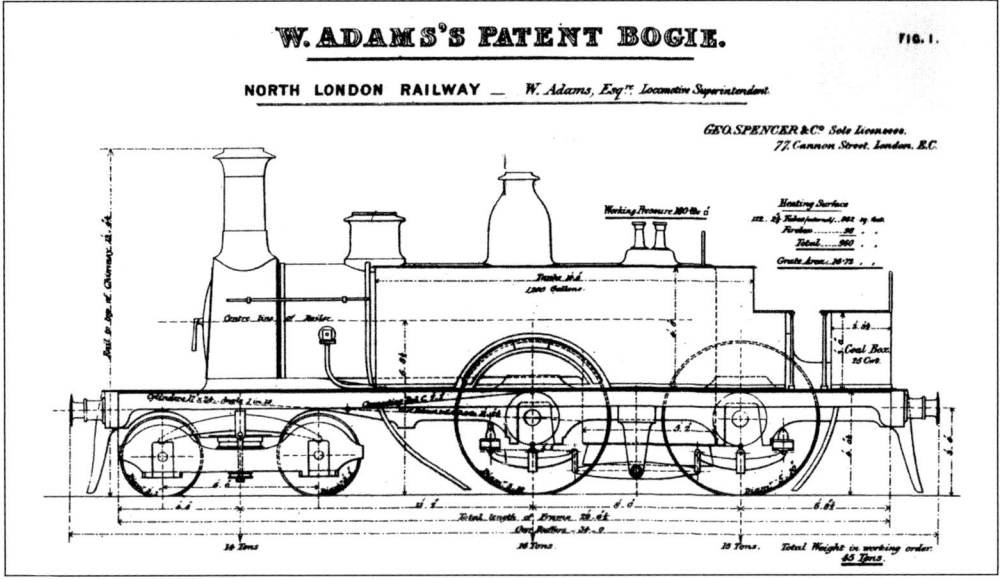

Above: George Spencer featured a drawing of the NLR's 51 class to promote sales of the Adams Patent Bogie. (NLRHS, Jim Connor collection)

Right: A contemporary advertisement placed by George Spencer, promoting a variety of rubber products for railway engineering applications, and also noting the licence held to promote the Adams bogie.

become interested in the use of vulcanised rubber as a shock absorbent material in railway applications, which led to the establishment of his own firm, George Spencer and Company in 1852, with the aim of supplying india-rubber springs to the railway industry. He took out several patents himself over a number of years, but also became licensee for the William Adams patent bogie.

The problem of effectively guiding locomotives around curves had exercised locomotive engineers for many years, and William Fernihough, who had been locomotive superintendent at the Eastern Counties Railway for several years in the 1840s, had suggested as early as 1845 that short wheelbase bogies with a fixed pivot would create unacceptable levels of oscillation and vibration, which could be dampened by the use of a large bearing surface. This was the basic principle applied not only in William Adams' later patented design, but quite independently also by J.D. Wardale, the chief draughtsman at the locomotive builder Robert Stephenson, who had prepared drawings for a proposed 4-2-2T which incorporated spring-controlled side-play within the bogie. This particular design, intended for the Metropolitan Railway, was not subsequently built, and neither was the bogie design patented, although it was incorporated in an 1864 order for 4-4-0 tank locomotives for the Buenos Aires Great Southern Railway, and clearly demonstrates that other engineers were working on solutions to the problem.

The class 51 locomotives were a refined design of the earlier class 43, with larger diameter driving wheels at 5ft 9in incorporating steel tyres rather than iron, plus the improved bogie, which also enjoyed a longer wheelbase than hitherto. Once again Adams employed compensating beams linking the springs of the coupled axles.

Zerah Colburn, the editor of *The Engineer*, and his colleagues were invited to ride on the buffer beam of one of the new engines on a particularly rough section of track and reported thus:

> We found the motion as easy as that of a first-class carriage. Vibration is completely taken up by the india-rubber blocks, and the engine, instead of jerking and grinding round curves, swings round them with an ease which, if not surprising under the conditions of its structure, is at all events unique.

The Society of Engineers discussed the relative merits of the William Bridges Adams radial axlebox, and the William Adams bogie in late 1865, with one contributor speaking of it as 'a far superior contrivance to the radial axlebox'. The outcome was general approval, with a number of reservations expressed about the efficiency of, and derailments caused by, the W.B. Adams approach; a reference to the earlier trials of the *White Raven* on the NLR.

This was part of the inaugural address of the president, the aforementioned Zerah Colburn, and a wider discussion relating to locomotive adhesion. Adams also spoke about his design of boiler mounted sandbox and its steam assisted operation, plus the installation of a sand drying kiln at Bow.

The subject of the December meeting, at which he was also present, was the Giffard injector, an innovation which he had embraced. He stated that the injector, an invention of 1858, allowed enginemen the opportunity of more efficient boiler management, rather than the reliance on feed pumps, and that he could demonstrate a small, but noticeable, decrease in coal consumption. The relatively high boiler pressure, 160lb, of the NLR locomotives would also benefit from the adoption of the injector, but intriguingly he also spoke of trials at 180lb.

The boilers of the new 51 class contained 120 tubes of a fairly generous 2¼in diameter, set in rows ⅞in apart, which Adams believed would improve circulation and aid steaming capabilities. However, experience showed that hot gases passing through the centre of larger tubes were largely wasted, and smaller tubes were fitted following overhaul. Adams also experimented with balanced, or equilibrium, slide valves, to designs by the unrelated Thomas Adams and a Mr Manico. Thomas Adams was a Scot, born in 1826, who enjoyed mixed fortunes from his slide valve, but went on to design a safety valve which he manufactured at the delightfully named Ant and Bee Works of Gorton, Manchester. He died whilst holidaying at Sandown, Isle of Wight, in 1882. The experimental slide valves were short lived, being replaced by more conventional components.

In May 1865, Adams was asked to visit the LNWR works at Crewe, to investigate any cost saving measures that could be applied to locomotive construction at Bow, but back in London his mother died on the 18th of that month, having been widowed some ten years previously. However, a more joyous family occasion could be celebrated in that same year with the birth of another son, Herbert. The following year Isabella lost her father, Charles Park, who had retired to Porto Venere, Florence, after which her mother, Catherine, returned to England. Yet another son joined the family in 1867, intriguingly with the given names George Spencer.

Despite earlier unfounded worries, William was now building locomotives at a lower unit cost than the last bought in examples of 1861. Those Slaughter Grüning engines had cost £2,690 each, whilst the unit cost for four 51 class engines built at Bow in 1866 was only £2,314 5s 11d.

In February 1868, Adams was asked by the board to prepare a report on the railway's locomotive fleet, to include ages and likely remaining life. Curiously, he was also authorised to sell any of the engines built between 1850 and 1855, even though a programme for further replacement had not yet been agreed. During the previous summer he had submitted a proposal and been authorised to build six new locomotives to replace older engines at a cost estimated as only £2,000 each.

He duly reported to the Locomotive Committee in June 1868, and the following month the board accepted its recommendation that it be adopted. The report outlined a building programme for the next five years. Adams stated that:

of the entire stock of sixty-six engines, thirty-six are of the standard pattern, and the remaining twenty-eight, of which twenty have been ordered to be sold as the opportunity arises, are of various types it is not intended to reproduce, but it is proposed to replace by others of the standard pattern during the next five years in the following manner:

8 engines in 1868	£14,000
7 engines in 1869	£14,000
4 engines in 1870	£8,000
4 engines in 1871	£8,000
4 engines in 1872	£8,000
Less value of old materials	£6,750
Total	£45,250

The 51 class was an undoubted success and would no doubt have been assumed to be the 'standard pattern' referred to, but Adams was already working on a new design, still a 4-4-0 wheel arrangement, but this time with outside cylinders, and an inside framed bogie. This would become the standard tank engine for the NLR, the No. 1 class, which first made its appearance in July 1868.

The principal dimensions were cylinders of 17in bore and 24in stroke, with 5ft 4in diameter driving wheels, and 2ft 9in diameter leading wheels located in a bogie with a generous wheelbase of 5ft 8in. The grate area of the new class was very slightly larger than the 51 class, with the boiler pressed to 160lb, whereas the boiler barrel was very slightly shorter, as it was no longer necessary to allow for the requirement of the inside crank axle and motion.

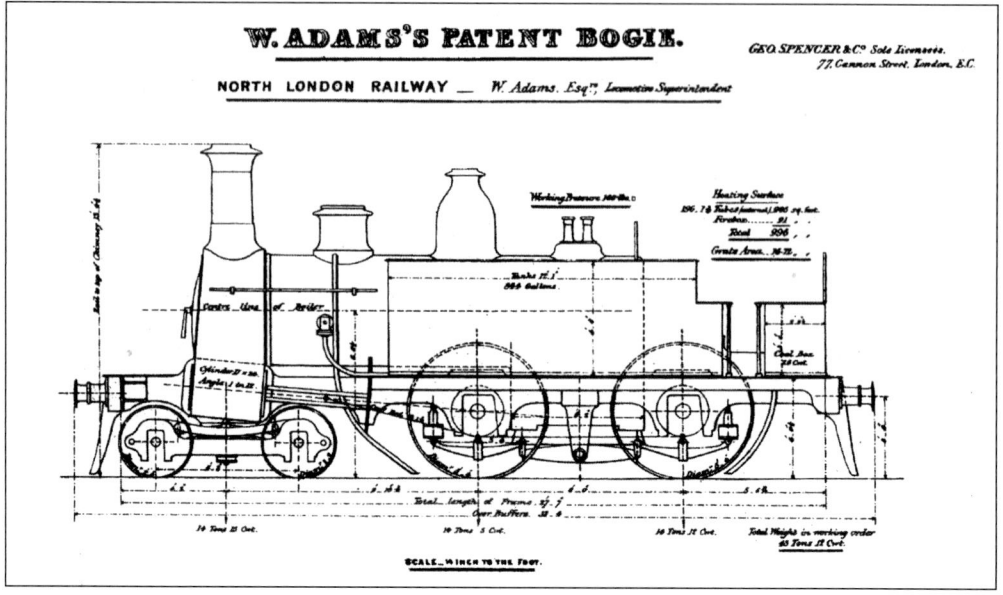

Spencer took advantage of the launch of the introduction of the No. 1 class for promotional purposes. (NLRHS, Jim Connor collection)

No. 1 class No. 27 when new, completed in January 1869 in works grey. Locomotives were repainted in the company livery after a period of running in. (NLRHS, Jim Connor collection)

Completed in June 1872, No. 1 class No.28 stands outside Bow Works in original condition. (NLRHS, Jim Connor collection)

The Innovative Years at Bow 59

Bow Junction circa 1870 with a No. 1 class locomotive, probably new ex-works in the headshunt, and one of the earlier Slaughter Grüning 4-4-0s outside the workshops. A Stothert & Slaughter 2-4-0 occupies the foreground. (NLRHS, Jim Connor collection)

The surging oscillating effect of the outside cylinders was reduced by the use of the patent bogie, and the cylinder design also eliminated the risk of crank axle failure, whilst also easing the daily lubrication routine for the driver. A total of thirty-four engines emerged from the works over an eight-year period, and from 1876 Adams' successor at Bow, John Park, continued with orders for another forty, with slightly larger cylinders of 17½in bore, and with 5ft 5in diameter driving wheels. Park would later report that each engine covered about 47,000 miles per annum, and whilst there had been crank axle failures with the earlier inside cylinder engines there had been no such problems with the No. 1 class.

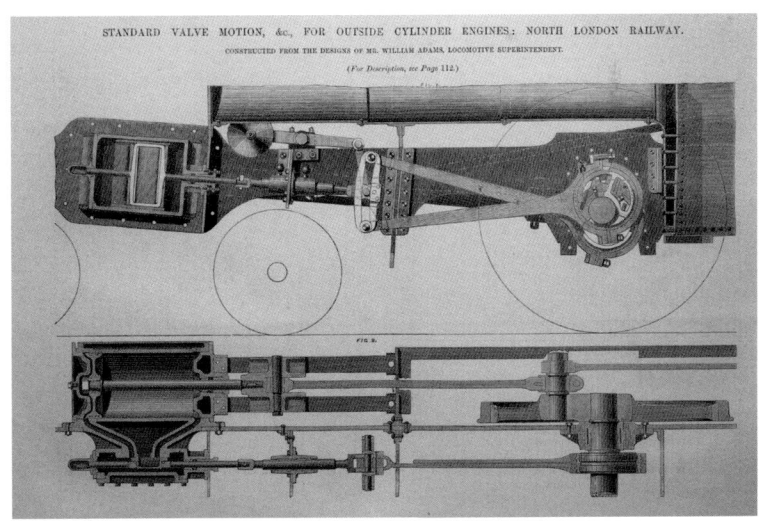

The valve motion of the No.1 class, from a review of the design by *The Engineer* in 1868.

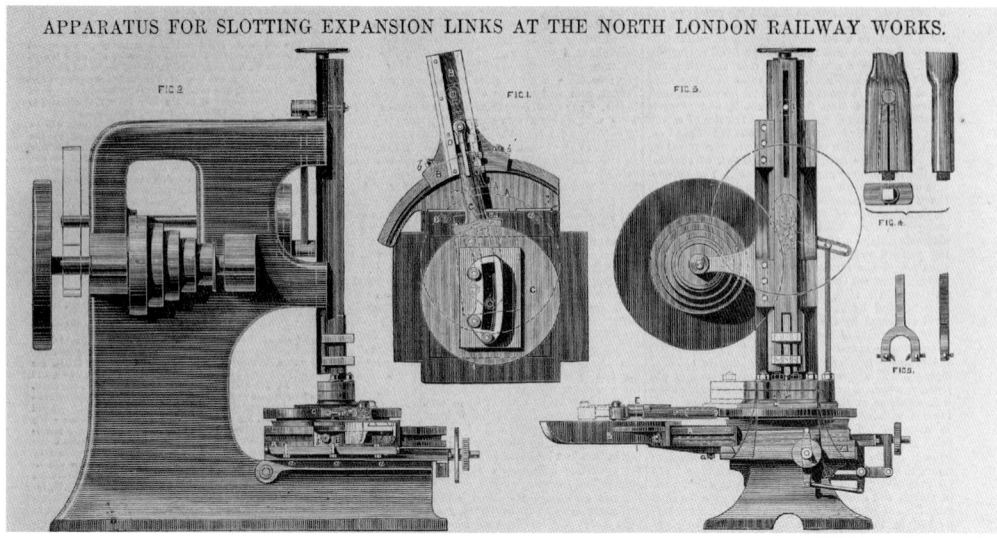

Amongst the equipment installed at Bow works was tooling for slotting locomotive expansion links. (Grace's Guide)

In 1889, during Park's tenure, apprentices at Bow built a one-eighth scale model of No. 60, which was exhibited at the Paris Exhibition that year, and subsequently displayed at Broad Street station for many years. Widely regarded as one of the finest and most accurate steam locomotive models ever built, it is now in the care of the National Collection.

The No. 1 class, with minor improvements, including the provision of a cab, continued to be built until 1907 under the then locomotive superintendent, H.J. Pryce. One of the last in service, by then numbered 6445, was sent to Derby for intended

The styling of the No. 1 class is shown to good effect in this view of No.48 at an unknown location. (John Scott-Morgan collection)

preservation in 1929, but was ordered to be cut up by William Stanier shortly after he took over at the LMS in 1932.

The first locomotives with the 0-4-4 wheel arrangement in Britain were outside-framed well tanks introduced by John Chester Craven of the London, Brighton & South Coast Railway and James Cudworth at the South Eastern in 1866, and two years later Adams rebuilt a pair of the Beyer, Peacock 0-4-2 saddle tanks, supplied eight years earlier, with a trailing bogie. This was probably an experiment to trial the patent bogie at the rear of the locomotive. The Cudworth engines were also derived from an existing 0-4-2 tank design, but that was a variation carried out primarily to increase coal bunker capacity. An earlier design of 0-4-4 tank locomotive had been patented and built in the USA by Matthias Forney in 1861, with flangeless wheels on the driving axle, and orders were completed for the elevated New York system and other city networks.

The modified engines numbered 38 and 41 were sold in 1874. The former, which had earlier been part of the W.B. Adams radial axlebox trial, passed to the Stafford & Uttoxeter Railway, where it was named *Ingestre*, surviving until 1882.

In 1858, the Manchester firm Sharp, Stewart built a four-coupled saddle tank locomotive for the N&SWJR to work the Acton to Hammersmith branch; it would be its only engine. Allocated works No. 1039, it featured inside cylinders of 13in diameter x 17in stroke, 3ft 10in diameter driving wheels, and a working boiler pressure of 120lb.

It was fairly soon taken over by the NLR, and allocated the number 37, although renumbered 29 in 1861. In 1872, by this time renumbered as 29A on the duplicate list, it was accepted into Bow works for conversion as a crane tank, to a design by William Adams. At this time, the concept of a crane locomotive was still fairly novel – the

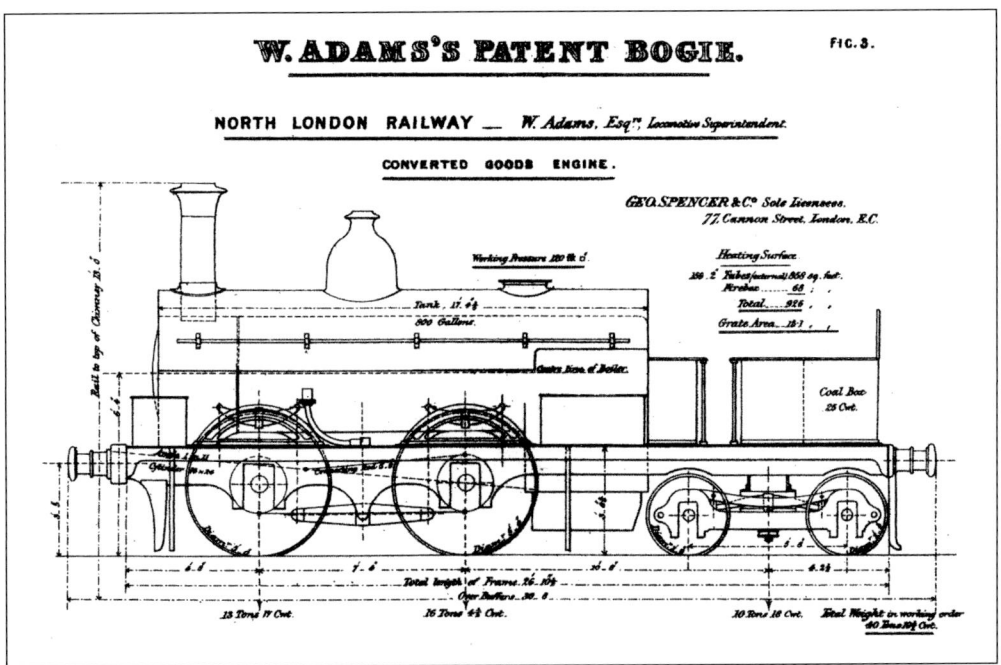

William Adams' first 0-4-4T, converted from Beyer, Peacock 0-4-2 saddle tank No. 38. (NLRHS, Jim Connor collection)

first recorded such rebuild was the conversion of a Francis Trevithick designed Crewe Goods by the LNWR in 1866, and the first purpose-built crane locomotive had emerged from the Glasgow works of Dübs and Company in 1868. The three-ton capacity steam-operated crane was fitted at the rear of the footplate above a new extended frame and trailing axle, which reduced the coal capacity to 8cwt. and, once outshopped, it was used primarily for shunting and lifting operations at the works.

It subsequently became LNWR number 2896, and then LMS 7217 after the grouping, with a further change in 1935 to 27217. At nationalisation, it was the oldest

The former North London Railway crane tank, as LMS No. 27217, at Devons Road shed c1938. (Paul Sankey)

27217 spent much of its life at Bow works, where it is seen in August 1937. (Paul Sankey)

locomotive to be taken over by British Railways, but only survived for a further three years, being withdrawn in 1951 as BR No. 58865 and scrapped at the ripe old age of ninety-three.

In the early 1870s, a variety of locomotive engineers were experimenting with steel fireboxes, initially with little success. William Adams conducted a trial with six fireboxes made from ½in Sheffield steel plates, but all had to be replaced after about 85,000 miles.

Another special project of 1872 was the construction of a directors' saloon which was built on a standard carriage underframe, but with buffers and conventional couplings at both ends. Facilities provided were a central saloon with tables and settees, a lavatory at one end (doubtless the only such on-board refinement on the NLR at the time), and a kitchen at the other.

Although William became a member of the Institution of Mechanical Engineers in 1859, proposed by one of its founding fathers, James Fenton, his relationship with it was somewhat complicated, as he resigned the following year, but re-joined in 1866. He was also granted membership of the Institution of Civil Engineers in 1869, when he resigned from the mechanical engineering body yet again. However, he re-joined in 1879, with his application on this occasion proposed by Louis Sterne, an American by birth, whose many engineering interests included an involvement with laying the first transatlantic cable, with Henry John Sillars Dübs, son of the founder of the Glasgow-based locomotive builder of that name, one of the seconders. He then retained his membership until retirement. He was also a member, and in 1870 president, of the Society of Engineers which had been established in 1854 by a small group of men who had been taught civil engineering at Putney College. Originally known simply as the Putney Club, it became the Society of Engineers in late 1857, and widened its membership base a few years later. His brother John would hold the presidency in 1875, followed by nephew Henry (son of John), in 1890. Henry Adams was by that time Professor at City of London College where he had founded a department of engineering. William also became a member of the London Association of Foreman Engineers and Draughtsmen, founded in 1852.

Two papers published in the *Proceedings of the Institution of Mechanical Engineers* in 1850 and 1851 have at times been erroneously attributed to our subject. Entitled 'Springs for Railway Carriages and Wagons' and 'On the Improvement in the construction of railway carrying stock', both were actually written and presented by one William Alexander Adams, son of William Bridges Adams, who was born in 1821 whilst his family were living in Chile. He later became a partner in his father's Fairfield Works enterprise. He subsequently entered into another partnership with George Allcock, engaged in the construction of railway rolling stock at the Midland Works, Smethwick, near Birmingham. He was elected a member of the institution in 1848, whereas 'our' William Adams did not seek membership for a further decade, and indeed was still engaged as a marine engineer in the Mediterranean at the time.

Apart from his professional and family life, Adams also appreciated music and the arts. Although not an instrumentalist, he was a talented amateur baritone and played a prominent role, along with John, in developing the Bow and Bromley Institute from the Working Men's Club in North Bow, becoming its President in 1872-3. Many of the men employed in his department became members, and the

Above: The 1866 application to re-join the Institution of Mechanical Engineers was proposed by Zerah Colburn, an American by birth who became editor of *The Engineer* but took his life only four years later at the age of thirty-seven. (Institution of Mechanical Engineers)

Left: William's third period of membership of the Institution of Mechanical Engineers was proposed by Louis Sterne in 1879. (Institution of Mechanical Engineers)

NLR Company allowed the use of the upper floors of a new enlarged Bow Station building, which opened in March 1870, to become the venue both for evening classes and performances, with a concert hall that could accommodate an audience of 1,200. George Bernard Shaw, as a young theatre critic, was sent to review a production, but was evidently so surprised to be asked to visit a venue unknown to him in the East End, that he felt obliged to carry his revolver. However, despite such initial misgivings, he reported that:

> The most accomplished English and foreign performers appeared, the charges for admission being sixpence and threepence. A means is hereby provided for enabling the humblest classes to become acquainted with at least one variety of the best music, performed in the best manner, at a nominal cost; and it is cheering to know that the movement has been attended by unqualified success.

In 1887, it became part of the East London Technical College, one of the early polytechnic institutions, and was later used by the Salvation Army before becoming a billiard hall. By now closed as a station, its final use was as a dance hall, the Bow Palais, until damaged by fire in 1956 and was later demolished.

Following the creation of the Volunteer Force in 1859, a part-time army of rifles, artillery and engineer corps, Adams enlisted in the Railway Rifles as a private, but soon gave it up because of his many other commitments. In 1874 he was tempted by freemasonry and was initiated into the Britannic Lodge No. 33 of the Ancient Order of Free and Accepted Masons but did not continue with his membership.

William Adams was instrumental in the formation of the Bow and Bromley Institute in 1879, housed in the upper floors of Bow Road station building. For a time, the family lived at Blenheim House adjoining the station. On the extreme right of the image is the Bryant & May Testimonial Fountain erected in response to the abolition of the match tax in 1872 following protests made by girls working in fairly dismal conditions at the nearby match factory.

The 1871 Census shows the family now living at Blenheim House, Bow Road, a property adjoining the station, with Adams' occupation given, perhaps surprisingly at this time, as civil engineer. George, aged four, and Sidney, just a year old, had joined the household which was assisted by two resident servants and a nurse.

After nearly twenty years with the NLR the time had come to move on, and Adams tendered his resignation on 28 July 1873, having accepted the position of Locomotive Superintendent at the GER. When he took over in 1854, the company owned 10 locomotives, but by 1873 the fleet had grown to a total of 66, a sizeable fleet for the mileage worked, plus a total of 422 carriages. With his successful work on the development of tank locomotives capable of rapid acceleration on steeply graded and sharply curved track and high capacity close-coupled four-wheel coach sets suitable for intensive suburban services with frequent station stops as well as his early advocacy of the continuous train brake, he could rightly be described as the father of the suburban train – an epithet so aptly made by E.H. Wilson in his study, *William Adams 1823 – 1904*, Transactions of the Newcomen Society 1986.

His eldest son, William John, had become an apprentice at Bow works, and he would remain there until 1876, when he left to join the Leeds firm of Tannett Walker and Company, a manufacturer of hydraulic pumps and equipment, joining as a draughtsman, but just one year later being promoted to the position of erecting manager, in which he supervised installations on site. In 1879, he entered into partnership with one Percival Everitt, trading as Everitt Adams and Company, agricultural and general engineers at St. Andrews Works, Great Ryburgh in Norfolk.

Everitt had been granted a patent for a ploughing engine the previous year, and although the firm was soon advertising other products such as the Eureka mower and a turnip thinner, the partnership was dissolved in 1882 and William John Adams moved on to become manager of the Vacuum Brake Company. Like his father, he was clearly fond of singing, as apart from their business activities, Messrs Everitt and Adams also made their mark as entertainers in the local community, performing for various charities, and a November 1879 report of an event in aid of the church restoration fund in Wells recorded that 'the very effective rendering of Offenbach's operetta by the duo was beyond all praise and highly appreciated by the audience'. In 1884 William John Adams went to Australia, and established William Adams and Company, initially working from a one room office in Bond Street, Sydney, which established agencies for a number of British railway engineering firms. Younger brother Alfred later joined him and opened a second office in Melbourne. The company claimed to supply 'everything for the engineer', and later expanded into heavy engineering itself, including the installation of steam turbines. In 1932, the company briefly even expanded into the manufacture of garden lawnmowers, using the brand name Presto – The Magic Mower, following the introduction of new tariffs which increased the cost of imported models. Although passing to new ownership in 1984, the company continues to thrive in the twenty-first century as William Adams Pty. Ltd., an agent and dealer for the Caterpillar brand. He also had an interest in the design and production of steel – rather than cast iron – axleboxes for railway wagons, and in 1891 the Patent Stamped Steel Axlebox Company was formed for their manufacture. However, the UK based company, which was located at Orchard Place, Blackwall, site of the Miller and Ravenhill shipyard, was wound up three years later.

EVERITT, ADAMS & Co.,
ENGINEERS,
St. Andrew's Works, RYBURGH, NORFOLK.

THE PATENT "UNIVERSAL" ENGINE.

For all systems of ploughing, this Engine is equally effective. For the Double Engine system one drum of wrought iron is mounted on the side of the boiler, and the rope led round a large pulley under tank to the plough or cultivator. The winding drum is driven **direct** from the crank shaft, thereby doing away with all clutches, bevil gear, coiling gear, and those parts about an engine most likely to get out of order, and also most costly to repair. For the single Engine systems two drums are used, one on either side of the boiler, and by means of leading pulleys on the tank and smoke box, the rope can be led away at any point in the compass. The Engine either remaining stationary or travelling along one headland.

For Traction or Thrashing purposes this Engine is equally efficient, as by a simple arrangement both drums can be taken off in a few minutes, and their weight dispensed with.

For heavy hauling, this Engine is admirably adapted, as the rope leads off parallel to the longitudinal axis of the boiler, so that the Engine can proceed the full length of the rope in advance of the object to be hauled, **paying the rope out in advancing,** and then set to work.

For Contractors' purposes, this Engine is also well suited.

Price £580.

The Everitt Adams 10hp Patent 'Universal' engine was advertised in 1880 at a cost of £580, together with an 8hp Contractor's engine for £500. (Peter Trent)

Adams actually left Bow in September 1873, to be succeeded by his brother-in-law, John Carter Park, who took over the following month. As a measure of how highly regarded he was, the *East London Observer* reported, in its edition of 1 November, that on his departure he was not only presented with a silver salver, plus a purse of one hundred guineas by the company, but fellow employees also subscribed to a silver epergne (an elaborate table centrepiece), a set of spoons, and an investment in railway stock. Isabella was also presented with a silver tea kettle. In its account, the newspaper also described how he had reduced costs during his time at Bow, and in particular the cost of building a locomotive had shrunk by one third.

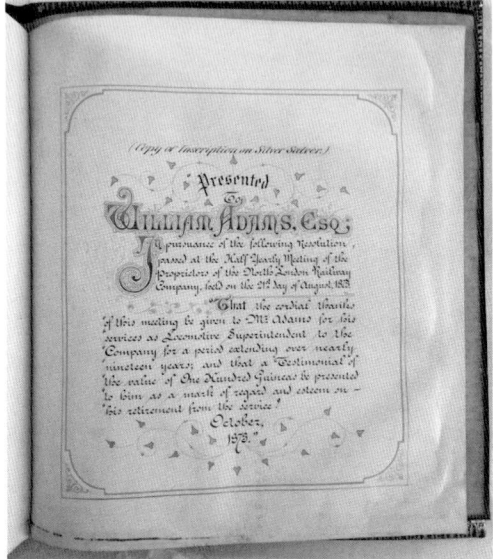

Left: A page from the illuminated testimonial title and book of subscribers presented to William on his departure from the North London Railway. (John Adams)

Below left and below right: William and Isabella in 1873. (Dr R.J. Adams)

Park was at the time Locomotive Works Manager of the Great Southern and Western Railway at Inchicore, Ireland, prior to which he had been locomotive superintendent of the Buffalo and Lake Huron Railway in Canada, from 1859 until 1864, when that company was taken over by the Grand Trunk Railway and his position made redundant. When William and Isabella had left Genoa, he remained with the Sardinian Navy, and served in the Crimean War, before returning to England. He then worked with the locomotive building firm Sharp, Stewart, until offered a post at the Longsight works of the London and North Western Railway by John Ramsbottom. He would remain with the NLR for twenty years, until ill health forced his resignation in January 1893. He retired to the south coast where he died at Christchurch three years later.

When he took over, most of the older, non-standard types of locomotive had gone, although one remarkable survivor was the old Rothwell 2-2-2WT, which was eventually withdrawn in 1877. He continued with the by now well-proven 4-4-0 tank locomotives for passenger work, with the Adams No. 1 class still being produced at Bow during the first three years of his tenure. Further locomotives were built from 1876 onwards, but with larger 5ft 5in diameter driving wheels and 17½in diameter cylinders, with the works also engaged in a steady programme of rebuilding and replacing earlier engines. From 1883, he adopted a new simple black locomotive livery with red, yellow and pale blue lining, and re-styled rectangular cast number plates which were broadly similar to the practice then favoured by Adams at the GER.

Like many other railway companies, the NLR renumbered engines as they were replaced, sometimes merely with an 'A' suffix to the original identity, but mainly in a separate three-digit (100) series, and it was not unusual for locomotives to be renumbered more than once. Those which lasted into the LNWR period of operation were renumbered once again by the larger company. The 1923 grouping resulted in the allocation of new numbers by the LMS, although not all the surviving former NLR engines actually carried them. A comprehensive tabulation of the myriad renumberings over the years is beyond the scope of this work, but the following examples are given.

The 1865 built prototype of the 51 Class was renumbered No. 109 in 1885. Standing on shed at Watford on 30 June 1923, it would be withdrawn two years later. (RCTS Archive, Collection John Vickery)

A view with more cab detail of No. 109 at Barking in April 1923. The LNWR had already allocated the new number 2874, but it would never carry its LMS allocated identity, 6435. (RCTS Archive, Collection John Vickery)

No. 1 class No.42 at Watford shed, c1920. The original No. 42, dating from 1874, was replaced by this locomotive, new in 1893. (RCTS Archive, Collection John Vickery)

No. 1 class No. 68 at Shoreditch, c1920. (RCTS Archive, Collection John Vickery)

Replacement of the old 43 class engines commenced in 1877, with Nos.43 and 44 being renumbered 43A and 44A as their original identities were allocated to new builds. Likewise, Nos.45 and 46 became Nos.103 and 104 in 1880, at which time Nos.43A and 44A were allocated Nos.109 and 110. To add further confusion these latter two were renumbered yet again just a few months later as Nos.101 and 102!

In a rather more straightforward process, Nos.47-50 became Nos.105-108 in 1883/4, and the four oldest engines of the class were withdrawn and scrapped in 1887. Nos.47 and 48 (as Nos.105/6) survived until 1915, and whilst the remaining pair, Nos.49/50, were still at work into the early years of the twentieth century, they were withdrawn in 1903 and 1908 respectively.

Likewise, the 51 class engines were renumbered as they were replaced by new build No. 1 class locomotives, with just three of the twenty-four strong class surviving long enough to be allocated LNWR and even LMS numbers, though the latter were never actually carried. Nos.51-56, dating from 1865/6, became Nos.109-114 as they were replaced in 1885, and Nos.11-14 followed on as Nos.115-118.

Park also continued to develop the works with the installation of new machinery and his desire to separate the running shed and workshop functions led to the opening of the Devons Road depot in 1884. However, he is doubtless best remembered for his own six-coupled outside-cylindered goods tank design, introduced in 1879, of which thirty were built, nearly half of them surviving into British Railways days. Several became well known in their later years as stalwarts of the Cromford and High Peak line in Derbyshire, and one example has been preserved at the Bluebell Railway.

A fine study of a No.1 class tank built by J.H. Pryce in 1906. Originally numbered 5 by the NLR, it is seen here in its final guise as LMS No. 6444. (Mike Morant)

Built by J.C. Park in 1876, LMS No. 6470 was nearing withdrawal in June 1928 when photographed at Potters Bar. (Mike Morant)

Chapter 6

A Move to Stratford

The GER had been formed in 1862 by a merger of the Eastern Counties, Eastern Union, East Anglian and other railway companies, to form a network that spread from London across East Anglia, serving cities such as Colchester, Ipswich, Norwich and Cambridge. In addition to the longer distance express services, it was also responsible, like the NLR, for an intensively worked suburban network from London.

Samuel Waite Johnson had been appointed Locomotive Superintendent of the Great Eastern in 1866, when he took over from Robert Sinclair who had held the reins at Stratford works for the previous ten years. In 1873 Johnson was appointed to the post of Locomotive Superintendent by the Midland Railway, at Derby, where he would remain until retirement in 1904. The attractive salary offered of £2,000 per annum was no doubt an inducement – the Great Eastern was not a railway known for generous remuneration. For Adams, the appointment as his replacement offered the challenge of providing locomotives for a wider variety of work, whilst being a very convenient move from a domestic aspect, with Stratford only a mile or two from Bow.

Stratford works had been in existence since the 1840s, originally built to serve the needs of the young Eastern Counties Railway, but it was by now unable to meet the needs of the enlarged system, with insufficient capacity for all locomotive and rolling stock construction. This was a factor not lost on the recently appointed chairman, Charles Henry Parkes, who sought self-sufficiency, although this would not be achieved for some years.

Although a proportion of locomotives would be constructed in-house throughout the Johnson and Adams years, this was hardly true for coaching stock, with virtually all new build contracts let to outside firms, with just a few design prototypes and special vehicles built at Stratford.

As early as March 1874, the board authorised its new department head the expenditure of £22,020 on a new boiler shop, extensions to other existing buildings and new machine tools. Later that year Adams also proposed other improvements to include a tramway for the conveyance of materials around the site, for which the board approved a figure of £890, to include new pits in the Tender Shop. Further developments quickly followed, as in April 1875 he was granted permission to double the size of the Foundry and extend the Locomotive Machine Shop, together with the requisite new tooling.

On taking over, he was immediately responsible for a varied locomotive fleet, the Y class 2-4-0 design of Robert Sinclair being the most numerous, with 110 examples on the books. The last of a class of thirty 0-4-4 side tanks designed by Johnson was just being completed, although construction was contracted out, orders being placed with both Neilson and the Avonside Engine Company. These were the first side tank locomotives with this wheel arrangement; other previous designs had used back tanks.

Given the experiment with the 0-4-4 conversions at Bow, this class would no doubt have been of particular interest. The T7 class 0-4-2T, intended for light passenger duties, was still in build at Stratford. Three had been completed in 1871, but the remaining twelve were outshopped between 1873 and 1875. Johnson had also been working on an inside-cylindered four-coupled tender design, the C8 class, of which two were built under his successor in 1874.

As designed, the T7 class had 500 gallon water tanks, but Adams increased the capacity on the later builds to 750, and some sported a stovepipe chimney, a feature which had been used on the GER by Sinclair but would later become a well-known Adams 'trademark'. The last five engines were fitted with Ramsbottom safety valves over the firebox in lieu of the Salter pattern of the original design used previously.

The two C8 class 4-4-0 tender engines, numbers 301/2, were designed for express passenger work, with 17in x 24in inside cylinders and 6ft 7in diameter driving wheels. The design featured the Adams bogie, but he also redesigned the cab and fitted Webb pattern injectors before they were completed. An elegant design, their appearance was somewhat marred by the use of second-hand Sinclair tenders. Apparently, they were initially fitted with iron fireboxes which required replacement with copper after only two years.

One of the first requirements from the locomotive department was for additional shunters for use in two London goods yards, Pepper Warehouses at Blackwall, and Devonshire Street at Mile End, both of which were subject to severe weight and size restrictions, with very tight curves. This was dealt with by an order placed with Neilson of Glasgow for a standard product of the company, a '12 inch Mineral Engine', with ogee-shaped saddle tank. Works number 1940 was delivered in 1874, with a second engine following a year later. They were allocated GER numbers 209/210. Two more followed in 1876, for use as Liverpool Street station pilots numbered 228/9. Subsequently rebuilt and reboilered two decades later, several survived into London & North Eastern days as the Y5 class, although number 229, which was sold off in 1918 for industrial use, has fortunately survived.

No. 306 was one of two C8 class 4-4-0 locomotives completed in 1874. Although a Johnson design, they were built with various Adams modifications, including his own bogie. (Tony Hisgett)

74 William Adams: His Life and Locomotives

Another priority was the need for more tank engines for suburban trains, especially with additional traffic generated following the opening of the new Liverpool Street terminus in 1874. Adams responded to this by following Johnson's example with a new 0-4-4 tank locomotive, the 61 class, of which fifty would be built between 1875 and 1878.

Samuel Waite Johnson introduced the first of a class of thirty 0-4-4 tank locomotives in 1872. They were the first side tanks of this wheel arrangement in Britain, and although later fitted with half type cabs by Adams, they offered minimal protection for the crew as built. No. 168 was a product of Neilson. (ETH archive)

Left: The 61 class to Adams' own design followed in 1875. With larger tanks, but smaller coupled wheels than the Johnson design, fifty examples were built, as exemplified by No. 74. (GER Society)

Below: No. 184 was one of the Kitson built engines, with various detail differences, for example the leading sandbox incorporated in the splasher. (GER Society)

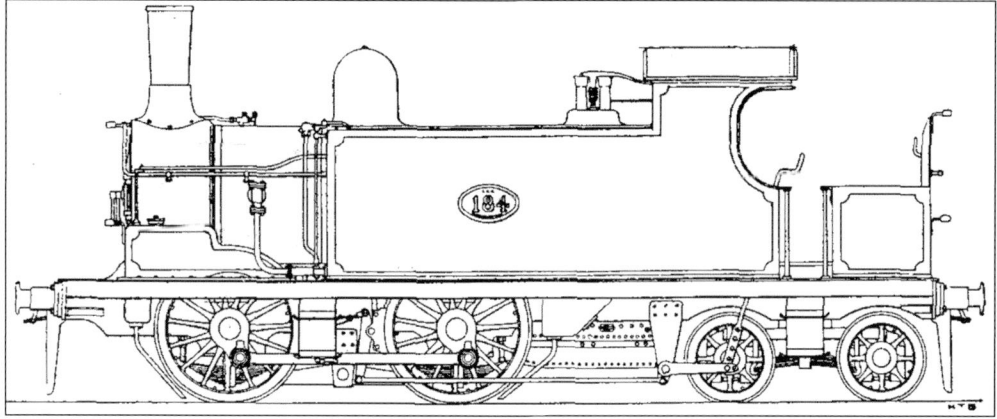

A Move to Stratford 75

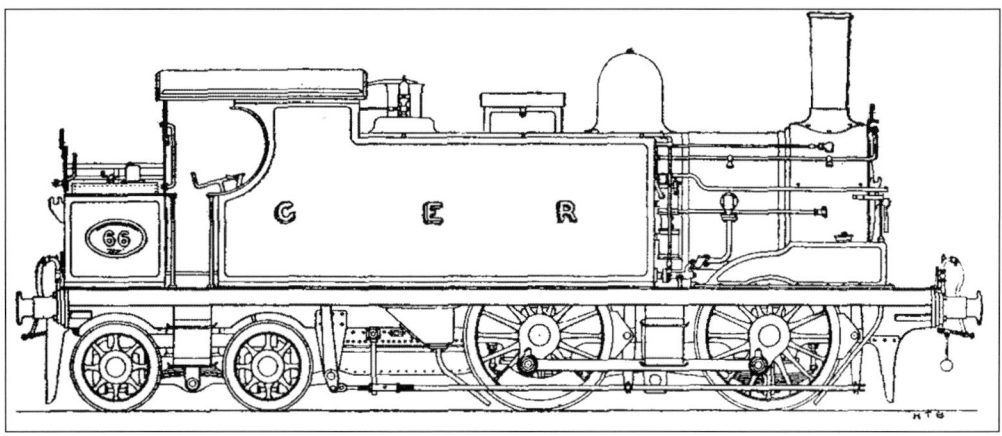

No. 66 as later rebuilt with enclosed cab and the Westinghouse brake. (GER Society)

61 Class No. 172, as rebuilt by Holden in 1891, heads a train from Epping/Ongar towards Liverpool Street at Stratford western junction, c1900. (Tony Hisgett)

Adams provided the Johnson 134 class with half-cabs and sandboxes, as exemplified by No. 193.

Of similar overall size, the Adams engines had smaller driving wheels of 4ft 10in diameter as opposed to 5ft 3in, which enhanced their acceleration, and increased water capacity. The construction was contracted out, with batches built by Neilson, Robert Stephenson and Kitson. They were numbered in three separate series, numbers 61-80, 170-184 and 211-225.

Although designed for suburban passenger work, some years later they were put to work hauling coal trains between Peterborough and London owing to a shortage of other more suitable locomotives. All were later reboilered and fitted with enclosed cabs, with some converted to oil firing, and the last of them survived in traffic until 1913. The Johnson 0-4-4Ts were also similarly rebuilt, with the last one withdrawn in 1912. Johnson had favoured a dark green locomotive livery, but William opted for plain black, with vermilion lining and buffer beams. Cast iron numberplates were rectangular in shape.

Adams next turned his attention to the need for engines for express work, and not only started design work on a new 4-4-0 tender locomotive, but set about planning a rebuilding programme, which would be done at Stratford, for the numerous Sinclair 2-4-0s which he had inherited.

There were in fact two classes of these Sinclair engines. The Z class, of which there were only six members, had been designed for goods traffic with 5ft 1in diameter driving wheels, introduced in 1858. These were not rebuilt – five were withdrawn in 1873 leaving just one, No. 306, to soldier on for two more years until it too met its end.

The other, much larger type was the Y class, of which no fewer than 110 had been built, Nos.307-416, between 1859 and 1866. They had been built by various firms including, unusually for a British railway, an order for twenty from Schneider et Cie at le Creusot in France. Sinclair had spent several years in France in the early 1840s as works manager for the Paris and Rouen Railway at Les Chartreux, a suburb of Rouen. Other batches built by R. & W. Hawthorn and Robert Stephenson featured an additional water tank below the footplate which was also intended to serve as a ballast weight. Although designed for freight traffic, like the Z class, they had been put to work, and proved themselves capable, on passenger services as well.

The most numerous locomotive type in the GER fleet when Adams took over was the 110 strong Sinclair 2-4-0 Y class. With a distinctively continental appearance, twenty had indeed been built at le Creusot in France. No. 374 is seen here in more or less original condition. (Tony Hisgett)

The engines had coupled wheels of 6ft 1in diameter, and 18in x 24in outside cylinders mounted horizontally. The tenders had wooden frames.

Most received new boilers during Adams' tenure, with pressure raised from 120 to 140lb, but twenty underwent a more substantial rebuilding, with the leading axle replaced by a four-wheel bogie, and driving wheel diameter increased by 2 inches. The 4-4-0 conversions were uprated as express passenger engines, and whilst withdrawals started in 1883, the last were not retired until 1894.

If the Y class rebuilds could be regarded as a success, Adams' own design for a new 4-4-0 was perhaps less so. Rather than continue with Johnson's inside cylinder concept of the two C8 engines, he chose to follow Sinclair with the use of outside cylinders – which of course had become the standard at the NLR. Known as the 265 class, but later widely known as Ironclads, twenty were ordered, ten from Dübs and Company in 1876, with the remainder from R. & W. Hawthorn the following year.

With large 18in x 26in cylinders, 6ft 1in driving wheels and a boiler pressure of 140lb, it has often been stated by historians that they were intended for express passenger work but were soon found wanting and relegated to freight duties. Indeed, E.L. Ahrons in his work, *British Steam Railway Locomotives, from 1825 - 1925*, wrote that many outside cylinder 4-4-0 designs of the period were unsuccessful, citing

Y class No. 0397 as rebuilt by Adams, but still a 2-4-0. (Tony Hisgett)

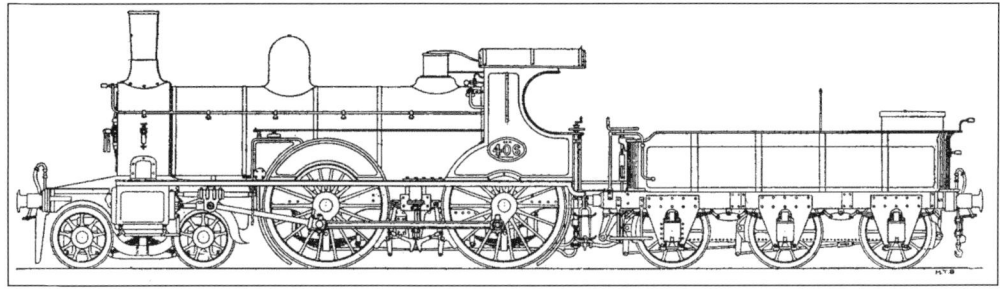

Sinclair No. 406 reboilered and converted with bogie to 4-4-0 configuration. Note also the Adams type single slide bar. (Great Eastern Railway Society)

Adams was of course very familiar with the 4-4-0 wheel arrangement at the NLR, but the 265 class of 1876/7 was, apart from the Sinclair rebuilds, his first such design for a tender locomotive. Known as Ironclads, No. 262 was one of ten built in Glasgow by Dübs & Co.

'an epidemic of large cylinders and small boilers'. E.H. Wilson, in his study of Adams' work, concludes that they had too low a power to weight ratio, being under-boilered, albeit with an overlong barrel, plus a lengthy, heavy frame which required additional bracing between bogie and leading driving wheels. This latter would be a recurring problem area with such designs. A more recent view is that they were intended for fast goods work from the outset, being fitted with a very powerful steam brake, but even if that were so, they still had a lower power to weight ratio than the Sinclair rebuilds, which were undoubtedly regarded as successful. Nevertheless, they gave steady service for nearly twenty years.

Adams designed a six-coupled tender locomotive with a leading pony truck intended for heavy freight trains of 700 gross tons, the first application of the 2-6-0 wheel arrangement in Britain, although not unusual in the United States. Trials conducted with trains of forty 10-ton wagons had shown that the existing 4-4-0 class was capable of handling such trains, although these engines experienced difficulties in adverse weather conditions, which no doubt led to the desire for greater adhesion. He ordered a total of fifteen from the Glasgow firm Neilson in 1878, but had left the GER before all were delivered, with modifications to cab and other details made by his successor. The first, No. 527, was named *Mogul*, and this became the generic name for this particular wheel arrangement.

This was the first six-coupled design by Adams, and it has been suggested that much of the detail design work was actually done by Deodatus Hilin Neale, who had been apprenticed to him at Bow, and subsequently held a position with Neilson, the chosen contractor, before returning to Stratford in 1878. Massey Bromley, who had been taken on as a pupil at Stratford by Johnson in 1869, very probably also had an input. Bromley had been to the USA in 1876/7, where he had the opportunity to inspect a 2-6-0 of the Baltimore and Ohio Railroad. Without a doubt, John Carter Park would have discussed his experience across the Atlantic with his brother-in-law, which may also have influenced the choice of layout. Certainly, the pony truck was the same as a design used on the Pennsylvania Railroad, and the cab had an American feel about it too. The earliest American 2-6-0 design dated from 1860, for the Louisville and Nashville railroad. In 1872, a paper on American locomotive design had been presented to the Society of Engineers by Vaughan Pendred, editor of the journal *The Engineer*, and in the discussion which followed, Adams acknowledged his interest in the subject. Early use in the USA of features such as the sandbox and bogie had influenced his own thinking and designs. He also referred to American practice in his own style of crossheads.

The coupled wheels were of 4ft 10in diameter, with those on the centre axle flangeless; the leading pony truck wheels were 2ft 10in diameter. Within a short period of their introduction, the flangeless wheels were replaced with flanged tyres. The outside cylinders, with the large diameter of 19in and 26in stroke, had Webb pattern circular slide valves, another unusual feature for an Adams design. Although the boiler had a total heating surface of 1,400 square feet compared to 1,109 square feet on the 4-4-0s, at slightly under 18 square feet the grate area was too small for the quantity of steam that the boiler would be required to supply.

No. 527 was the first of the 2-6-0 class, named *Mogul*, which became the generic name for the wheel arrangement. (Alon Siton)

Although an attractive design, the locomotives were essentially underpowered, and enjoyed short working lives. (ETH Archive)

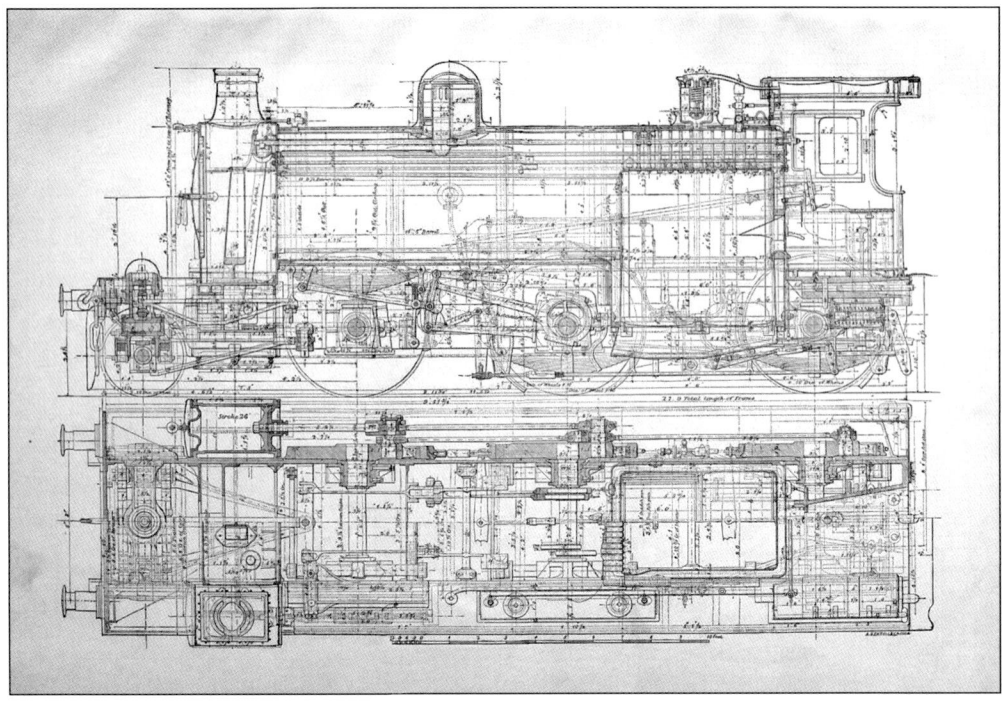

An 1879 drawing of the Mogul design. The first five 2-6-0s built were fitted with sandboxes on top of the boiler, but these were soon removed. As built, the class had flangeless driving wheels which were also replaced with conventional tyred rims.

Although powerful engines, they were soon found to be very heavy on coal consumption, and shed fitters were soon reporting trouble with the steam feed pipes to the cylinders, which were constantly working loose and proving difficult to keep steam tight. This was a problem which was never fully resolved – partly due to the difficulty in accessing the confined space occupied by the steam pipes within the frame structure. They were also prone to heavy condensation within the cylinders, and the rather complex design of the pony truck was less than effective. However, the boilers did not steam well, and the 2-6-0s were found to be less efficient and economical than the earlier Johnson 0-6-0 types on the heavy coal trains between Peterborough and London, which was after all, their raison d'être, and the entire class, Nos. 527-541, were withdrawn and broken up after only six to eight years of service in 1887.

In 1881 the Belgian State Railway ordered a copy of the 527 class from Neilson, numbered 512, and also known as *Mogul*, which it set to work on the Jemelle-Arlon section of the route between Namur and Luxembourg. However, no further orders were forthcoming, and in 1894 it was fitted with an experimental boiler, the invention of M. Docteur, an engineer at the railway's Luttre works. The firebox of the Docteur boiler was made of refractory brick surrounded by air, not water, and with a separate cylindrical steam reservoir atop the main boiler barrel instead of a steam dome. The modified engine was trialled until 1906 when withdrawn and scrapped, by which time it was the last surviving Adams Mogul.

One further 2-6-0 was built by Neilson for the Belgian State Railway in 1881, numbered 512 and later fitted with an experimental boiler by M. Docteur. (PFT archive)

The Docteur boiler featured a firebox lined with refractory brick, with a separate steam reservoir above the main barrel. However, it outlived the GER class, and survived until 1906. (PFT archive)

The next requirement was for a number of smaller tank engines for lighter passenger duties, and the result was the 0-4-2T K9 class, ten of which were built at Stratford in 1877-8, and were the only new locomotives built in-house during Adams' tenure. Allocated the numbers 7-10 and 20-25, they were perhaps not the most elegant Adams design, and utilised a number of parts which were available in store, including trailing wheels which had once formed leading wheels of the rebuilt Sinclair Y class, plus 4ft 10in diameter driving wheels from withdrawn former Eastern Counties engines. They had 15in x 22in inside cylinders and a working boiler pressure of 140lb. Weight in working order was 38 tons. They proved reliable, useful engines, with the last one withdrawn in 1907.

There was one further addition to the locomotive fleet, a vertical boiler tram engine bought from Messrs Kitson in 1878 for working the Millwall Extension Railway

Not, perhaps, William Adams' most attractive design, the K9 0-4-2T was intended for branch line work. No. 25 was photographed at Norwich. (Manchester Locomotive Society)

A total of ten K9s were constructed at Stratford in 1877/8. The trailing wheels came from some of the Sinclair Y types which had been rebuilt as 4-4-0s. An unidentified locomotive is seen here on the Waveney Valley line. (David Bousfield)

K9 class No. 23, completed in June 1878, is shown here as later fitted with the Westinghouse automatic air brake. (Manchester Locomotive Society)

which ran from Millwall Junction to North Greenwich. Kitson works No. T4, it was allocated GER No. 230. The use of conventional locomotives through the dock areas had been resisted, and it was acquired to replace a small former Eastern Counties 2-4-0T *Ariel's Girdle* which had worked the short line since its opening in 1872. However, only two years later the dock companies were persuaded that the fire risk from steam locomotives was not as great as they had perceived and the Kitson was redundant. It remained at Stratford for several years until it found an unusual new use as the operating mechanism for a new works traverser.

When reviewing the success of the Ironclads and Moguls, it must be remembered that Adams left the company within two years of the introduction of the former, and the first 2-6-0 did not arrive until after he had gone. Had he stayed he may well have reboilered the Moguls with a larger firebox, and reworked the steam passages to the cylinders, although this may have required completely new design and castings. A revised, simpler design of pony truck would also have helped. But of course, all of this work would have been very expensive, reliant upon sufficient available workshop capacity, and it would have been necessary to keep the modifications within the acceptable overall weight limit. The engines as built weighed 46 tons 12cwt.

Beyer, Peacock built a number of 2-6-0 locomotives for the New South Wales Government Railways in Australia, and two of this design were supplied to the Midland and South West Junction Railway in 1895 – the next use of the wheel arrangement in Britain. One of the pair survived in colliery use until the 1940s, but several Australian engines, built by both Dübs and Beyer, Peacock, have been preserved, the oldest dating from 1881. These were followed by an order for a total of eighty bar-framed engines from United States builders Baldwin and the Schenectady Locomotive Works for the Midland, Great Northern and Great Central railways. With 18in x 24in cylinders and 5ft 1½in coupled wheels, they also had a relatively high boiler pressure of 175lb. It was necessary to seek new locomotives from overseas builders because of a backlog of orders amongst British firms exacerbated by a strike in the engineering industry, but none of the American locomotives enjoyed a particularly long life either, with the last ones withdrawn by 1915. Intriguingly, John Henry Adams would become responsible for a fleet of British-built 2-6-0 tank locomotives in South America in the late 1880s.

In a view dating from the late nineteenth century, various Adams design and later locomotives are awaiting their next turn in Stratford Jubilee yard. (Tony Hisgett)

Until 1880 the London, Tilbury & Southend Railway's (LTSR) services were worked by locomotives provided by the Great Eastern Railway, but in June 1879 the LTSR placed an order for thirty 4-4-2 side tank locomotives with Sharp, Stewart, the first of which were delivered the following year, at a cost of £1,970 each. The design of these locomotives is normally associated with the name of Thomas Whitelegg, but it should correctly be attributed to William Adams. Whitelegg had been an apprentice and chargehand erector with Sharp, Stewart, and worked on contracts for the construction of locomotives for the GER at Ruston & Proctor, but was later employed in the Stratford drawing office. He left in 1879 to become the first locomotive superintendent of the LTSR. However, Arthur Lewis Stride, who had been appointed General Manager and Engineer in 1875, engaged Adams as consultant design engineer for the locomotives, and also in regard to the company's new works at Plaistow. The contract for the first locomotives was let to Sharp, Stewart in July 1879, several months before Whitelegg took up his new position at Plaistow.

The LTSR, like the NLR, operated a very intensive passenger service, but over longer distances with fast running, and Adams produced an essentially enlarged North London tank design, with a modified William Bridges Adams trailing axle.

These were the first 4-4-2 tank locomotives in the country, denoted class 1 by Plaistow, but soon dubbed Tilbury Tanks, and were joined by an order for a further six examples built by Nasmyth Wilson in 1892. They were numbered 1-36 by the LTSR, and all were named after places served. Principal dimensions were 17in x 26in outside cylinders, with 6ft 0in diameter driving wheels. Boiler pressure was 160lb, with a grate area of 17 square feet, 1,300 gallon water tanks and a total gross weight of 59 tons 12cwt. They were withdrawn between 1929 and 1935.

The LTSR subsequently built three successor classes with the same wheel arrangement, which maintained the bulk of passenger services until the last was withdrawn in 1960.

During the Adams years at Stratford, the carriage fleet increased from about 1,500 to 2,000 vehicles, consisting mainly of four-wheel stock, but with the introduction

Prior to 1880, London, Tilbury & Southend Railway services were run by the GER. No. 3 *Tilbury* was the third of a class of thirty-six engines built for the company, a design by Adams, although officially attributed to Thomas Whitelegg. The builders had offered an alternative lipped chimney, but Adams preferred to retain his own stovepipe design. (Alon Siton)

The majority of the LTSR Class 1 locomotives were built by Sharp, Stewart. However, No. 31 *St Pancras* was part of an order placed with Nasmyth Wilson. New in 1892, it remained in service until 1933, by then renumbered 2061. (Alon Siton)

of six-wheelers for longer distance express services, carriages could be allocated for specific use. He essentially continued with earlier Johnson styles, still based on wooden underframes, but with solebars strengthened with ⅜in steel flitchplates. The first steel underframes followed in 1879. Frederick Attock was appointed Carriage and Wagon Superintendent in 1874, taking over the role from his father, George, to whom he had been apprenticed at Stratford. In 1877, Frederick Attock departed to take on a similar position with the Lancashire and Yorkshire Railway.

In 1875/6, five six-wheel family saloons were constructed at Stratford, an innovation for the GER, which featured a first-class saloon, lavatory, a third-class compartment for accompanying servants, and generous luggage space. At the same time, the standard length of new four-wheel coaches was increased from 26 to 27 feet.

Having used gas lighting on the NLR, he introduced a similar system to replace oil lighting of GER suburban carriages in late 1877, towards the end of his tenure at Stratford. This time he opted for a system invented by Julius Pintsch, which was based on the use of a compressed gas obtained from distilled naphtha and which had been trialled by the LNWR. In September that year, he negotiated an arrangement with the Berlin-based firm Pintsch Pischon & Company to construct an oil gas plant at Stratford, which would produce enough fuel to supply 230 carriages, plus four purpose-built gas tank wagons. The first gas-lit carriages were used on services to Enfield, Walthamstow and Palace Gates. In May 1878, a new British entity, Pintsch's Patent Lighting Company, was set up in London to market the system.

Adams was an early advocate of continuous train brakes whilst at the NLR, but it was not until 1870 that the first trials were undertaken by Johnson at the GER, not only with the Clark chain brake, but Barker's Hydraulic and Fay's Manual systems too. Adams also trialled the Westinghouse air brake and the Smith vacuum brake in 1874. Whilst the vacuum brake was thought to be the more suitable for suburban trains, trials continued with the Westinghouse system, which led to the inconvenient use of two systems until the air brake was adopted as standard in 1882, after Adams' departure.

A new opportunity presented itself in 1878 and Adams resigned from the Great Eastern to be succeeded by Massey Bromley who had been at Stratford since commencing his pupillage with Johnson in 1869, and works manager since 1874. His salary on appointment to his former chief's role was £800 per annum. Perhaps surprisingly, before embarking on his railway engineering career, Bromley had graduated from Brasenose College, Oxford, in 1869, being awarded his Master's degree three years later.

Despite improvements carried out at Stratford in the Adams years, the works did not yet have sufficient capacity to build all the railway's new locomotives in-house, and it would still be necessary to rely on outside contractors until well into the next decade, with the last external contracts placed in 1883. Hamilton Ellis, in *Twenty Locomotive Men,* described the works at this time as 'being full of old-fashioned machines with poverty stricken stores'.

It would be fair to say that the Adams designs of the Great Eastern era met with mixed success, and to quote from Hamilton Ellis once again, 'he shone with a slightly impaired brilliance' at Stratford. He departed with presentations from his staff of a silver champagne cup, a silver tea tray and a large, ornate bracket clock.

Railway author and artist Cuthbert Hamilton Ellis wrote a series of articles featuring 'Famous Locomotive Engineers', including Adams, for the *Locomotive Magazine* in the late 1930s and 40s, many of which were later published in book form entitled *Twenty Locomotive Men.* Ellis also tried his hand at writing fiction and his 1948 novel *Dandy Hart* includes many scenes and genuine incidents from railway history in the mid-nineteenth century. Although much is centred around the London, Brighton & South Coast Railway, other railways and characters are introduced, as, for example, William Adams supposedly writes from the NLR's Bow Works on 15 March 1865 'My Dear Hart, I enclose letters of introduction to my father-in-law, Mr Park, of Genoa …' Hamilton Ellis was acquainted with Adams' son Charles, and also recalled seeing the GER clock, which he described as 'having a regular madrigal of chimes' in Charles's London office: unfortunately the clock's subsequent fate is unknown.

Massey Bromley clearly saw the merits of the 0-4-4T classes of both of his earlier bosses, and promptly placed an order for sixty to a design of his own, but for express work he opted for a 4-2-2 single driver arrangement rather than perpetuate the four-coupled layout. Bromley's tenure in charge at Stratford was short lived, as he resigned in 1882 in order to practise as a consulting engineer. He was tragically killed two years later in a railway accident at Penistone at the age of thirty-seven.

Chapter 7

To the South Western

For over twenty years, Joseph Hamilton Beattie held the position of locomotive engineer with the London & South Western Railway at its Nine Elms works. A highly regarded and competent man, he succumbed to diphtheria in October 1871 aged sixty-three, to be replaced by his 30-year-old son, William George, who had been employed in his father's drawing office for most of the previous nine years, latterly looking after the company's hydraulic machinery. However, despite the directors' hopes that he would exhibit similar qualities to his father, William Beattie's tenure leading the department was rather less than successful, both in terms of engineering and management competency, to the extent that he found himself obliged to tender his resignation in December 1877, on the grounds of ill health. Three years later, he also resigned his membership of the Institution of Mechanical Engineers, and retired into engineering oblivion.

The Locomotive Committee considered the various applications for the consequent vacancy on 16 January 1878 and invited William Adams to attend at Waterloo Bridge the following day. After 'discussion and explanation' he was appointed to the post of Locomotive and Carriage Superintendent, at the annual salary of £1,500, with the company entitled to free use of all his patents. At its next meeting on 6 February, it was noted that he would commence work at Nine Elms the next day.

The Nine Elms site was established close to the original London terminus of the London and Southampton Railway at Vauxhall before the extension to the new station at Waterloo was opened in 1848. The works had initially been built on the north side of the running lines but was relocated to the southern side in the 1860s, and in 1876 a semi-circular roundhouse running shed had been added.

Like the Great Eastern, the LSWR was responsible for a network of suburban services, this time serving the area around south west London, with longer distance passenger services to Portsmouth, Southampton, Salisbury and Exeter, plus freight traffic to and from Southampton docks.

Archibald Scott, the General Manager at the time of Adams' appointment, had previously managed the traffic department – a role he had assumed in 1852, and Adams, with his broader experience gained at the NLR and GER, rapidly became frustrated by many of Scott's working practices, which he regarded as outdated and unfit for purpose in an increasingly complex railway, and which undoubtedly had a significant impact on the profitability of the company. As the new locomotive chief developed and improved his own department's management, plus the capability and efficiency of Nine Elms works, his opinions were often favoured by the wider Court of Directors (as it preferred to style itself) in preference to those of Scott, whose inefficient style of management resulted in excessive operating costs.

The Locomotive Superintendent at this time was also in charge of the Carriage and Wagon Department and Adams was concerned at the lack of any coherent programme to replace and update worn out or obsolete rolling stock. Much of the blame for this can be laid at the doorstep of Scott, the General Manager, who for years had pursued a programme of minimal carriage replacement and renewal. He preferred to maintain old carriages just enough to keep them in service, with the result that the image of and quality of service offered by the LSWR no longer compared favourably with rivals such as the Great Western Railway on the main line to the south west. A year or two after Adams' appointment, the board attempted to separate the responsibility of the Carriage and Wagon Department from the Locomotive Superintendent, a move which was opposed by both Adams himself and Scott – one occasion on which the two men did agree!

Oversight of the combined department was a heavy burden in view of the scale of renewal and upgrading required, and it is entirely possible to sympathise with the directors' view that passenger and freight stock would be better managed separately, but for the time being the status quo remained.

The primary task was to assess the condition of the existing fleet and evaluate the future requirements of the railway. As at Stratford, the company did not have sufficient works capacity to build for its own needs and was heavily reliant on private locomotive builders, and part of the review process was to consider the modernisation and future capabilities required of Nine Elms works.

He was surprised to discover that Nine Elms did not keep a supply of spare boilers ready to be exchanged at overhaul, which led to the hopelessly inefficient practice of protracted overhauls as the boilers of individual locomotives were repaired whilst they were in the works, not only resulting in excessive downtime for engines, but a waste of valuable workshop space. Towards the end of his first year at Nine Elms, he was able to take the members of the Traffic Committee on a tour of the works to demonstrate that a combination of new equipment and replacement of skilled labour by unskilled where possible, for example in the foundry, had already reduced repair costs of locomotives per train mile by nearly ten per cent.

Adams inherited a variety of locomotive types, predominately 2-4-0s in tender and tank form, plus six-coupled engines for freight work, and a batch of 4-4-0 tanks of the Metropolitan Railway's A class design.

A year after taking office, Joseph Beattie had introduced an inside cylinder 2-4-0 for express passenger work in 1851, followed by an outside-cylindered design for fast goods work in 1855, and his Canute class of single drivers a year later. An innovative engineer, he had pioneered the use of coal, rather than coke, as a fuel for steam locomotives and was an advocate of feed water heating.

Excessive smoke caused by the inefficient burning of coal in early locomotives with poorly understood draughting arrangements led to the use of coke, a less suitable and more expensive fuel, but a solution to the emissions problem. Beattie was not alone in seeking a remedy, as James Cudworth at the South Eastern Railway and the LNWR's James McConnell were busy experimenting with their own ideas too.

In essence, all three developed a form of double firebox, with two separate grates, divided either longitudinally or laterally, sometimes combined with an additional combustion chamber extending into the boiler barrel. The Beattie double firebox consisted of two grates, separated laterally, each fired via its own firehole door, the rearmost grate (backhead end) fired with coal, which then allowed smoke and volatile gases to pass over the hot front end grate fired with coke, which resulted in further combustion and a significant reduction of smoke. The smoke problem was eventually neatly resolved following a series of experiments conducted between 1856 and 1860 by Charles Markham and Matthew Kirtley at the Midland Railway, with the installation of a brick arch at the front of a single firebox, below the rear tubeplate, a deflector plate, or baffle, above the firehole door, and an adjustable damper. This allowed the further combustion of volatile gases during their passage to the firetubes, and with careful use of the damper, a high degree of control. Enginemen of today will recognise this as standard practice, but Cudworth and Beattie still chose to continue with their own more complex arrangements and resultant higher maintenance costs.

His next class of outside cylindered express 2-4-0s introduced in 1859 were the first British engines with 7ft diameter coupled driving wheels. The railway also operated a large fleet of 2-4-0 well tanks on its suburban network.

The last order for new engines before William Adams took office was for twenty 4-4-0 tender locomotives in 1876/7 from Sharp, Stewart to a design by William George Beattie. They were poor performers, being indifferent steamers, and like Adams' own 4-4-0 design at Stratford, the cylinders were very large at 18½in diameter bore and 26in stroke. Also problematic were piston valves, which led to a litany of broken valve spindles caused by trapped water, plus other faults blamed on poor workmanship and quality of build.

Joseph Beattie had favoured feedwater heating, with boilers supplied by pumps, and Adams embarked on a gradual programme of replacement with injectors, often initially retaining one pump, whilst removing the hot water provision and installing just one injector. Where appropriate, the by now outmoded Beattie model of the double coal burning firebox was replaced by a conventional firebox as locomotives were overhauled, but withdrawals of the remaining single drivers and earliest classes of 2-4-0 commenced shortly after Adams took over.

In his first weeks of office, Adams took No. 348, one of the poorly performing W.G. Beattie 4-4-0s, out of general service, using it for testing purposes over the following months to formulate a rebuilding scheme. Eventually it and five others were modified with conventional fireboxes, smaller 17½in diameter cylinders with slide in lieu of piston valves, and injectors replacing pumps and feedwater heaters. Ten years later, 348 was the first to be fitted with an Adams boiler, and was eventually one of the last to be withdrawn in 1905.

Within months of taking over, Adams ordered ten spare boilers from Beyer, Peacock, which would be suitable for several classes, and in 1885 he produced a new boiler to his own design for the Vesuvius class 2-4-0 of 1869-75, which were still highly regarded as good performers. The rebuilt engines were outshopped with new cabs and standard Adams stovepipe chimneys, and in 1886 two of the earlier 231 class 2-4-0s dating from 1866 were also fitted with new Adams boilers. Other Centaur class 2-4-0s were rebuilt in 1888 with refurbished boilers from withdrawn Single Frame Goods engines, but with Adams pattern cabs.

The standard class of 2-4-0 well tank, consisting of no less than eighty-eight locomotives, handled the bulk of London suburban services. Like other classes, the

Eight of the poorly designed and built W.G. Beattie 348 class were rebuilt in the Adams years, including No. 351 seen here as modified. (John Scott-Morgan collection)

No. 353 was similarly rebuilt and was one of the class to be withdrawn in 1905. (John Scott-Morgan collection)

old Beattie fireboxes were gradually replaced, and in 1878 Adams ordered two new spare boilers, but by 1882 it was apparent that large numbers would soon be replaced by new engines, and it was decided to overhaul half the class with new boilers, but withdraw others as repairs became due. Although reboilered, the well tanks were not always suitable for the work found for them as they were cascaded around the network, and a total of thirty-one were rebuilt as 2-4-0s with second-hand tenders, giving them

To the South Western 91

No. 365 received only minor modification and shows the original cab styling. The engine was withdrawn in 1898. (John Scott-Morgan collection)

The Vesuvius class of 2-4-0 express locomotives was Joseph Beattie's final design, and No. 280, formerly named *Persia*, was rebuilt and reboilered by Adams in 1886. (ETH Archive)

a much-improved range. The remaining well tanks were gradually withdrawn, but in 1893 one, No. 248, was sent to the Bodmin and Wadebridge Railway, a journey undertaken by sea because of the then isolated nature of the line, and by 1899 only three of the celebrated Beattie well tanks remained on the books. With Adams boilers and cabs they became synonymous with the china clay trains of the Cornish branch, and with a further later reboilering by Drummond, continued to work the line until withdrawn in 1962.

As the Double Framed Goods 6-coupled engines were replaced in the mid-1880s, Adams considered rebuilding twenty-four as 0-4-4 tank engines, but the cost of such a proposal was uneconomic, and it was therefore decided to build new tank locomotives, and simply

No. 329 was one of the celebrated trio of Beattie well tanks which survived working north Cornwall china clay traffic until 1962, and was rebuilt with an Adams boiler from withdrawn 2-4-0 No. 195 in 1892. (John Scott-Morgan collection)

No. 0196 was one of thirty-one Beattie well tanks rebuilt as tender locomotives between 1883 and 1887. Although some of the converted engines retained their original boilers, 0196 has received an Adams type with stovepipe chimney, and the 0 prefix indicates that a new O2 class locomotive has taken its original number, thus relegating it to the duplicate list. (John Scott-Morgan collection)

To the South Western 93

reboiler only the best of the goods class. Adams boilers were also fitted to some, but by no means all, single-framed Beyer, Peacock and Ilfracombe Goods six-coupled classes.

W.G. Beattie had also ordered a batch of outside cylinder 4-4-0 tank locomotives from Beyer, Peacock, to a design supplied to the Metropolitan Railway, which became known as its Class A. Delivered in 1875, they proved problematic on the south western routes for which they were intended, and were transferred to the London area for

Single Framed Beyer Goods No. 162 was one of a batch ordered by W.G. Beattie in 1877. It is seen here as reboilered by Adams, and with Drummond chimney. Renumbered 162A in 1916, it was withdrawn in 1924. (John Scott-Morgan collection)

No. 287 was a member of the Beyer Double Framed Goods class ordered by Joseph Beattie, and delivered in 1873. It was rebuilt with Adams boiler and cab in June 1895, in which form it worked for another nineteen years. (John Scott-Morgan collection)

suburban work. In an attempt to improve the riding quality, one engine, No. 318, was in fact fitted with an Adams bogie, but it remained the only example so treated.

After only three months in post, Adams presented drawings for a new 4-4-0 tank locomotive to the Locomotive Committee, with a request for approval to construct 'at the least a class of twelve new bogie tank engines'. This was subsequently granted in June 1878, but as there was a lack of capacity for any construction in-house, the

Classmate No. 273 was similarly rebuilt and renumbered 273A in 1917, by which time it carried a Drummond chimney. (John Scott-Morgan collection)

Metropolitan tank No. 318 was modified with an Adams bogie – the only member of the class altered in this manner. (ETH Archive)

The additional length of the Adams bogie can be appreciated when compared to this view of a Metropolitan tank with original design. (ETH Archive)

contract was let to Beyer, Peacock at a cost of £1,995 each. By midsummer he had also proposed the scrapping of ninety-three old carriages, and had won approval to order thirty new composites, with a request for a further twenty-two second-class coaches under discussion. New woodworking machinery for the Carriage and Wagon workshops was on order, and his in-tray had also included, amongst many other things, a claim for infringement of the 'Sheeham Process for Steelyfing Iron' patent rights – rejected by Adams and the Locomotive Committee.

The long summer days were memorable for an important family occasion too, as eldest daughter Catherine married Dudley Maitland on 12 June 1878, at St John's Church, Hackney, with William and Isabella's first grandchild, Leslie George, being born on 18 March the following spring. He was joined by a younger sister, Isabella, in August 1880. Apart from membership of the various engineering professional bodies, Adams had also become involved with the London and Suburban Railway Officials' Association, taking on the role of president in 1879-80.

The new locomotive design was the first 4-4-0 tank since North London days but was slightly larger and heavier than the earlier No. 1 class with larger cylinders and driving wheels, yet with a smaller grate area and total heating surface. The following table compares the basic dimensions of the new design, which became known as class 46, with the old NLR No. 1 class, and the Metropolitan tanks also in the LSWR fleet.

Class 46 No. 123 as built in 1879.

Comparative main dimensions of NLR No. 1, LSWR class 46 and Metropolitan 4-4-0 tank locomotives:

	NLR No. 1	LSWR 46	Metropolitan
Cylinders	17 x 24in	18 x 24in	16 x 20in
Leading wheel dia.	2ft 9in	2ft 6in	3ft 0in
Coupled wheel dia.	5ft 6in	5ft 7in	5ft ½in
Heating surface	1,015sq ft	983.75sq ft	912.60sq ft
Grate area	16.62sq ft	16sq ft	17.40sq ft
Boiler pressure	160lb	160lb	120lb as built
Water capacity	844gallons	1,000gallons	1,000gallons
Axle loading	14.25 tons	17.65 tons	15.475 tons
Weight (working order)	43.60 tons	50.80 tons	42.80 tons

The new locomotives were numbered 46, 123/4/30/2/3, and 374-9. The latter series were fitted with circular slide valves of Church's pattern, which suffered lubrication problems leading to rapid wear, and were soon replaced with a conventional pattern. These sturdy machines, with their rather small solid disc bogie wheels, which soon attracted the nickname Ironclads, were set to work in the London area. Within a few years the civil engineer complained about their weight, which resulted in them being rebuilt as 4-4-2 tanks. Although the civil engineer wanted a maximum tank locomotive weight of 52 tons, the rebuilt engines, although with a stated axle weight of 17.30 tons, still exceeded the total by 3.75 tons – and that is thought to be an optimistic figure.

However, despite the misgivings about their weight, the engines gave steady, reliable service, each averaging around 32,000 miles per year until withdrawn between 1921 and 1925. No. 376 was actually sold in 1914 via the dealer Bute Works and Supply

46 class No. 374 after rebuilding in 1886 as a 4-4-2T. (John Scott-Morgan collection)

No. 44 with Drummond chimney circa 1905. Note the solid bogie wheels which led to the nickname Ironclads. (John Scott-Morgan collection)

Company to the Brecon & Merthyr Railway, where it was found to be unsuitable on such a steeply graded line, and the hoped-for sale of further examples fell through.

The class 46 led to the design of a comparable mixed traffic tender version which was duly authorised in November 1878, and a contract for the construction of twelve locomotives was let once again to Beyer, Peacock. Designated the 380 class, they were allocated numbers 380-91 and, as before, the solid bogie wheels attracted a nickname, hence they were more generally known as Steamrollers. Wheels and cylinders were the same as the class 46 tanks, but the boiler was slightly larger, and with a bigger firebox provided a total heating surface of 1,126 square feet, with a grate area of 17 square feet. A further trial was made with Church's circular slide valves fitted to half of the order, but once again the shortcomings of the design led to their replacement within a year or two. Several of the new engines were allocated to Southampton (Northam) and Salisbury where they were found to be too heavy for certain duties. Reallocated to Nine Elms, several were later transferred to Devon. In the Edwardian years, they were often relegated to goods duties. Most were laid aside for withdrawal in 1913, but five were reinstated and returned to traffic with the last working examples being condemned in 1924.

The first of the many 4-4-0 designs at Nine Elms was the 380 class. No. 384 is seen in the mid-1890s in holly green livery. (John Scott-Morgan collection)

Like the 46 class tanks, the 380s were fitted with solid bogie wheels, and they soon acquired the nickname Steamrollers. No. 381 is seen at Strawberry Hill MPD. (Mike Morant)

No. 380 is seen on a goods duty at Exeter St David's in 1904. (John Scott-Morgan collection)

The 135 class was the first express design by Adams for the South Western, with Beyer, Peacock contracted to build twelve, numbered 135-46, in 1880. Coupled wheels were of 6ft 7in diameter, powered by 18in x 24in cylinders. With a boiler pressure of 160lb, heating surface of 1,216 square feet and a grate of 17.8 square feet, the total engine weight was 46½ tons. They proved to be an excellent investment, with each engine recording a mileage of about 36,000 in 1882, but once again the civil engineer was not entirely happy about their weight. The entire class was laid aside in 1913, but like the 380 design, several of the better engines were reinstated and continued to work into the next decade, although only one, No. 139, by then renumbered 0307, ran in the first months of the Southern Railway regime, being withdrawn in December 1924.

In 1882, Beyer, Peacock received an order for four 4-4-0 locomotives for the Lynn and Fakenham Railway, to a design which was in essence a lighter version of the LSWR 135 class, with 6ft 0in diameter driving wheels and 17in x 24in cylinders, with a heating surface of 1,083 square feet, the locomotive without tender weighing in at 38.35 tons. It has been suggested that William Adams was engaged as a consultant for the design (Brian Reed, *150 Years of the British Steam Locomotive*, 1975), and whilst there is certainly an Adams influence, there are still recognisably Charles Beyer features, common to other Gorton Works products. If it were entirely his work, Adams would almost certainly have continued his preference for single slide-bars for example. The Lynn and Fakenham had become part of the Eastern and Midlands Railway before its engines were delivered, but the class eventually totalled fifteen, with the remainder delivered in 1888. The Eastern and Midlands in turn became part of the Midland and Great Northern Joint Railway in 1893. All were later rebuilt with Midland Railway C type boilers, which had larger fireboxes and smaller barrels than hitherto, and were

The 135 class, with 6ft. 7in. coupled wheels, was designed for express work, and No. 141 approaches Talbot Woods bound for Basingstoke in August 1902. (John Scott-Morgan collection)

No. 146 when new in 1881. Note the shunter's footsteps and handrails on the tender. (ETH Archive)

henceforth designated as class A. Generally known by staff as Peacocks, they were gradually displaced from 1894 onwards from front line to secondary duties, but they were well enough regarded for eight of them to be rebuilt a second time between 1914 and 1927. The boiler was slightly higher pitched in the Class A rebuilds, which, with an extended smokebox, Great Northern style chimney, and modified cab, all contributed to an altered appearance, disguising the Adams origin. Only five of the class A Rebuilds were still in service when the London and North Eastern Railway took over in 1936, with three more withdrawn shortly afterwards. The class became extinct in 1941.

Perhaps more intriguingly, the New South Wales Government Railways class H.373 (later Z17) of 1887 also bore an uncanny resemblance to both the LSWR class 135 and Lynn & Fakenham designs, but were built by Vulcan Foundry. One of the Australian engines has been preserved at Thirlmere, albeit fitted with a later boiler with Belpaire firebox.

When William Adams first took up his position at Nine Elms the family were living at Stormont House, Downs Park Road, Lower Clapton, and did not move immediately, but on 24 May 1880 they moved into a new home at Salisbury House, Upper Richmond Road, Putney. Stormont House later became a school for blind boys, and a Red Cross Hospital during the First World War. Although the building was destroyed by enemy action in the 1940s, the name is still retained by a new special needs school built on the site. William and Isabella now had a family of ten children, with Amy the youngest at just six years old, and two years later on 25 April 1882, their eldest son, William John, by now 29, married Alice Slater at St. Olave's Church, Bermondsey. The next year William John and his wife departed for a new life in Australia, and thus William and Isabella's grandchildren Dorothy, Alice and Dudley were born many thousands of miles away in New South Wales.

Despite his initial analysis and assessment of future requirements, as early as 1881 Adams was faced with a locomotive shortage, created in part by an increase in demand for suburban passenger traffic, and he proposed that the railway urgently needed thirty new tank locomotives and twenty-four engines for goods work. The immediate shortage could be addressed by lengthening boiler washout cycles and delaying minor repair work, but this was only a very short-term measure which would

Bearing a marked resemblance to the 135 and 380 designs for the LSWR, the Lynn and Fakenham Railway ordered a lightweight 4-4-0 from Beyer, Peacock, with the first locomotives delivered in 1881. (ETH Archive)

inevitably only store up problems for the future. He also submitted a report stating that with the limited site available, Nine Elms locomotive works could only be expanded by relocating the carriage and wagon department elsewhere, and the space thus vacated could form a new erecting shop. The re-equipped works would then be capable of building twenty-five locomotives each year, as well as performing eighty overhauls and 100 casual repairs. In August 1881, another William Beattie, a nephew of Joseph Beattie, was appointed as Adams' assistant, an office he held for less than eighteen months as he died on 19 December the following year at the age of only forty-six. He had been born in Liverpool in 1836 and began his career as an apprentice farrier to his father before moving on to Dallam Forge in 1852, a Wigan-based firm which had recently been awarded a gold medal at the Great Exhibition of 1851 for 'excellence of iron and of railway plant'. He joined the LSWR in 1855, to serve under his uncle in the Nine Elms drawing office, to be followed a few years later by his younger brother Francis.

Two former apprentices from Great Eastern days at Stratford who followed Adams to Nine Elms also played key roles in planning and managing the extensions and improvements to the works. Gilbert Henry Garrett had initially been articled at Bow in 1871, but then followed his boss to Stratford, before being appointed as a draughtsman at Nine Elms in March 1878. During his time at Stratford, he had managed the gas works and overseen the installation of carriage gas lighting. His colleague Ralph Archbould had commenced his Stratford apprenticeship in 1874, again relocating to Nine Elms four years later. Adams must have been well satisfied with them, as he proposed them both for membership of the Institution of Civil Engineers in 1881, whilst two years later Garrett married his daughter Isabella. Archbould subsequently went to America for a few years, returning to manage an electrical engineering firm. After a period in Glasgow as manager of Louis Sterne's engineering company, which manufactured refrigeration equipment amongst a range of products, in 1885 Garrett went on to manage the locomotive building works of Robert Stephenson at Newcastle. Tragically, both men died in their early thirties, in Garrett's case leaving William Adams a widowed daughter and two young granddaughters.

In 1882, Adams also expressed his concern about the railway's insufficient quantity of carriage stock and inadequate renewal programme, and the resulting difficulties in keeping the fleet in good repair, as carriages needing attention were often required to be kept in traffic, or prematurely returned to service, which led to increased maintenance costs later. Furthermore, the high numbers of obsolete wagons awaiting or under repair was causing unacceptable delays to carriage maintenance. In March the following year, he stated that just over half of the company's total stock of 2,485 carriages were 'obsolete types', and followed this a few weeks later with a letter to directors which claimed that a comparative survey of twelve major railway companies showed that the LSWR was one of three which did not have a proper, standardised renewal programme for rolling stock. He sought permission for a renewal rate of four per cent of the carriage stock per annum, but this was rejected by the Traffic Committee.

Adams also became increasingly critical of the traffic department and its provision of services, plus methods of train control. Following a serious derailment in June 1884 between Downton and Breamore resulting in four fatalities, the Board of Trade inspector Colonel Rich, in his subsequent report, roundly condemned many of the outmoded operating practices of the LSWR, thus highlighting Adams' concerns.

The locomotive strategy was a long-term plan, but although it was well received by the board, he was only granted funds and authorisation for a total of twenty-four new locomotives, to be split equally between passenger tank and six-coupled goods engines.

He tackled the passenger tank problem with a new 4-4-2T, using experience gained with the Tilbury Tanks and the rebuilt 46 class to produce a design with shorter side tanks, and an extended bunker which incorporated an element of water space, supported by a trailing Webb type radial axle.

Beyer, Peacock was once again awarded the contract, with locomotives to be delivered in late summer and autumn 1882, at a cost of £2,350 each. Unlike the 46 class predecessor, the new Radial Tanks, as they would become widely known, had conventional spoked bogie wheels, though larger at 3ft 0in diameter. The coupled wheels remained the same size at 5ft 7in, but the cylinders were slightly smaller at 17½ x 24in, and a marginally increased total heating surface of 1,053 square feet was provided. Despite the smaller side tanks, water capacity was still a respectable 1,000 gallons with the rear tank space included. The overall wheelbase was 29ft 5in, but with 2½in side-play allowed by both bogie and radial axle the engines proved themselves very versatile, with the result that orders for a further fifty-nine locomotives were placed with a variety of builders between July 1882 and July 1884.

Beyer, Peacock did not win any further orders for this particular class, which was designated 415, but Robert Stephenson were awarded orders for a total of twenty-eight in two separate orders, with the rest constructed in Glasgow, twenty by Dübs and the remaining ten by Neilson. The later orders differed slightly, with larger water tanks and deeper fireboxes. The engines were employed across the network, but with a majority

The first order for twelve radial tanks was placed with Beyer, Peacock in 1881, and 424 was delivered in October the following year. Note the short tanks, which together with the rear tank beneath the bunker gave a total capacity of 1,000 gallons. (Alon Siton)

Built by Dübs in 1885, No.518 is seen in as built condition, before the later addition of coal rails. (ETH Archive)

No. 486, photographed by the builder Neilson before delivery in March 1885. (ETH Archive)

in and around London. Later, as they were gradually replaced on suburban duties, they were cascaded to country areas, and in 1913 they were trialled on the Axminster-Lyme Regis branch, a line which had proved notoriously difficult to operate with tortuous curves and light axle loading, but with bogie and axle side-play relaxed beyond the normal adjustment, the Radial Tanks proved instantly successful and became synonymous with the branch for the next half century. Widespread withdrawals of the class took place the same year, but during the First World War one, No. 488, was sold for government service, later finding its way to the East Kent Railway, whilst four were loaned to the Highland Railway in 1918. Eventually, only two remained to work the Lyme Regis branch, but following the Second World War, 488 was repurchased by the Southern Railway to provide a third, which duly rejoined its sisters in rural Dorset.

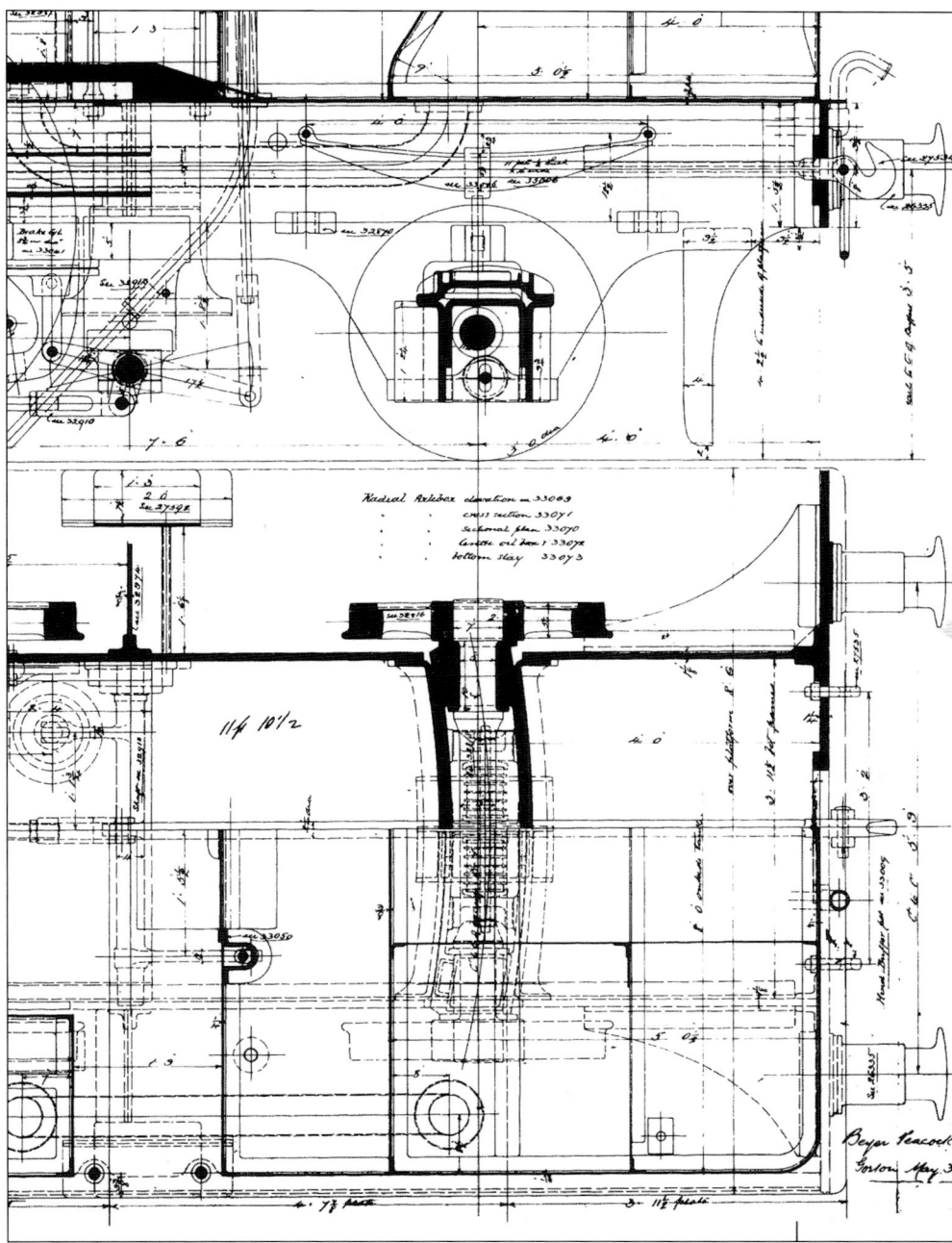

Arrangement of the trailing axle of the class 415 tank, which clearly indicates the lateral movement permitted by the radial axlebox.

This venerable trio, the only three to pass into British Railways ownership, renumbered 30582/3/4, remained at work until replaced by Ivatt 2MT 2-6-2Ts in 1961. At the time of their withdrawal, both 30582 and 30584 had each clocked up over two million miles in service – a commendable record.

On 10 April 1960 Radial tanks Nos. 30583/4 were rostered for a ballast train, seen here between Combpyne and Cannington Viaduct. (Roger Joanes)

Drummond boilered No. 30582 leaves Cannington Viaduct with a typical single coach Lyme Regis branch train on 2 April 1959. (Roger Joanes)

A through train from Lyme Regis to Waterloo on 3 September 1960 was diagrammed as a double header. 30582 and 30583 are seen here near Combpyne. (Roger Joanes)

To address the goods locomotive requirement, Adams produced drawings for the 395 class, a six-coupled design, with 17½in x 24in cylinders, 5ft 1in diameter wheels, a total heating surface of 1,177 square feet and a grate area of 17.75 square feet. Surprisingly perhaps, boiler pressure was only 140lb, although several locomotives were later raised to 160lb.

The authorised order for the twelve locomotives was let to Neilson in June 1881, at a price of £2,250 each, and over the next four years further orders followed, which brought the class total to seventy. Neilson won all five contracts for them but, intriguingly, in 1884 Adams wanted to invite tenders from one or two American firms, including the Baldwin Locomotive Company and Vulcan Iron Works, an idea that was met with short shrift from higher authority. The later engines were slightly longer than the early deliveries, and were also fitted with single, heavier slide bars. One aspect of the design was a sloping smokebox front and door, which could be considered an anachronistic style for the time.

Apart from freight duties, the 395 class, although rough riding, also acquitted itself well on secondary passenger duties, and were regularly returning an annual average mileage of around 30,000.

During the First World War no less than fifty engines of the class were requisitioned by the government for use by the Railway Operating Division of the Royal Engineers and sent to the Middle East. Five engines were sent to Salonika, and no less than thirty-six went to the Palestine Military Railway. Of these, ten were subsequently shipped on to Mesopotamia, to join the remaining nine which were sent there directly in 1917. Following the end of the war, those in Mesopotamia became part of the stock

Delivered in January 1886, No. 515 was part of the last batch of 395 class locomotives built by Neilson. It remained in the UK to be finally withdrawn in June 1933. (ETH Archive)

No. 434 was sold to the government in 1916 and ended its days with Iraq State Railways after a period in Palestine. (John Scott-Morgan collection)

of the Iraq State Railway, whilst the Palestinian engines were overhauled at Cairo, and remained at work for a further decade until most were sold for scrap, with just seven remaining in service until 1937/8.

A shortage of spare boilers for those that remained in the UK resulted in three being fitted with those from withdrawn London, Chatham & Dover Railway class M3 4-4-0s in the late 1920s. Eighteen survived to be taken into British Railways stock at nationalisation, but were withdrawn progressively from 1953 onwards, and although three were given general overhauls in 1954, the last one was scrapped five years later.

A First World War period scene of an unidentified 395 class 0-6-0 of the Palestine Military Railway, hauling an ambulance train of former LSWR carriages, in the Judean Hills, on the line between Jerusalem and Jaffa. (Alon Siton)

Still in LSWR livery, No.28 waits with a train of Egyptian coaches at Jerusalem station, shortly after the British took over the city from the Ottoman Army. (Alon Siton)

Ex-LSWR 395 class No. 508 outside Haifa-Kishon works in January 1945. The locomotive had been withdrawn eight years earlier. (Alon Siton)

The 445 class was built by Robert Stephenson and featured 7ft 1in diameter coupled wheels. No. 449 was delivered in June 1883 and was withdrawn two years into the Southern Railway era in 1925. (ETH Archive)

In 1881, Adams also faced a shortage of shunting locomotives, as the railway was still heavily reliant on horse shunting at this time, a problem he dealt with expediently by an order for twelve from Beyer, Peacock, to a standard saddle tank design similar to engines ordered earlier by W.G. Beattie.

The next 4-4-0 order, the 445 class, numbered 445-56, featured larger 7ft 1in diameter coupled wheels, designed specifically for the Waterloo-Salisbury route. Again,

No. 445, new in April 1883, is seen alongside Eastleigh coaling stage on 28 May 1921. (Mike Morant)

twelve were ordered, in October 1882, but this time Robert Stephenson won the contract, quoting a price of £2,970 each. William Jacomb, the civil engineer, would have been pleased to note the engine weight of 44 tons, even though the combined engine and tender weight of 74½ tons still exceeded his stated limit of 70 tons!

Shortly before Adams' arrival at Nine Elms, W.G. Beattie had conducted trials with the Clark chain, and Newall's wheel and chain continuous brakes, using two locomotives fitted with a steam brake over the route between Clapham Junction and Windsor. As a result the continuous mechanical brake systems were discarded, but a decision was made to use the steam brake for goods trains. An offer made by the Vacuum Brake Company in April 1878 to fit a locomotive and several carriages with its simple vacuum system, free of charge, for a trial period, was accepted, and at the end of the year, two 2-4-0 locomotives and the requisite number of carriages were ready for a daily return trip between London and Portsmouth.

It was not long before the Westinghouse Brake & Signal Company responded with a similar offer to trial its own air brake, and accordingly two more 2-4-0s and seven further carriages were equipped for the alternative trial, once again working a daily return service to Portsmouth.

Further trials using both the automatic vacuum and Westinghouse brakes were undertaken on main lines and also between Clapham Junction and Windsor to gain experience with suburban stop start working.

After such extensive testing, Adams was able to carefully assess the merits and costs of each alternative, with the result that he recommended the adoption of the automatic vacuum brake. The Locomotive Committee accepted the estimated cost of £45,000 and

Classmate No. 455 was photographed at Eastleigh the following year. Although still bearing the original number, it had been placed on the duplicate list some years earlier as No. 0455. (Mike Morant)

endorsed Adams' proposal in May 1881. The fitting of the necessary equipment to over 400 locomotives and 1,500 carriages would inevitably take time, but it was reported in June 1887 that the task was virtually complete.

The first experiments with a compound locomotive can be dated to 1850 when James Samuel and John Nicholson took out a patent and converted two locomotives at the Eastern Counties Railway. In the early 1880s, Francis Webb of the LNWR built a class of three cylinder 2-2-2-0 locomotives which had two high-pressure outside cylinders driving the rear axle, exhausting into an inside third low-pressure cylinder which drove the centre axle. The driven axles remained uncoupled. The claims of economy and efficiency attracted the attention of senior management at the LSWR, with the result that Crewe built No. 300, appropriately named *Compound*, was loaned to Nine Elms for trial in May 1884, and compared against the 445 class on a variety of duties, with mixed results. Having also inspected a newer and more powerful LNWR Dreadnought class, Adams was authorised to convert No. 446, using the Webb-Von Borries system, at a cost not exceeding £200. Fitted with a new right-hand low-pressure cylinder of 26in bore, No. 446 re-entered service, and further trials were conducted for comparison with No. 448, which remained in original condition. The cost saving reported to the Locomotive Committee in late 1890 was too small to be regarded as a conclusive result and so, having run over 60,000 miles as a compound locomotive, 446 was returned to original condition later in the following year. The 445 class continued to work Salisbury and Southampton expresses, the latter later extended to Bournemouth when the new direct line superseded the old Castleman's Corkscrew route via Ringwood, with the added prestige of Pullman cars provided on certain

No. 446 ran as a two-cylinder compound from 1888-91, retaining its original 18in diameter high pressure cylinder on one side, and fitted with a 26in diameter low pressure cylinder on the other. In forty-two years of service, it ran a total of 1,300, 968 miles. (John Scott-Morgan collection)

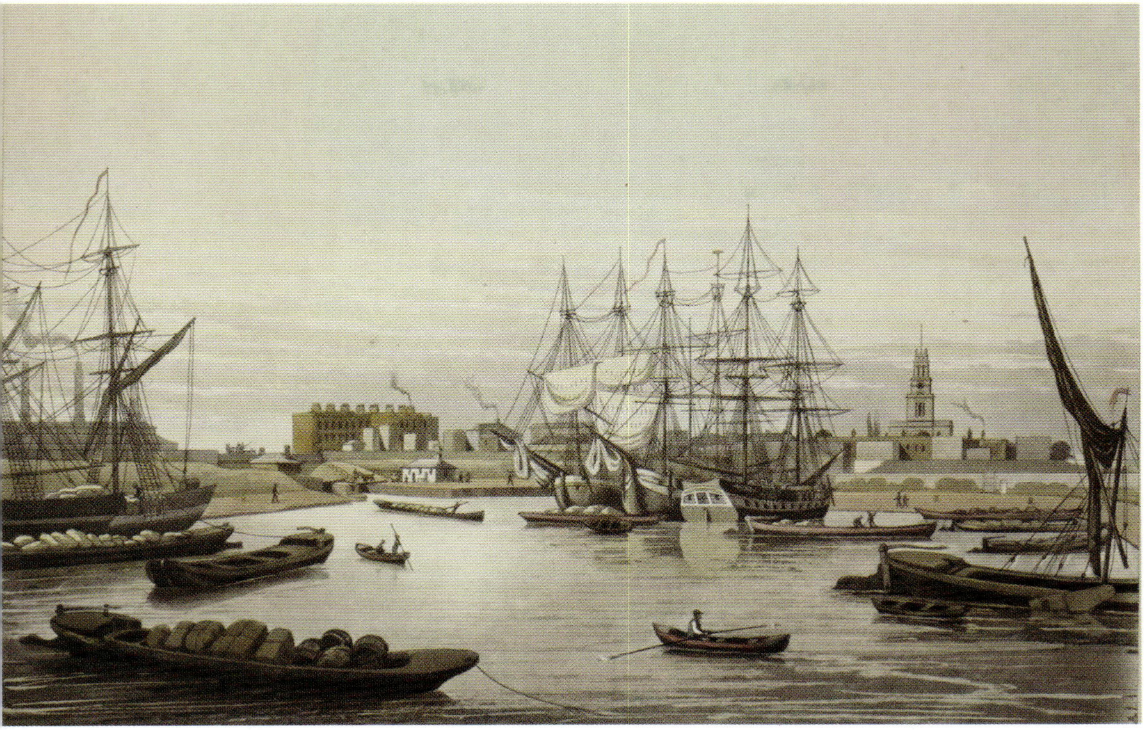

A scene which would have been familiar to the young William, Limehouse Basin, otherwise known as Regent's Canal Dock, dated 1827 by Thomas Hosmer Shepherd. Mill Place is on the far side of the dock, with St. Anne's church beyond. The entrance to Regent's Canal is visible centre-left. (Science Museum)

This Indenture Witnesseth, That William Adams, son of John Samuel Adams of the West India Docks in the parish of All Saints Poplar in the County of Middlesex Gentleman with the consent of his said Father testified by his being a party hereto doth put himself Apprentice to Joseph Miller and Richard Ravenhill to learn their Art, and with them, (after the Manner of an Apprentice,) to serve from the day of the date hereof until the full End and Term of Five — Years from thence next following, to be fully complete and ended. During which Term, the said Apprentice his said Masters faithfully shall serve, their Secrets keep; their lawful Commands every where gladly do. He shall do no damage to his said Master, nor see it to be done of others, but that he to his power shall let, or forthwith give Warning to his said Master of the same. He shall not waste the Goods of his said Master, nor lend them unlawfully to any. He shall not commit Fornication nor contract Matrimony within the said Term. He shall not play at Cards, Dice, Tables, or any other unlawful Games, whereby his said Master may have any Loss. With his own Goods or Others, during the said Term, without License of his said Masters he shall neither buy nor sell. He shall not haunt Taverns, or Playhouses, nor absent himself from his said Master's Service, Day or Night unlawfully. But in all Things as a faithful Apprentice, he shall behave himself towards his Master, and all his, during the said Term. He shall give a true and just account of his said Master's Goods, Chattels, and Money committed to his charge, or which shall come to his hands, whenever required so to do by his said Masters. And the said Joseph Miller and Richard Ravenhill their said Apprentice in the Art of a fitter of Machinery which they use, by the best means that he can, shall teach and instruct, or cause to be taught and instructed; ~~finding unto his said Apprentice sufficient Meat, Drink,~~ ~~lodging and all other necessaries during the said Term~~ and shall pay him Wages after the following rates per week of 6 days and ten working hours in each day, that is to say after the completion of the first year for which no wages will be given, six shillings per week the second year, seven shillings per week the third, eight shillings per week the fourth year and nine shillings per week the fifth and last year of this agreement.

And for the true Performance of all and every the said Covenants and Agreements, either of the said Parties bindeth himself unto the other by these Presents. In Witness whereof, the Parties above-named to these Indentures have set their Hands and Seals, the twenty first Day of April in the fourth Year of the Reign of our Sovereign Lady Victoria, by the Grace of God of the United Kingdom of Great Britain and Ireland, Queen, Defender of the Faith, and in the year of our Lord One Thousand, Eight Hundred and forty one

Signed, Sealed, and Delivered (being first duly stamped) in the presence of . . .

Geo Staley

William Adams

John S. Adams

Joseph Miller

Richard Ravenhill

9.3.41

Soldby J. Waterlow, Law Stationers, 24, Birchin Lane, and 23, Threadneedle Street, London.

William's apprenticeship indentures with Miller and Ravenhill, dated 12 April 1841. For a sixty-hour week, he received a wage of six shillings per week in the second year, rising to nine shillings weekly in the fifth and final year. (Dr R.J. Adams)

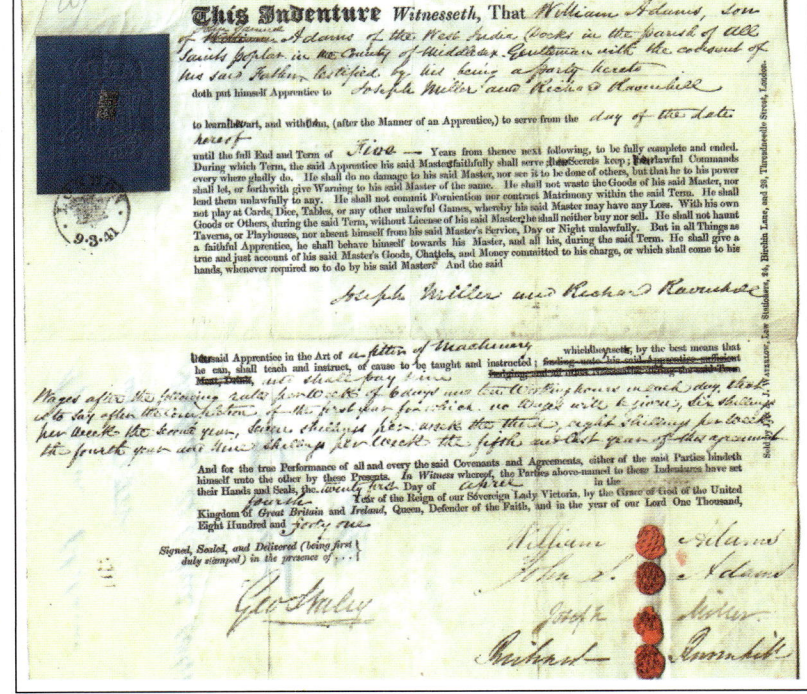

The shipyard of Miller and Ravenhill is clearly seen in the background of this river scene depicting the paddle steamers *Meteor* and *Prince of Wales* leaving Brunswick Wharf, Blackwall, in 1844, a painting by Robert K. Thomas, dedicated to the directors of the London and Blackwall Railway Company. (Yale Center for British Art)

The iron hulled paddle steamer *Prince of Wales* was built by Miller and Ravenhill but was damaged during an unsuccessful launch in 1843. Despite a twisted bow and other problems, repairs were completed in only four days. (Royal Museums Greenwich)

The first steamship to join the Royal Sardinian Navy fleet was *Gulnaro*. Laid down at the Thames shipyard of Thomas Pitcher in 1832, she was launched in December 1834, and arrived at Genoa in the following May. (Klaus Krick)

An 1850 view of the Terrazio di Marmo, or marble terrace, Genova, by the artist Carlo Bossoli.

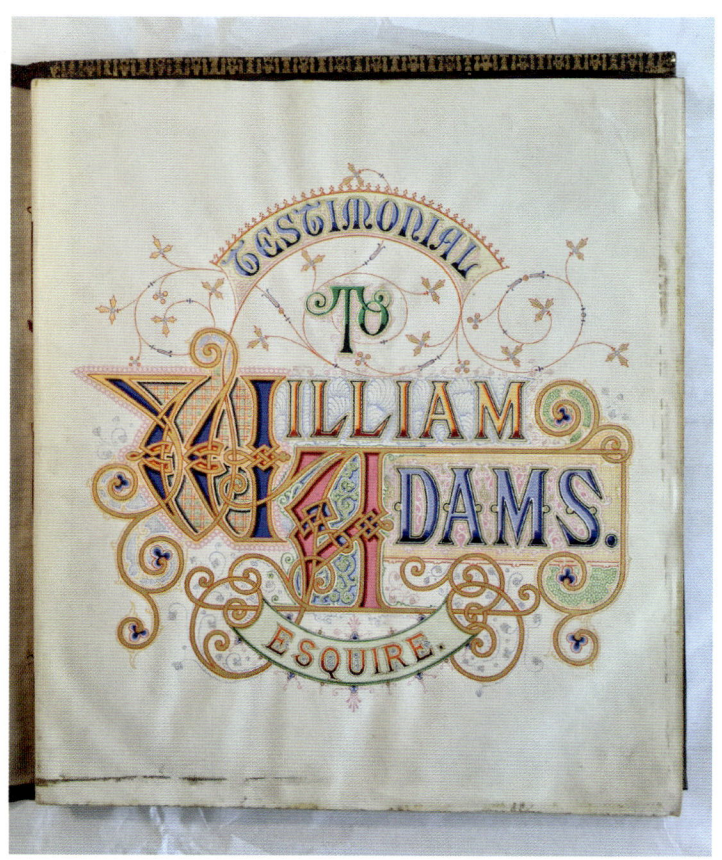

Left, below left and below right: The illuminated testimonial title and pages from the book of subscribers presented to William on his departure from the North London Railway. (John Adams)

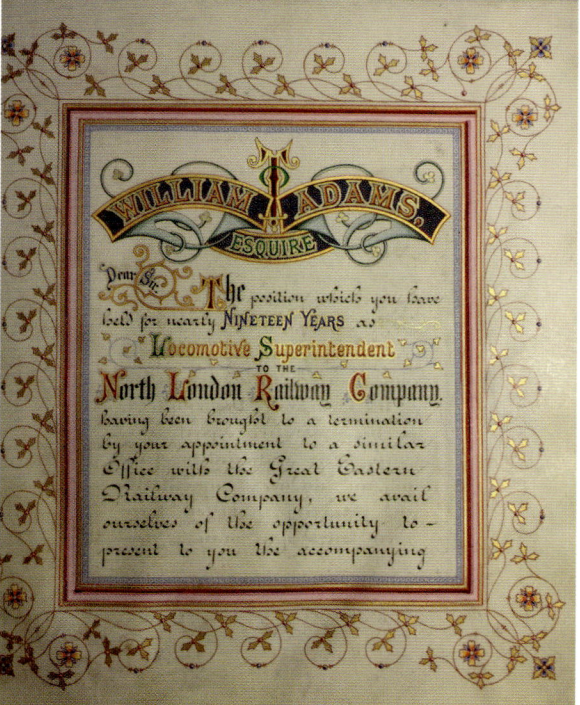

The Adams lined black Great Eastern livery is shown to good effect by this delightful model of a K9 0-4-2T built by Mike Edge. (David Bousfield)

LSWR class X2 No.584 new in 1891, in pea green livery with wide splashers bearing a large LSWR monogram. (John Scott-Morgan collection, colour by John Faulkner)

The Adams bogie of LSWR T3 class No.563 showing the block which slides laterally on the bogie frame, with the lateral springs each side. (Nathan Au)

W14 *Fishbourne*, originally LSWR No. 178, dating from 1889, and at the time the oldest locomotive at work with British Railways, has just arrived at Shanklin in the winter afternoon sunlight of 31 December 1966, the last day of steam services on the Isle of Wight, suitably adorned with wreath and headboard. (Roger Joanes)

In 2011, preserved T3 class No. 563 was shipped to Canada for use in a stage production of *The Railway Children*, by E. Nesbit. It is seen here at Toronto, on the turntable of the John Street Roundhouse, which became a temporary theatre. (Stephen Gardiner)

Above: Shortly after transfer to the Swanage Railway in 2017, 563 was used for an after dark photo charter at Corfe Castle. Although non-operational, an authentic period scene was created. (Calum Hepplewhite)

Right: New L class No. 2 represents a John Henry Adams design in preservation. Although built after his death, it was one of several sold for further service in industry. Now based at the Foxfield Railway, appropriately in Staffordshire.

After a number of years on display at Butlins Holiday Camp, Skegness, preserved LSWR B4 class No. 102 *Granville* moved to the Bressingham Steam Museum, where it is now displayed with cut away cab. (Bob Passmore)

In March 2019, O2 class W24 *Calbourne* visited the Bluebell Railway, which enabled three of the surviving Adams locomotives, all in British Railways livery, to be seen together. Bluebell residents 30096 and Radial tank 30583 join the O2 at Sheffield Park. (John Faulkner)

Above left: Pride of the Isle of Wight Steam Railway's locomotive fleet, O2 class W24 *Calbourne* at Smallbrook Junction, shortly after repaint in April 2016. (John Faulkner)

Above right: The WA monogram from the North London Railway presentation testimonial. (John Adams)

trains from 1889 – a Pullman car had been unsuccessfully trialled earlier in 1880 on the Waterloo-Exeter service. In their later years, these well-regarded locomotives were inevitably cascaded to secondary local services, and all were withdrawn by the end of 1925, each having run in the order of 1.2-1.3 million miles.

Following the 445 class came the general purpose 460 class, another 4-4-0 design, but with 6ft 7in coupled wheels, for which, after some trading over the usual weight concerns with the civil engineer, approval was granted in July 1883. Orders were placed with the firms Robert Stephenson and Neilson for delivery of ten locomotives each, numbered 147, 460-478. They were essentially a variation of the 445 class, and were well liked because of their wider route availability, and hence the range of duties that could be covered. Within a few years annual mileages approaching 40,000 were being recorded. Robert Stephenson actually built an eleventh as its choice of display at the 1887 Jubilee Exhibition in Newcastle, which was sold to the LSWR at the close of the event. Because of its high standard of finish, No. 526, as it became, was Nine Elms' choice for Royal trains and other high profile turns. The LSWR had often promoted itself as 'The Royal Road' because it was regularly used by Queen Victoria travelling between London or Windsor and Gosport en route to the Isle of Wight and her beloved Osborne House. The entire class was still on the books at the grouping, but withdrawals commenced the following year, with the last two condemned in April 1929.

A general purpose design with 6ft 7in coupled wheels, the 460 class was ordered in 1883. No. 464 was delivered by Neilson in October 1884. (ETH Archive)

No. 477, built by Robert Stephenson in 1884, shunting at Andover Junction, 27 May 1922. (Mike Morant)

No. 526 was specially built by Robert Stephenson for display at the 1887 Newcastle Jubilee Exhibition in addition to the original order for ten locomotives placed by the LSWR. (John Scott-Morgan collection)

Chapter 8

Master of his Art

In 1885 Scott retired, to be replaced by a new General Manager, Charles Scotter, with a mission to improve both profitability and efficiency of the company. He had previously been employed as Chief Goods Manager at the Manchester, Sheffield & Lincolnshire Railway under the forward thinking and progressive Edward Watkin, and his experience had included several years seeking new business around continental Europe. He set about improving the management structure, including increasing accountability of the various department heads, including Adams.

When Adams had taken office, the Traffic Committee oversaw the work of the Locomotive, Carriage & Wagon Department, but this responsibility passed to the Engineering Committee in 1880. However, under the new General Manager, the Locomotive Committee finally gained its independence, being formed of two members each from the Traffic and Engineering committees.

Whilst Adams had successfully resisted earlier attempts to create separate locomotive and carriage & wagon departments, Scotter recognised that the division was necessary, as the responsibility with such a wide remit was now too great for one person. It would seem that Adams now recognised this too, and from January 1886 he was in charge of the Locomotive Department, with William Panter taking command of the carriage and wagon function. The latter, who came to Nine Elms from the London & North Western Railway's Wolverton Works, rapidly embarked on an extensive carriage building programme.

Despite improved methods of working in the Traffic Department, heavier train weights and faster schedules were noticeably increasing costs in the locomotive department. Adams attempted to establish what measures other railways took to establish and test fuel efficiency, but apart from the Great Northern which had a laboratory facility, most of the major concerns reported to him that they did not do so. Amongst other cost saving measures considered were footplate crew bonus payments, feedwater heating and, perhaps surprisingly, lower boiler pressures. Premium payments to enginemen for efficient driving were in fact introduced in 1887 – or more correctly, reinstated, as the idea had earlier been used by Joseph Beattie but later abandoned by his son.

In September 1885, the Locomotive Committee authorised the trial of the vortex blast pipe in two locomotives, No. 403 of the 395 class, and 4-4-0 No. 463, in order to assess its impact on fuel economy. The vortex blast pipe was an invention of William Adams and his nephew Henry, and they jointly patented it that month. Both had considered ideas for improvements to locomotive draughting and blast pipe design many years earlier when Henry was apprenticed to his uncle at Bow. A conventional blast pipe was of cylindrical section, but it was reasoned that by using an annular section, with a scoop placed close to the lower smokebox tubeplate, a more even passage of hot gases through all the tubes of the boiler, particularly the lower ones, would be encouraged. The trials showed a noticeable fuel saving of around twelve per cent with the goods engine, and nearly nine per cent with the faster passenger services, which pleased the Locomotive Committee to the extent that they ordered that the innovation should be fitted to all new tender engines. The LSWR trial was not the first use of an annular blast pipe per se; it was a concept which had been used for the previous decade by Charles Brown, founder of the Swiss Locomotive Works at Winterthur. Intriguingly, in a later paper to the Institution of Structural Engineers, Henry described how Adams was initially unwilling to adopt the principle, thinking it 'only a juvenile idea', and also later

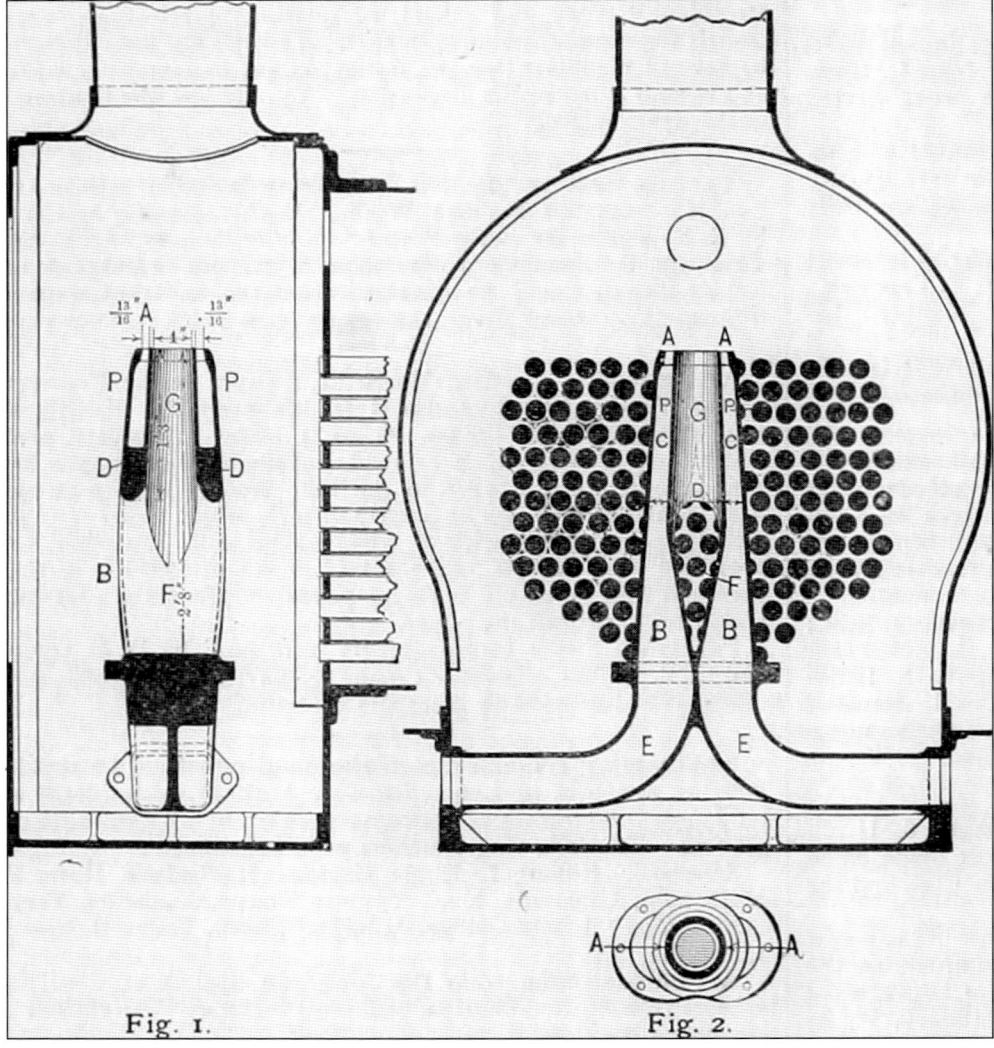

Longitudinal and transverse sectional drawings of the Adams vortex blast pipe, from the *Railroad and Engineering Journal* of July 1887. The annular orifice at the top, level with the uppermost row of tubes, is clearly demonstrated. The opening F) to the rear of the pipe allows combustion gases to be drawn into the partial vacuum created in the inner tube G) by the locomotive's exhaust blast, thus permitting a more even distribution across the entire tubeplate.

resisted forming a company to market their patents, resulting in missed opportunities subsequently exploited by others. Uncle William was apparently persuaded to patent the idea whilst he and Henry were both on holiday at Herne Bay. The advantage of the vortex blast pipe was clearly demonstrated at the LSWR by a cost saving in coal of £60,000 in seven years, whilst the various efficiency measures together reduced average coal consumption per train mile from 31.20lb to 26.90lb.

In 1887, an eminent Professor of Chemistry, Edward Frankland, was engaged to analyse the quality of water used by the LSWR's locomotives, and his subsequent report prompted Adams to trial Maignen's Patent water softening process on ten selected engines. Frankland had previously been employed to investigate the quality of oils, paints and other consumables, with the aim of obtaining the best quality yet cost effective materials, and towards the end of 1883 regular reporting of 'Analysis of Stores' had been introduced at the meetings of the Engineering and Stores Committee.

In March 1886, William Frank Pettigrew was appointed Manager at the recently refitted Nine Elms Works. He had started his career in 1874 as an articled pupil of Adams at Stratford, and then under his successor Massey Bromley, leaving at the end of his term in 1879 to work firstly on hydraulic cranes at Millwall, then finding employment in Scotland with his father, who worked with marine engines. He then returned to Stratford as assistant works manager, serving Thomas Worsdell and James Holden, before finding a promotion with his old boss at Nine Elms.

An advertisement for Maignen's water softening equipment, trialled by the LSWR, from 1888.

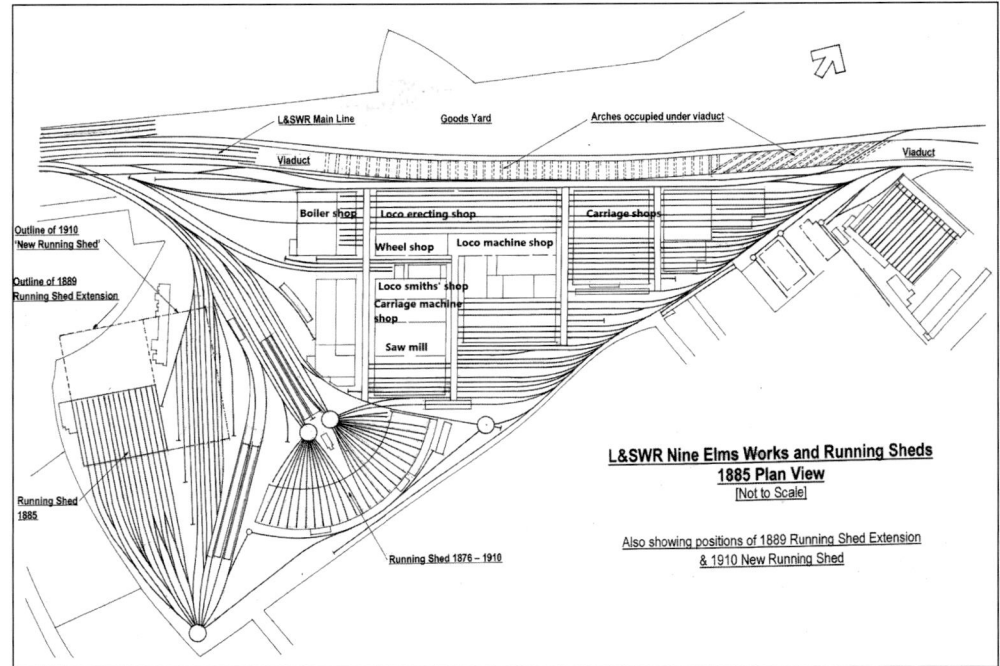

Plan of Nine Elms Works and running shed 1885. (Drawn by Philip Hayward)

As described above, it was self-evident that Nine Elms works had outgrown the available area, and a decision was made to move the entire carriage and wagon department to a new site at Bishopstoke, about five miles north of Southampton, in order to allow for expansion of the locomotive works. Bishopstoke was the site of the junction where the routes from London to Southampton and Gosport via Fareham diverged, and a large site was identified to the east of the main line.

The new works was opened in 1891 under the supervision of Carriage & Wagon Superintendent William Panter, who relocated, together with virtually his entire workforce, from London to what, a year or two earlier, had been a sleepy hamlet, but was now a growing railway town, with a new name – Eastleigh. It is probably fair to say that many of the displaced workers were not entirely happy with their enforced change of circumstances, and lack of facilities and amenities, but Mr Panter played a key role in the establishment of the LSWR Institution in the new town centre. The site provided scope for much further expansion over the following two decades, firstly with the relocation of the locomotive running shed from Northam, Southampton, and finally by the closure of Nine Elms locomotive works and its transfer to Eastleigh.

In 1876, during William Beattie's tenure in charge, construction of a new Nine Elms running shed was authorised, which took the form of a twenty-six road semi-roundhouse, accessed by two turntables, together with a two-storey office block graced with an elegant clocktower. By 1885 this facility had been joined by a new fifteen road running shed, but this time a linear arrangement rather than a roundhouse, and this building was doubled in length from 180ft to 360ft in 1889. This vast new shed could however only be accessed by a turntable in a corner of the site, which must have made shunting movements somewhat awkward. However, it remained in use until the end of steam operation in 1967. The roundhouse when built could accommodate 100 engines, but as larger designs were introduced this overall number was reduced. A pattern of working emerged whereby main line tender engines were shedded in the new straight building, whilst smaller tank engines engaged on suburban and shunting duties were allocated to the roundhouse, which was also used for a certain amount of repair work, plus the storage of stopped engines awaiting works attention.

The relocation of the carriage and wagon works to Eastleigh immediately opened up the potential to expand the locomotive works further. However, the company promptly embarked on a scheme to widen the adjacent main line to and from Waterloo from four to six tracks, which caused some degree of disruption, and some of the C&W buildings were taken over by the adjoining Goods Department. The locomotive erecting shop was extended into the main C&W shop which involved the removal of a steam operated traverser previously used for access, and the creation of two bays each with three tracks and 750ft in length by 57ft wide. Two 30 ton overhead travelling cranes were installed. It was now possible to accommodate over eighty engines for overhaul/repair, and between ten and twenty new builds at any given time, and consequently reduce the reliance on additional workshop capacity in the roundhouse. At the time of Pettigrew's arrival, some locomotives were still being overhauled at Northam and Exeter depots, but from 1891 this practice was gradually phased out so that three years later all general repairs could be accommodated at Nine Elms.

The pea green livery is undoubtedly the colour scheme most generally associated with the Adams period, and with black borders edged with fine white lining and vermilion buffer beams suited his designs admirably. This did not actually appear until 1885 when he repainted a class 135 4-4-0 in a pea green livery – apparently, he sought Isabella's advice and she did not find favour with his first choice of a darker Brunswick green. Nephews Thomas and Henry noted that William was often led by his wife, whom they described as a 'diplomatist', so perhaps this was one such occasion!

The directors, keen to improve the image of the railway, agreed with Isabella and from July 1885 the Nine Elms paint shops were kept busy repainting not only locomotives, but coaching stock as well, for which a smart new salmon pink and brown livery was approved. For goods class locomotives a darker holly green livery was approved, with black borders with a light green lining.

William Adams had first proposed a livery change in June 1878, when it was agreed that two locomotives working passenger trains should be repainted in two contrasting schemes to potentially replace W.G. Beattie's rather sombre brownish-purple finish. A month later the directors were duly presented with the choice of an umber or dark green livery, with the former gaining approval for new build and rebuilt/reboilered locomotives. Unfortunately, the umber livery did not weather well, hence the quest for a suitable alternative seven years later.

In the early Adams period, new engines carried brass numerals which from 1887 were replaced with cast brass oval numberplates applied to cab or tank sides. From mid-1890, LSWR monograms began to be applied to leading splashers of express locomotives.

William had no doubt taken a keen interest in the four-coupled express tender engines, fitted with a trailing axle rather than leading bogie, recently introduced by

William Stroudley at the neighbouring London, Brighton & South Coast Railway. His renowned Gladstone class, with 6ft 6in diameter driving wheels, appeared in 1884, and was a development of a very similar design of six years earlier. In March 1885, Stroudley presented a Paper to the Institution of Mechanical Engineers explaining his reasoning for, and assessment of, the design in which large diameter leading wheels were guided on curves by a trailing axle.

In June 1886, the works was ready to accept an order for twenty locomotives to a new design, a mixed traffic 0-4-2 tender locomotive, which, with an engine weight of only 42 tons, would permit an extensive route availability. This was the first new construction at Nine Elms since Adams' appointment and, in fact, for over a decade. With the first examples of the new A12 class completed in 1887, they were nicknamed Jubilees in honour of Queen Victoria's fifty-year reign. It became the practice for all new-build locomotive works orders to be designated by a letter and single digit number, with the class generally being known by the order designation of the first batch, so it is perhaps odd that the first such order should be recorded as A12, i.e., with two digits. The Locomotive Committee was happy to authorise the in-house construction when assured by Adams that it would represent an annual saving of around £5,700.

The A12 was a compact design with 18in x 26in cylinders, 6ft 1in diameter coupled wheels, a total heating surface of 1,248 square feet, grate area of 17 square feet and boiler pressure at 160lb. No new tenders were included in the order for the new engines which were allocated the numbers 527-546, and they were paired with old tenders from withdrawn Beattie locomotives, except for the last three which enjoyed the privilege of new-builds.

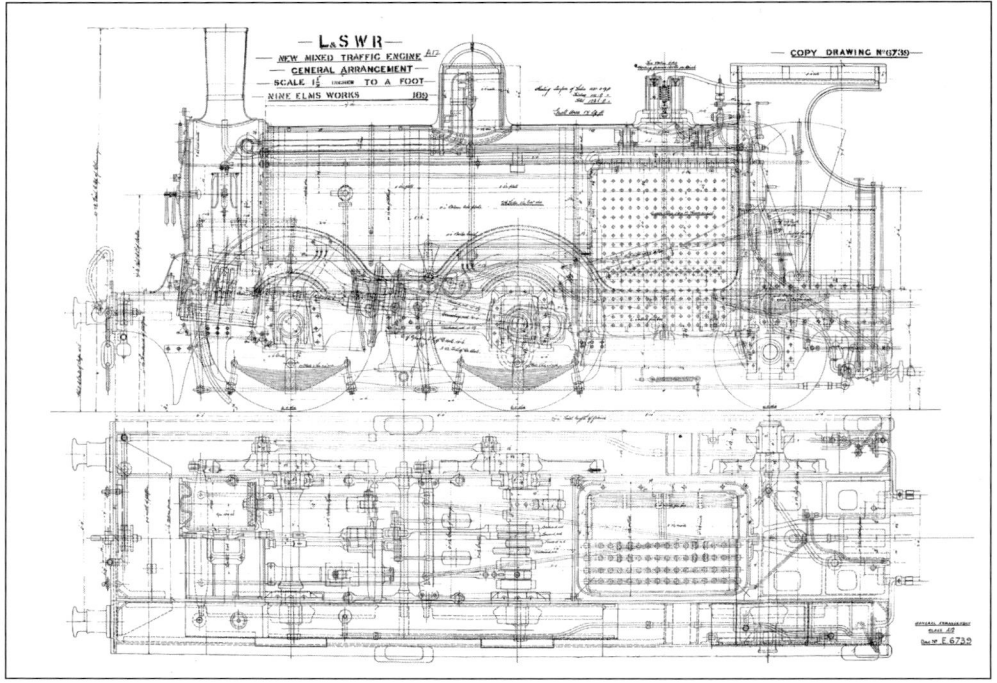

A Nine Elms general arrangement drawing for the A12 Jubilee class. (Dr R.J. Adams)

The A12 was a mixed traffic design introduced in 1887. No. 539 was built at Nine Elms the following year, as part of order E1 for a batch of ten locomotives. (ETH Archive)

The A12 design was influenced by William Stroudley's success with the 0-4-2 type, epitomised by Gladstone class No. 175 *Hayling*. (Tony Hisgett)

Although the first A12s were the first engines built at Nine Elms in over a decade, some construction had to be contracted out, and No. 636 was delivered by Neilson in 1893. (ETH Archive)

The tender of No. 530 is rather well loaded at Salisbury in August 1897. (John Scott-Morgan collection)

Jubilee No. 630 stands by the coaling stage at Eastleigh, in 1922, the last year of the independent LSWR. (John Scott-Morgan collection)

A12 class No. 651 shunting at Guildford on 24 September 1921. Built in 1895, this engine would last until withdrawal in 1933. (Mike Morant)

The class would eventually grow to a total of ninety locomotives, with Nine Elms constructing a further thirty in three batches over the following seven years, and a large order placed with Neilson in April 1892 for the remaining forty. There were minor detail differences between various orders with, for example, the first Nine Elms-built locomotives provided with screw reversers and valves below the cylinders, rather than between, whilst those built later had reversing levers. Apart from the first batch, all were fitted with vortex blast pipes, except one of the Neilson engines which had an experimental variable blast pipe. Various other experiments carried out by Adams to A12 class engines included a water softening plant on the tender of No. 602, a deeper firebox for No. 553 and Westinghouse air brake for six others.

Although intended for mixed traffic duties, the loss of fifty locomotives of the 395 class during the First World War resulted in their increased use on freight duties. All were still in use at the time of the grouping, but withdrawals commenced in 1928 with only four examples remaining on the books at nationalisation in 1948. These too were withdrawn during that year, although one, No. 612, managed to survive until 1951 as a stationary boiler at Eastleigh. During the Second World War, several locomotives were temporarily transferred to the Longmoor Military Railway, whence two were sent further afield to the Melbourne Military Railway in Derbyshire.

When an order for further suburban tank locomotives was required in 1887, Adams produced an 0-4-4T design which used many components common with the A12 Jubilees, including cylinders and boiler, although with smaller 5ft 7in diameter driving wheels and 3ft 0in diameter bogie wheels. It is known that consideration was also given to an enlarged radial tank, and also the conversion of twenty-four Double

Framed Goods six-coupled engines as 0-4-4Ts before committing to an order of twenty engines of the new T1 class. Like the first A12s, the initial T1 order had steam chests incorporated below the cylinders, rather than in between. The first locomotive, No. 61, was completed and trialled several months ahead of the rest of the batch, but having proved themselves, a further forty were ordered in 1893-5, although not all were delivered before their designer retired. In later life they were dispersed around the system, and in 1915-17 were trialled on motor train working but were not as successful as the O2 and Drummond M7 classes – the trials were probably not helped by the outmoded system of cables and pulleys employed by the South Western. The first withdrawals took place in 1931, and although some were reprieved by the outbreak of the Second World War, the last two succumbed in 1951.

T1 class 0-4-4T No. 71 in as built condition, before the addition of coal rails. (ETH Archive)

T1 class No. 8 at Nine Elms shed on 6 May 1922. Built in August 1894, this locomotive was withdrawn from Eastleigh shed in May 1949. (Mike Morant)

Even Adams locomotives occasionally came to grief! In 1907, T1 class No. 65 found itself in an undignified position on the side of an embankment at Camberley, Surrey. (Howard Webb collection)

No. 65 was righted and then hauled back up to the main line by three locomotives. (Howard Webb collection)

T1 class No. 75 awaits its next turn at Plymouth Friary shed. A Ford model TT one ton truck can be seen behind the engine. (John Scott-Morgan collection)

Another smaller, more compact 0-4-4T design, the O2 class, followed in 1889, with its main dimensions remarkably similar to the Stratford Class 61 of some fifteen years earlier. They were designed to replace Beattie well tanks, and a total of sixty were built in five orders between 1889 and 1893, with one final order for a further ten cancelled after William Adams' retirement.

Comparative principal dimensions of GER 61 and LSWR O2 class 0-4-4 tank locomotives:

	GER 61 Class	LSWR O2 Class
Cylinders	17 x 24in	17 x 24in
Driving wheel diameter	4ft 10in	4ft 10in
Trailing wheel diameter	2ft 10in	3ft 0in
Wheelbase	21ft 7in	20ft 4in
Heating surface	1,084sq ft	987.5sq ft
Grate area	15.3sq ft	14.83sq ft
Boiler pressure	160lb	160lb
Water capacity	1,000gallons	800gallons
Weight	49 tons 4cwt	44 tons 11½cwt

Nicknamed Flittermice, the O2s soon proved themselves to be very versatile and useful engines, and in 1890 No. 185 was selected for a special duty in connection with the opening of the Brookwood-Bisley Camp branch on 14 July 1890, adorned with the arms and feathers of the Prince of Wales. It subsequently carried the name *Alexandra* on the side tanks, until removed by Adams' successor.

As noted above, O2s later took part in various motor train trials, in which they acquitted themselves well, and were used as such on the Yeovil Town-Pen Mill shuttles and Plymouth Friary-Turnchapel trains.

Shortly after the grouping in 1923, the Southern Railway equipped two with air brakes and sent them to the Isle of Wight, where the ageing locomotive fleet was in dire need of new investment. They proved ideal for the job, although on some routes, notably the Newport-Freshwater line, the permanent way required upgrading in order to accept them. The Southern transferred twenty-one in total between 1923 and 1947, with the final pair dispatched by British Railways in 1949. In an attempt to improve their range before servicing, A.B. McLeod, the manager of the island system 1928-34, designed a new enlarged bunker, which was trialled on one locomotive, and whilst the initial version was not pursued, a redesigned version was adopted which doubled bunker capacity from 1½ to 3 tons. The island engines were renumbered in a separate sequence, W14-36, and named after local towns and villages. It is interesting to note that apart from the island engines, and for a short time O2 No. 185 *Alexandra* described above, Southampton docks shunters were the only Adams locomotives to carry names. Although certain classes had been named in the Joseph Beattie era, none of the Adams express designs was, although it was a common practice with the neighbouring Great Western and Brighton companies. Indeed, the latter named virtually its entire locomotive fleet.

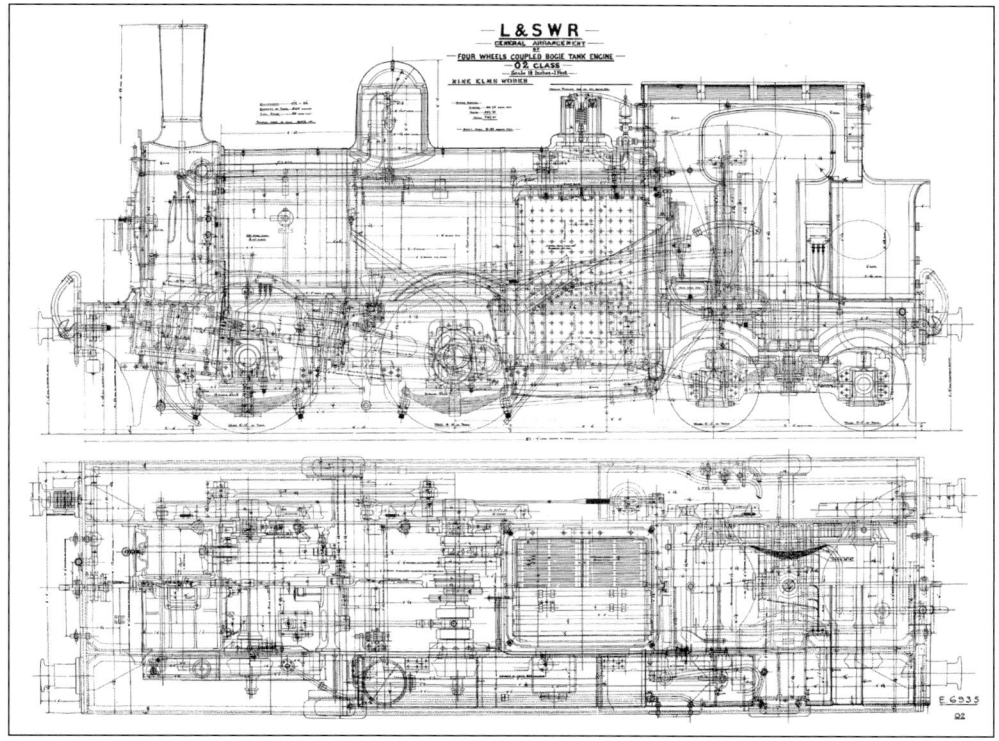

General arrangement drawing for the 0-4-4T O2 class. (IWSR)

O2 class No. 208 awaits departure from Bournemouth West in August 1902. This locomotive was sent to the Isle of Wight in 1930 to become W17 *Seaview*. (John Scott-Morgan collection)

The cab roof brackets and pulleys for the cable worked motor train equipment favoured by the LSWR are clearly visible on O2 class No. 201, with Drummond livery and chimney. No. 201 was also sent to the Isle of Wight in 1947 as W34 *Newport*, where it survived for only eight years. Taken into Ryde works for overhaul in 1955, it was found to be beyond economic repair and consequently scrapped. (John Scott-Morgan collection)

The mainland engines could be found at work into the 1950s as regular motive power on the Bere Alston-Callington branch, and the Portland branch in Dorset, with the last examples withdrawn in 1962.

O2s remained at work in the Isle of Wight until 31 December 1966, when regular steam services between Ryde and Shanklin ended, to be replaced by former London

Master of his Art 129

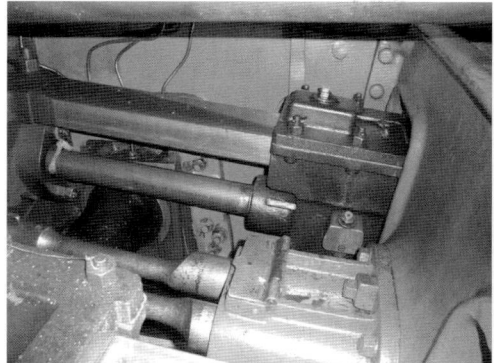 

Above left: The Adams preference for a single heavy slidebar is demonstrated by O2 class W24 *Calbourne*.

Above right: The left-hand side crosshead and slidebar of W24.

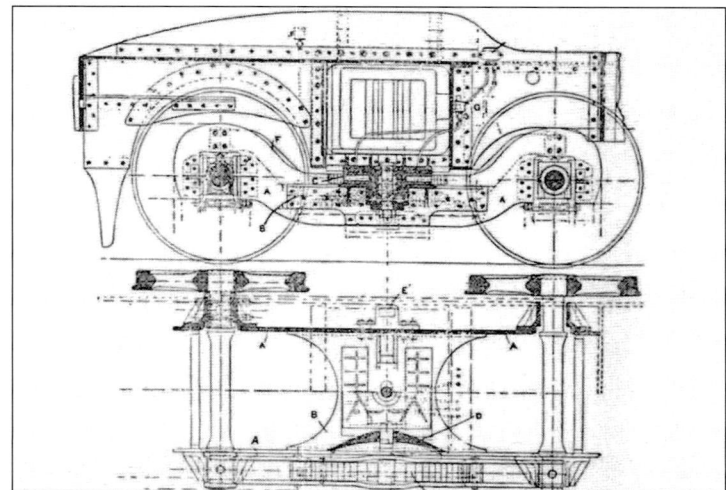

A Nine Elms drawing of an Adams type bogie for the O2 class. (Andy Summers, IWSR)

The bogie centre pin of O2 class W24 *Calbourne*, demonstrating the allowance for lateral sideplay.

The first O2 class locomotives transferred to the Isle of Wight by the Southern Railway were still in LSWR livery. No. 211, which later became W20 *Shanklin*, is unloaded from the floating crane at Ryde Pier Head on 4 May 1923. (IWSR Archive)

The versatile O2s proved very suitable for working the Bere Alston to Callington branch. Drummond boilered No. 30193 arrives at the branch terminus on 6 May 1961. (Mike Morant)

Transport tube stock, although two locomotives were retained for engineers' trains for a further three months. The island's network had been gradually cut back since 1952, with a consequent reduction in the number of locomotives required, but in 1964 fourteen engines were still required for the busy Summer Saturday schedule which was, in those last few years, and for only a few weeks each year, the most intensively worked steam service in the UK. When it is considered that no major spare components had been manufactured since 1936, it is a commendable achievement that the small works at Ryde, albeit with the support of Eastleigh, kept the O2s in traffic for so long. A crisis developed in the spring of 1964 when ultrasonic testing condemned the dangerously thin cylinder walls of four locomotives. Mainland depot stores were scoured and two new unused cylinder blocks were located at Exmouth Junction and Eastleigh. It is also a testament to their designer that in their seventh decade, they were still well capable of maintaining the type of intensive service for which they were designed, with up to six-coach train weights of 150 tons, and a testing, lengthy 1 in 70 gradient on the Ryde to Ventnor road. On that fateful day in December 1966, W14 *Fishbourne*, originally LSWR No. 178 built in 1889, and by then the oldest engine working on the BR system, became the last Adams locomotive to work a main line passenger train, with a total recorded mileage at withdrawal of 1,411,809.

A six-coupled design for freight and shunting, the G6 class shared many components with the O2 class. Ten were ordered in June 1893, and the class eventually numbered

Ryde works continued to repair the remaining O2s until July 1966, and in April of that year, W28 *Ashey* received attention to 'bottom end' bearings. Although earmarked for withdrawal in 1964, she remained in traffic until the final day of Isle of Wight steam, 31 December 1966. (Andrew Southwell)

The footplate of O2 class W28 *Ashey*, originally LSWR No. 186, at Ventnor in April 1964. (David Christie)

On the last day, no less than eight of the remaining O2s were steamed. The Locomotive Club of Great Britain arranged a special train, using now preserved W24 *Calbourne* and Drummond boilered W31 *Chale*, the last double header with two Adams locomotives. Although all the other remaining engines were withdrawn the following day, these two were retained for a few more weeks for engineering trains. W24 had received a general overhaul just eighteen months earlier, whilst earlier in 1965, W31 had been fitted with new cylinders. (Roger Joanes)

thirty-four, the remainder actually built by Drummond following Adams' retirement, largely using spare boilers taken from withdrawn reboilered Beattie engines, and one of only two classes perpetuated by his successor. Once again, the design fulfilled expectations not only with goods duties, but at times used for station pilot and banking duties at Exeter. As boilers were replaced in later life the locomotives often found

The last steaming of an Adams locomotive by British Railways occurred on 18 April 1967, when O2 class W27 *Merstone* was used to shunt eight of her sisters into position for breaking up in Newport yard. The engines had been stored in the platforms of the by then closed station for the previous three months.The boiler is filled with assistance from the local fire brigade, as driver Roy Rodwell and his colleagues prepare to light up. (Iain Whitlam)

Originally LSWR No. 184, W27 was actually the property of the scrap merchant H.B. Jolliffe at the time of her final duty, and the firm's crane and lorry are already in attendance. Within days most of the non-ferrous fittings had been stripped from the locomotives. (Iain Whitlam)

themselves with Drummond pattern spares, as new Adams type boilers were fitted in preference to the O2 class. The first withdrawals commenced in 1948, with the last two survivors transferred to Departmental Stock as DS 682/3152 for use at Meldon Quarry. Finally replaced by a USA tank, DS 682 was withdrawn in 1962.

Left: G6 class 0-6-0T, with BR identity 30238, ended its career on shunting duties at Meldon Quarry renumbered DS 682. (Roger Joanes)

Below: G6 class No. 273 was not built until 1898, after Adams had retired; a view thought to be at Strawberry Hill shed. (John Scott-Morgan collection)

G6 class 30266 in ex-works condition at Brighton in March 1952, shortly before return to service from its allocated shed at Basingstoke. (Mike Morant)

To cater for the increasing need for smaller yard shunters, Adams designed an outside-cylinder four-coupled side tank, designated B4 class, and an order was placed for twenty locomotives in August 1890. Although the railway had the 330 class Beyer, Peacocks, and an assortment of small Manning Wardle tanks, the provision of purpose-built shunters, with just four coupled wheels making them more adaptable in tightly curved environments, was considered a worthwhile investment. With 16in x 22in cylinders, 3ft 9¾in diameter coupled wheels, and a wheelbase of 7ft 0in, they weighed 33 tons 9cwt. After the LSWR absorbed the Southampton Dock Company two B4s were transferred to the subsidiary in 1893. With modified cutaway cabs to improve visibility, Nos. 81 and 176 were named *Jersey* and *Guernsey*. So successful were they that ten more followed.

1891 built B4 class No. 86 was named *Havre* by the Southampton Docks dept, and is seen here outside the docks shed. (ETH Archive)

Britanny, sporting a Drummond chimney, with linseed oil filter visible behind the dome. No. 97 was one of five engines sold to David R. Zeiler & Co. in 1949, a firm engaged on the construction of Bilton Iron & Steel works in Staffordshire. (ETH Archive)

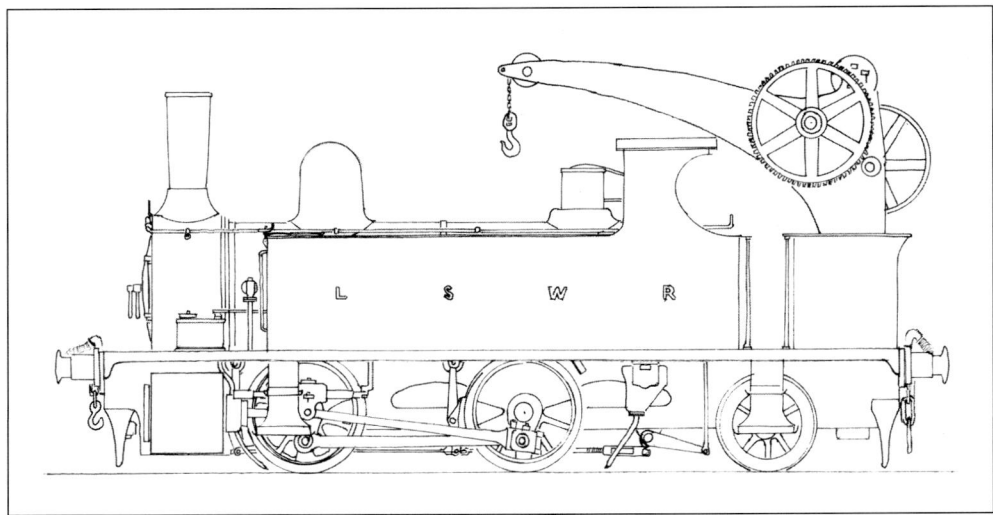

The crane locomotive conversion at Bow Works had clearly proved its worth, as Adams designed a similar crane variant of the B4 dock tank. The intention was to build three, but the order was cancelled and proprietary self-propelled locomotive cranes were used instead.

In 1894, Adams produced a crane tank variant with a lengthened frame and a pair of trailing wheels. In November of that year an order was placed for three engines, to cost £1,485 each, for use at Nine Elms Works, Northam (at that time a major locomotive depot) and Wimbledon. However, it was subsequently decided that the intended work could be done more cost effectively by self-propelled yard cranes, and the order was cancelled.

Drummond actually built five more B4s in 1907, with his own pattern boiler. They were numbered 82-4, and 746/7, and 84 had the honour of being the last locomotive to be built at Nine Elms, with 746/7 turned out by the then new works at Eastleigh.

By 1948, many of the class were redundant, the Southampton Docks fleet replaced by former US Army six-coupled tanks, nearly new engines which the Southern had managed to obtain as war surplus at a very advantageous price. A number of engines were offered for sale, with eleven finding new industrial users as far north as Northumberland, whilst others were sent outside south western territory, finding work at locations such as Dover Docks and Chislet Colliery in east Kent. When No. 96 was withdrawn as BR No. 30096, it was sold in late 1963 to P.D. Fuels, for use at Dibles Wharf, Southampton, where it continued to work, named *Corrall Queen*, until 1972, by which time it was the very last Adams locomotive in commercial service.

Shortly after celebrating his sixty-fifth birthday in 1888, William Adams considered building further class 445 express locomotives but, despite their size and power, increased train weights and demands for tighter schedules indicated the need for something more powerful still. Six months later, in May 1889, the design of a new class X2 enlarged express locomotive with 7ft 1in driving wheels was approved, and an order placed for twenty, the first being delivered in June 1890.

They had 19in x 26in cylinders and a larger boiler than the 445 class, with a grate area of 18 square feet, a total heating surface of 1,367 square feet and boiler pressure

One of several B4 class dock shunters sold for industrial service in 1949, Taylor Woodrow's No. SL1 worked for a year or so at Waun Wen opencast coal site near Blaenavon before resale to Blaenavon ironworks. It had originally been built under Drummond as No. 747 *Dinard* in 1908. (Mike Morant)

The last Adams engine in commercial service was B4 dock tank, BR No. 30096, seen here shunting Eling Wharf, Southampton. Bearing the name *Corrall Queen*, it remained in use with her owner P.D. Fuels until 1972, latterly with the cab roof reprofiled. (Anthony Storey)

of 175lb. No. 577 was the first to be completed and while it was being tested, concerns were raised over several issues including whether its small firebox size and tender water capacity of 3,000 gallons would be adequate for the heavier duties. These were the result of misunderstanding in the drawing office, rather than inherent design flaws. Adams was able to substitute 3,300 gallon tenders, but the firebox design was less simple to remedy, as many boilers had by now been built.

X2 class No. 577 as built, with coupling rod splashers and narrow cab. (Tony Hisgett)

584 once again, showing the 3,300 gallon tender. (John Scott-Morgan collection)

X2 class No.588 awaits departure from Bournemouth early in the Edwardian era. (Mike Morant)

Master of his Art 139

An X2 class locomotive, No. 582, sister to No. 579, was chosen by Adams and Pettigrew for a series of trials in July 1891. (ETH Archive)

X2 class 593 prepared for the photographer, probably shortly after delivery 1893. Note the piston tail rods, later removed. (ETH Archive)

In July 1891, Adams and Pettigrew conducted a comprehensive series of trials with an X2 class locomotive, No. 582, on the main lines from Waterloo to Bournemouth and Exeter. The test runs are summarised below.

Table A. Trial journeys

Test No.	Date	Journey	Distance
1	9 July 1891	5.50 am Waterloo-Bournemouth	111 miles
2	9 July 1891	1.55 pm Bournemouth-Waterloo	111 miles
3	10 July 1891	11.00 am Waterloo-Exeter	171½ miles
4	11 July 1891	12.54pm Exeter-Waterloo (Note a)	171½ miles
5	13 July 1891	2.40 pm Waterloo-Salisbury	83½ miles

Note:
a) The trial was aborted at Woking because of delays, apparently the result of the local racing calendar and a review of troops at Wimbledon! Therefore, the distance over which meaningful measurements could be taken was 147 miles.

The results, which are thought to be the most detailed and comprehensive study carried out in the Victorian era, were presented in a paper entitled 'Trials of an Express Locomotive', submitted to the Institution of Civil Engineers. Table B gives a brief summary of measurements taken and data gathered, which extended to nearly seventy categories, enabling the authors to calculate the overall boiler efficiency of the locomotive as 66.54 per cent, and the overall efficiency (boiler and engine) of No. 582 as 7.34 per cent. The paper won both co-authors a Telford Premium and George Stephenson Medal and is recorded in the Institution's Proceedings Volume 125 of 1895/6. An abridged version is included as Appendix B.

Table B. Summary of test results

Trial No.	1	2	3	4	5
Mean load tons (note a)	180	136	168	199	138
Intermediate stops	11	4	3	5	3
Maximum speed mph	68.50	67.00	78.00	81.00	75.00
Mean speed excluding stops mph	37.00	45.20	46.10	44.45	46.70
Average boiler pressure lb/sq in	167.50	167.20	171.70	169.40	170.80
Coal burnt lb per train mile	30.50	28.10	28.40	32.98	28.16
Water evaporated, lb per train mile	296.28	246.90	251.30	260.90	262.60
Maximum Indicated hp	684.10	610.10	803.60	804.30	626.10
Efficiency of engine %	9.8	9.55	10.7	11.02	9.61
Efficiency of boiler %	77.50	70.00	71.10	66.60	75.50
Overall combined efficiency of boiler and engine %	7.70	6.68	7.60	7.34	7.25

Note:
a) On certain journeys the train formation altered during the course of the trial. For example, in test 1, the train left Waterloo with a train load of 239 tons exclusive of locomotive and tender, but this had reduced to 116 tons by the time that it departed from Brockenhurst. Hence a mean train load is given.

Earlier, in July 1890, the company was asked by the President of the International Congress on Railways for permission to appoint William Adams as one of its 'reporters' for the next such event, to be held in St Petersburg in 1892. The conference would cover a wide range of topics, with Adams allocated the subject of high-pressure boilers, along with two continental European counterparts, M. Parent of the Chemin de Fer de l'État Français and M. Carcanagues of Chemin de Fer Paris à Lyon et la Mediterranée. The two Frenchmen invited submissions and prepared a paper relating to the practice of compounding, whilst Adams was responsible for every other aspect of the development and use of high-pressure steam locomotive boilers. His fluency in at least two other European languages doubtless served him well, not only in seeking responses around the world, but also with the preparation of the final paper, and the results of the 1891 trials would have proved of great value too. Yet, for all the work involved, he was not one of the delegates to attend the actual meeting.

The X2 was followed by the T3, which was designed for duties to Portsmouth and services west of Salisbury, with 6ft 7in driving wheels. Adams seized the opportunity to lengthen the locomotive, with a 6ft 10in firebox, which gave a grate area of 19¾ square feet, and a total heating surface of 1,320 square feet. The first of twenty T3s appeared in 1893 as construction was delayed by a full order book at Nine Elms. The design changes incorporated undoubtedly produced a masterpiece, and one of the finest express locomotives of its day.

The T3 class was intended to replace the older 460 class locomotives. No. 571, new in August 1893, was initially allocated to Fratton shed. It was the last of the class to receive an overhaul in 1938 and remained at work until withdrawal in 1943. (ETH Archive)

579, withdrawn in May 1932, was, within a few months, being dismantled in Eastleigh works, alongside T1 and 395 class locomotives under repair. The freshly painted tank covers in front of No. 579 are probably for Stroudley E1 class locomotives being prepared for transfer to the Isle of Wight. (John Scott-Morgan collection)

X2 class No. 578 pilots T3 class No. 560 on a Reading bound parcels train through Basingstoke in Southern days. (Mike Morant)

Master of his Art 143

The increased dimensions of the T3 were then incorporated into a further order in October 1894 for ten locomotives, numbered 677-86, with large 7ft 1in diameter driving wheels, which became the T6 class. Just one month later, another order was placed for ten more engines, numbered 657-66, with 6ft 7in driving wheels, which became the X6 class, but construction of both designs only commenced after Adams had retired.

These four locomotive classes were the pinnacle of a distinguished career, robustly constructed, yet elegant, capable performers; they remained in charge of express duties until gradually displaced by Drummond-designed engines. Withdrawals commenced in the early 1930s, and the last one in use was X6 class No. 658, ending its days on shunting and light goods duties, being finally condemned in December 1946.

T6 class No. 682 new in December 1895, photographed in works grey livery. (ETH Archive)

The final 4-4-0 design was the X6 class. No. 658 was completed by Nine Elms works in December 1895 after Adams' retirement, and was the last example withdrawn exactly fifty-one years later. Classmate No. 657 found fame in 1937 with a role in the Will Hay film *Oh! Mr Porter*, filmed on the recently closed Basingstoke and Alton line. (John Scott-Morgan collection)

A special duty for an unidentified class X6 locomotive, with a Waterloo & City Railway tube car sandwiched between two match wagons, at Esher, shortly before the opening of the line in 1898. The American built tube stock was shipped to Southampton Docks in knocked down form and was assembled at Eastleigh works prior to delivery to London. (John Scott-Morgan collection)

In October 1889, the first meeting of the Association of Railway Locomotive Engineers was held, which was in effect a reincarnation of the Association of Locomotive Engineers in Scotland, an organisation which had become dormant some years earlier, but was now reconstituted to include England, Wales and Ireland as well. William was unable to attend this meeting, but he was present at the next one on 15 January 1890. His brother-in-law John Park did attend the inaugural meeting which saw Samuel Johnson and Dugald Drummond elected chairman and vice-chairman respectively, although within months the latter departed for an interlude in Australia.

Early in 1887, the Adams household moved to Carlton House, Carlton Road, Putney, and two years later son John Henry married Theodora Carter at St Luke's Church, Hackney. He had briefly returned home from an overseas post, but the newlyweds returned to South America before the birth of granddaughter Winifred the following year at Imbituba, in the southern Brazilian state of Santa Catarina. In 1877, the 17-year-old John Henry had commenced an apprenticeship with his father at Stratford and followed him to Nine Elms the following year. His subsequent railway career is described separately in the following chapter.

It is inevitable that not all proposals and designs put forward by a locomotive superintendent would result in orders for new engines for a wide variety of reasons, and in 1886 one such idea was for a more powerful radial tank. The existing 415 class featured a lengthy bunker with water space below, but it was reasoned that if this was replaced by 1,200 gallon side tanks and a shorter bunker, the resulting additional overall length of a more powerful engine with 18in x 26in cylinders and a correspondingly larger boiler could be kept to a minimum. In the event the concept was not pursued, to be replaced by the T1 class 0-4-4 tanks introduced two years later.

Although William Adams had experience of Sinclair's single driver express engines during his time at the Great Eastern, it is perhaps rather surprising that it was only in the last years of his career that he embarked upon a proposal for such a type, intended for fast, non-stop working between London and Bournemouth. Having fallen out of favour because of poor adhesion, and low tractive effort with increasingly heavier trains, there was a resurgence of interest in the concept in the 1880s. A further batch of Patrick Stirling's famous 'eight footers' was ordered for the Great Northern Railway in 1884, and a new design by Samuel Waite Johnson introduced to the Midland Railway in 1887. Indeed, further examples of both types were built as late as 1896 and 1899 respectively.

Adams visited Derby works in June 1893 to evaluate the Johnson-designed locomotives, following the presentation, three months earlier, of his own drawings to the Locomotive Committee, whose members would have doubtless expressed a degree of surprise at the proposal before them.

Adams was clearly impressed by the economy and performance of the Johnson engines, and arrangements were made for the LSWR to trial one of the MR engines, No. 1872, on its own metals, an idea that eventually foundered when the civil engineer discovered the axle loading of the single and vetoed the scheme.

Axle weight loading would eventually kill off any prospect of a South Western single, another victim of the constant battle waged between those responsible for the requirements of the traffic, locomotive and civil engineering departments, in an attempt to keep designs for more powerful engines within acceptable weight limits. The LSWR civil engineer stipulated that any such design must not exceed an axle loading of 17½ tons, whereas the locomotive proposed by Adams resulted in a driving axle weight of 19 tons. The design also featured driving wheels of 8ft 0in diameter, cylinders of 19in diameter and 28in stroke, the largest of any Adams locomotive, with a boiler of similar dimensions to the T6 class, pressed to 175lb.

There then followed a design for another express 4-4-0, which would have been the ninth class with this particular wheel arrangement produced by Adams for the LSWR.

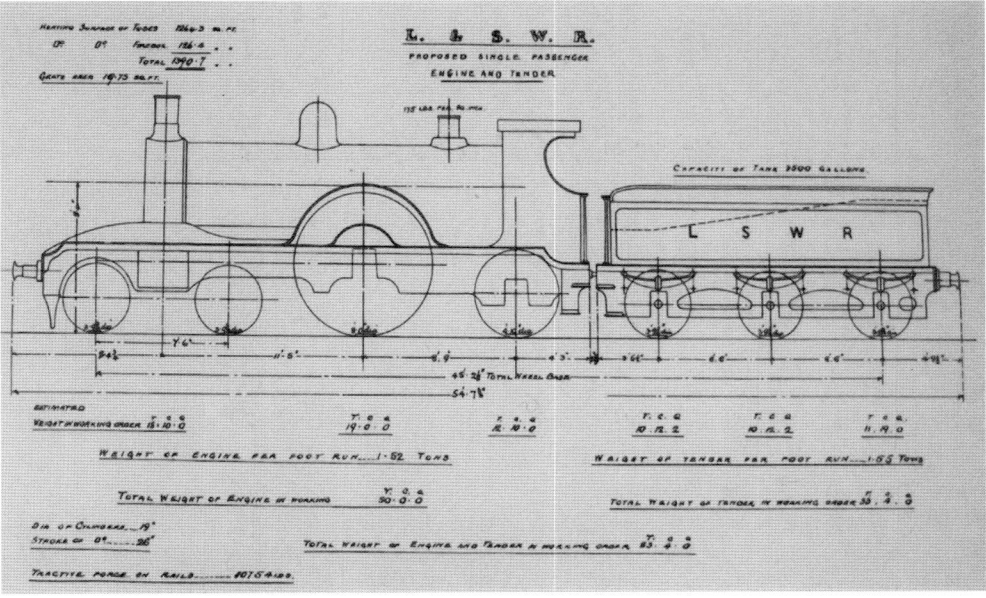

Towards the end of his career, Adams became interested in the possibility of a new single driver design and presented a sketch design to the Locomotive Committee in April 1893.

He subsequently arranged for the loan of an 1853 class 4-2-2 locomotive from the Midland Railway – a class introduced in 1891 by Samuel Waite Johnson, his predecessor at the GER – but the proposed trial was rejected by the Civil Engineer on weight grounds. (Tony Hisgett)

With the same-sized cylinders as the proposed single, the new four-coupled engines were drawn with 7ft 7in diameter driving wheels. The leading coupled axle bore a loading of 16¾ tons, within the limits imposed by the civil engineer, but the idea was abandoned as the proposal for a new T6 class, with 7ft 1in driving wheels, was drawn up. It was envisaged that the T6, with slightly smaller wheels, would be more useful over a wider range of routes, particularly the more tortuous line between Salisbury and Exeter.

Although the Great Eastern Moguls had not been a success, the idea of a 2-6-0 design for freight work was in many respects eminently sensible, and when the need for a more powerful goods engine became apparent in 1894, Adams proposed a new class which could utilise a range of existing components and patterns.

The outside cylinders were 19in x 26in, the same size as the GER Moguls, but the coupled wheels were slightly larger at 5ft 1in diameter. Whilst the firebox had a larger grate area of 19.75 square feet, as opposed to 17.8 square feet of the earlier engines, the overall heating surface was only 1,268 square feet compared with the figure of 1,400 square feet for the Stratford class.

The design would almost certainly have been built at an estimated cost of £2,380 per locomotive, were it not for lack of immediate capacity at Nine Elms works, followed by Adams' retirement before an order could be placed. His successor, Dugald Drummond, showed no interest in continuing with the project which was quietly shelved, with no opportunity of proving the design.

What was probably the only narrow-gauge engine for which William Adams became responsible was a small tramway locomotive operated by the National Rifle Association at its Bisley ranges. The NRA had previously built a 3ft 6in gauge tramway for its shooting ranges at Wimbledon Common, worked by a small Merryweather steam tram engine named *Wharncliffe*, but had relocated to Bisley in 1890. The line was relaid at Bisley, still to 3ft 6in gauge, and the LSWR agreed to take over maintenance and operation in 1893.

The LSWR and NRA enjoyed a close relationship, and in 1894 *Wharncliffe* was taken to Nine Elms for overhaul. Drawings prepared at the time have given rise to the theory that it was actually designed by Adams, but they do in fact show the Merryweather product. In Adams' time it sported a blue and cream livery, but it was later reboilered by Merryweather, and bore a red and cream colour scheme with its appearance altered by the removal of the tramway skirts.

Wharncliffe was not the only oddity associated with the LSWR, as seven assorted locomotives were taken over with the acquisition of the Southampton Dock Company in November 1892. Although the older engines were retained, with one, *Canute*, which had been supplied by Dick & Stevenson in 1870, finding a new use as a stationary boiler, four were officially taken into stock, all four-coupled saddle tanks. The newest two were 1890 products of Hawthorn, Leslie, named *Clausentum* and *Ironside*, which were allocated the numbers 457/8, whilst the other pair, *Vulcan* and *Bretwalda*, had been built by Vulcan Foundry in 1878, and these were numbered 118 and 408 respectively. Soon displaced at the docks by B4 tanks, *Bretwalda* and *Clausentum* were set to work on the Southampton Royal Pier tramway, whilst the other two were found employment as shunters in the Bournemouth and Poole area.

William Adams also acquired a number of second-hand Manning, Wardle saddle tanks for various specific purposes over the years, the first arrival in December 1879 being a standard I class six-coupled design, bought at a cost of £380 for use on the

Perhaps the only narrow gauge locomotive for which Adams was responsible was *Wharncliffe*, the Merryweather steam tram operated by the National Rifle Association at its Bisley Tramway. It was overhauled at Nine Elms in 1893 but is seen here after a subsequent reboilering by its builder. (Christopher Bunch)

Clapham Junction-Wimbledon widening project. Named *Lady Portsmouth*, and dating from 1862, it gave good service and was considered worthy of a new boiler and cylinders in 1885. In the same month, another opportunity presented itself to acquire a third Shanks tramway locomotive to share the Royal Pier tramway duties with the existing pair of engines, *Cowes* and *Southampton*, which had been supplied in 1877. It had been employed on a contract at Cuxhaven harbour and retained the name *Ritzebuttel* throughout its South Western days.

Two smaller four-coupled E class Manning, Wardles were purchased in 1881 for the harbour branches in the Plymouth area. As numbers 407/8, *Pioneer* and *Jessie* were joined by a sister, No. 457 *St Michael*, two years later. *Jessie* was broken up in 1892, but her boiler survived to provide hot water for boiler washing at Nine Elms works.

Later in 1883, two more I class 0-6-0STs were found for use at Nine Elms goods yard, where horses were widely employed for shunting, and it was estimated that each locomotive would replace ten animals and five men, as well as significantly speed up operations. Dating from 1862/3, the two engines were named *Jumbo* and *Sambo*.

Apart from *Jessie* and *St Michael*, all were still on the books when William Adams' successor took over, having proved their worth on a variety of duties across the network.

Since 1857 the civil engineer's department had maintained a separate fleet of locomotives for its own use, but following the unexpected and sudden death of its chief, William Jacomb, in 1887, his successor Edmund Andrews agreed with Adams that it would be more expedient for the locomotive department to take over this work, and thus he found himself responsible for a further fourteen assorted engines, the oldest of which were long-boilered 2-4-0s by George England of Hatcham Ironworks, dating from 1857/8. As they became due for heavy repair they were withdrawn and replaced by displaced locomotives from the running fleet.

When Adams joined the LSWR, he was responsible for a fleet of 386 locomotives working approximately 9,000,000 train miles annually, but by 1895 that total had risen to 664 engines working roughly double the mileage. He had undoubtedly modernised and improved working practices and consequently efficiency at Nine Elms. An American journalist, John E. Sweet, writing for the magazine *Machinery*, who visited in 1895, was impressed by a 'Locomotive boiler made tight without calking [sic], in fact a boiler shop where both drift pin and calking tool were prohibited was a new thing to me, as was the whole boiler construction'. However, colleagues were gradually becoming aware that their chief was increasingly absent-minded and at times rather vague, and it fell to William Pettigrew as works manager to keep the locomotive department running properly. It was also apparent that his informal style was now leading to a reduction in overall efficiency of the department, and a gradual tacit acceptance of dubious practices such as drinking by enginemen. It is perhaps a measure of his decency and sense of fairness that there are many records in the Locomotive Committee minutes of his requests for sick pay or other financial aid for men unable to work through illness or workplace injury. Although such requests were often granted, his presentation of a petition by enginemen in July 1893 for one-week annual leave 'without stoppage of pay' was given short shrift by the committee and dismissed. In time, the symptoms of what today would be recognised as the early stages of dementia became a matter of concern to the board, and 'Old Daddy Adams' as he had become

Adams' residence in retirement, Hill Rise, in Amersham Road, now renamed Mercier Road, Putney. (Rob Dembrey)

known tendered his resignation on 29 May 1895, which was accepted by the board a fortnight later. In retirement he remained in Putney, albeit moving to a smaller house, Hill Rise, Amersham Road (today renamed Mercier Road), just around the corner from Carlton Road, in February 1896.

His wife died in 1898, but daughter Isabella and teenage granddaughter Nancy, together with a nurse, remained at the house with him, where he died early in the morning of 7 August 1904, by which time his condition had deteriorated to the point where he no longer recognised friends and family. His funeral took place on 10 August, followed by burial at Putney Vale Cemetery. The mourners included his son William John, who had returned from Australia. In his very lengthy and detailed will, a document which, with three codicils, extended to some fourteen pages, he made bequests to the many members of his family. His estate, which totalled nearly £64,000 (equivalent to some £8 million in 2022), included a number of residential properties in Kenninghall Road, Clapton, plus a variety of investments in railway companies, both at home and abroad. His love of music is demonstrated by the specific bequests of his pianos, including a grand by Steinway, plus bound volumes of Italian operas.

Although it had a very capable and competent potential successor in 37-year-old William Pettigrew, the board decided to cast the net wider in search of a replacement, perhaps still conscious of the need to bring in an external candidate as they had done with Adams himself and later Scotter. Their choice was a much older man, Dugald

Left: The gravestone at Putney Vale Cemetery, where William and Isabella are buried. (Marion Turner)

Below: A second memorial stone erected by the enginemen of the LSWR in William's memory. (Mike Fell)

Drummond, by now in his mid-fifties, whose career had included spells with the North British and Caledonian railways, plus a brief, fairly disastrous, interlude in Australia, and a something less than successful venture into business since his return. He was actually appointed at a salary of £1,500 per annum, the same figure that his predecessor had commanded on taking up his appointment nearly two decades earlier, and furthermore, less than his earlier salary at the Caledonian. Adams was known for his calm, easy going, gentlemanly personality, but his replacement was a man with a very different temperament, and a gruff, uncompromising manner. Some years earlier, in 1885, Adams and his brother-in-law John Carter Park had sponsored Drummond in his application for membership of the Institution of Mechanical Engineers.

Although Drummond continued to build further G6 and B4 class locomotives, he was eager to make his own mark, and over a period of time removed a number of Adams features from his locomotives, including the vortex blast pipe and compensating suspension beams. An order for a final batch of ten O2 class engines was cancelled by the new chief, a decision apparently made without reference to the Locomotive Committee, whose members expressed their concern and displeasure. Drummond was also an innovator, and developed a cross-tube firebox, and a smokebox steam drier, which was at best an indifferent attempt to develop an alternative form of superheater. His four-coupled designs were reasonably capable locomotives, but the heavy six-coupled machines developed towards the end of his career were somewhat less than successful. Earlier in his professional life he had been an assistant to William Stroudley and retained his former chief's enthusiasm for feedwater heating with boiler feed pumps. Although he was not interested in pursuing Adams' idea of a single driver express locomotive, he did develop the concept of the 'double-single', with two independently driven axles, perhaps inspired by the LNWR's 2-2-2-0 compound locomotives designed by Francis Webb. However, the concept of the 'single' was not yet dead, as witnessed by his famous inspection saloon, the 4-2-4T which appeared in 1899 becoming well known as *The Bug,* and subsequently 0-2-2 designs used in railmotors and the small C14 class locomotives.

The Adams designs which were completed after Drummond took office were finished in what he termed a 'royal' green livery, darker than the pea green but not as dark as the holly green which he retained for the goods engines.

Under his stewardship, in the early years of the twentieth century, Nine Elms locomotives works was closed and transferred, along with staff, to join the carriage and wagon works at Eastleigh, whilst Nine Elms remained a major steam locomotive depot until the end of Southern Region steam operation in July 1967.

William Pettigrew had clearly enjoyed an excellent relationship with his old boss, who very probably regarded him as his natural successor, but he did not remain at Nine Elms for long, and was appointed chief mechanical engineer of the Furness Railway, a post he held until his retirement in 1918.

Pettigrew's departure led to the appointment as works manager of Robert Urie, who had previously held a similar position with the Caledonian Railway at St Rollox under Drummond. A fellow Scot, he later went on to succeed his boss, becoming the last CME of the LSWR in 1912.

CHAPTER 9

The Two Protégés, John Henry Adams and W.F. Pettigrew

Two of William Adams' apprentices went on to become locomotive designers in their own right, his son John Henry at the North Staffordshire Railway, plus GER apprentice and later Nine Elms colleague, William Frank Pettigrew, further north at the Furness Railway. It is therefore worth studying both their careers in a little more detail. It is also interesting to speculate whether son-in-law Gilbert Henry Garrett, having attained a senior management position at the Robert Stephenson works, would have found a similar opportunity had he not died at such a young age.

John was the third son of William and Isabella, born on 10 September 1860, and he grew up to pursue a notable career in railway engineering. He was educated at Brighton Grammar School, which had at the time just moved into a new purpose-built building in Buckingham Road, followed by Thanet Collegiate School in Margate, and finally in Brussels with a private tutor, Rev A. K. Havlock. He then commenced an apprenticeship under his father in the Drawing Office at Stratford in June 1877. He followed William to Nine Elms a few months later, and upon completion of his formal engineering training he gained valuable experience working on the footplate. In an article for the *Railway Magazine* published in 1904, John Adams described how:

> following the routine common to all engineering aspirants, working in erecting shop, brass and iron foundry, pattern shop, turnery, smithy and running shed [he was] desirous of becoming proficient in the practical handling of a locomotive, and served as a fireman on goods and passenger trains for nine months. I then passed the Inspector's test for an engine driver, and had charge of trains running between London and Exeter during a period of fifteen months.

Then came a move northwards to Leeds, where he was employed by Tannett Walker & Company, a firm specialising in the manufacture and installation of hydraulic pumps and associated machinery, where older brother William had also earlier been employed, in order to gain further experience in another aspect of mechanical engineering.

In July 1887 he was appointed Locomotive, Carriage and Wagon Superintendent of the Donna Thereza Christina Railway in Brazil, named after the Italian Princess Donna Christina Maria de Bourbon, the wife of Brazil's last Emperor, Dom Pedro II. This was a British-built metre gauge line about seventy miles in length, opened in 1884, and essentially intended for coal traffic between the mines at Lauro Müller in the southern state of Santa Catarina, and the port of Imbituba. Construction took nearly four years, and works included the Cabecuda viaduct, nearly a mile in length. Worked by 2-6-0 tank locomotives supplied by Hunslet and Nasmyth Wilson, John Adams arrived just as the railway suffered major damage by flooding, with consequent repairs to some bridges not completed until as late as 1890.

The country finally announced the formal abolition of the slave trade in 1888 which led to a wave of immigration from Europe, and more rapid development of the economy with the aid of foreign investment. However, the railway's base at Tubarao became the centre of a rebellion in 1893, resulting in revolutionaries working the line for several months. The projected financial returns failed to materialise, largely because of the poor quality of coal mined in the region, and British investors withdrew, resulting in nationalisation of the operation in 1902. The British built 2-6-0s were withdrawn in the 1920s, but larger replacement 2-10-4 locomotives were still active in the late 1970s.

A portrait of John Henry Adams of 1904. (Mike Fell)

After a little over ten years in post, John Adams resigned in September 1898, returning to England to be appointed the following January as Assistant Manager at the Ashford Works of the newly formed South Eastern & Chatham Railway. The new company, a merger of the perpetually squabbling London, Chatham & Dover and South Eastern railways had, in advance of the Act of Parliament authorising the merger, agreed a new strategy to concentrate locomotive building and repair work at Ashford, and run down the old LCDR works at Longhedge in south London. The South Eastern Railway had first established its locomotive works at Ashford in 1847, with a carriage and wagon facility opening three years later, and by the early 1880s the site employed over 1,300 men.

The locomotive superintendents of both the SER and LCDR, James Stirling and William Kirtley respectively, retired at the start of the merged operation, with Harry Wainwright taking overall control as the new Locomotive, Carriage and Wagon Superintendent. The new assistant works manager took up his position as Wainwright embarked on a programme of modernisation and expansion of the works.

On 25 March 1902 John Adams was one of four previously short-listed candidates interviewed for the position of Locomotive, Carriage and Wagon Superintendent of the North Staffordshire Railway. He proved to be the board's choice for he was duly appointed as successor to Luke Longbottom, whose death had created the vacancy, at an annual salary of £400, plus a house, rent and rates free. Thus, he and his family, now with three daughters, left their home in Christchurch Road, Ashford, in the Garden of England and headed northwards to Stoke-on-Trent and the heart of The Potteries. In the same year he was elected to membership of the Institution of Mechanical Engineers, proposed by Dugald Drummond, his father's successor at Nine Elms, and seconded by Samuel Waite Johnson.

The North Staffordshire Railway, colloquially known as 'The Knotty', operated a network of lines, around 200 route miles in total, within an area very roughly bounded by Macclesfield, Stafford and Crewe. Apart from largely local passenger trains, it conveyed large quantities of manufactured pottery and china goods, plus the more usual coal traffic. Despite being surrounded by larger concerns, and within a heavily industrialised area, it survived various merger proposals and remained independent until the grouping in 1923.

The engineering base was centred at Stoke-on-Trent, and within a few months John Adams had persuaded a former Ashford colleague, the Chief Locomotive Draughtsman Basil Kingsford Field, to join him at Stoke as the new Works Manager. However, he only stayed for a very short period before being succeeded in November 1902 by another ex-Ashford man, John Hookham, who had just returned from a brief interlude in Brazil as John Adams' successor at the DTCR.

The Stoke works had constructed most of the NSR's new locomotives since 1875, but at the time of Adams' appointment was engaged in a rebuilding programme initiated by Longbottom.

During his first year in office, he oversaw the completion of nine such rebuilds, mainly tank and tender six-coupled types, plus one 2-4-0. In the following year, twenty more were outshopped, and he also adopted a new livery of madder lake, lined in yellow, which was first applied to a 2-4-0 ex-works in September 1903. The NSR board must have been pleased with their man, as his salary was now increased to £500 per annum.

Conscious of the urgent need for new, powerful locomotives, the first three engines built at Stoke in 1902 were DX class 0-6-2 tanks to an existing Longbottom design.

The erecting shop at Stoke works, with a variety of classes evident. Note the pile of coupled wheel castings in the foreground. (Mike Fell)

However, in that first year six more 0-6-2 radial tanks, the new L Class, were authorised, and an order placed with Vulcan Foundry for their construction. Bearing NSR numbers 165-170, they were intended for heavy mixed traffic duties and, with thoughts towards standardisation, Adams claimed that many parts could be fitted to older engines. Just as the stovepipe chimney had become a trademark of his father at the South Western, Adams introduced his own design at the NSR, first carried by the L Class, which would become a familiar feature on all his subsequent locomotives, although it has been said to have originated at the desk of Basil Kingsford Field. He also took heed of paternal thinking in regard to boiler design, utilising reasonably sized boiler tubes with ample water circulation space. Another South Eastern feature imported from Ashford was the steam-operated reversing gear.

Adams then embarked on an 0-4-4 tank locomotive design, the M class, the NSR's first class to utilise a bogie which was, unsurprisingly, to his father's patented pattern. The first two, numbered 9 and 11, were built at Stoke works in 1907, with three more, numbers 12, 41 and 42, completed in the following year.

However, before the first of the four-coupled tanks appeared, three more 2-4-0s were built at Stoke in 1905/6, an old design but paired with a new Adams design tender, a feature of which was improved bearing design. The early Edwardian period is also associated with a rapid growth of interest in the concept of the steam railmotor and its economy of operation, an idea that was not lost on the NSR's General Manager, William Douglas Phipps, faced with declining passenger numbers caused by competition from new electrified tramways. The railway therefore ordered three units, with 0-2-2 locomotive portions built by Beyer, Peacock. These were to a standard

In 1907, John Adams built two 0-4-4 tanks at Stoke, to a new design, designated class M. They were, in fact, the first NSR locomotives to feature a bogie, which was to his father's design. (ETH Archive)

The following year saw the completion of the first four 0-6-2 tanks to Adams' new L class design. No. 93 was part of the second batch dating from 1909. (ETH Archive)

Many railways experimented with steam railmotors during the Edwardian era, and the NSR too attempted to exploit the potential cost savings offered by their use. The only new motive power not built at Stoke by John Adams, the three railmotors were delivered by Beyer, Peacock in 1905, part of a batch of eight designed and constructed by the Manchester firm. (Mike Fell)

design of the Gorton manufacturer, which presumably did not involve Adams and his team at Stoke. A total of eight was built, with the remainder supplied to the London, Brighton & South Coast Railway and the United Railways of Havana, Cuba.

A further development of the 0-6-2T design produced the NEW L variant, of which sixteen were built in three batches between 1908 and 1913. The last batch differed slightly in carrying Belpaire, rather than round-topped, fireboxes.

After production of the 1908 batch NEW L class, attention at Stoke turned to a new six-coupled goods tender engine, the H class, which bore a remarkable similarity to the SECR C class, and four examples were constructed at Stoke in 1909. They not only proved their worth on longer freight workings but could also be found on passenger diagrams too.

No. 96 was a New L class, but part of a 1913 batch which featured a slightly larger heating surface area. (ETH Archive)

John Adams had improved the efficiency of Stoke works within the physical constraints of the site, such that all new locomotives were built in-house, including the next, and possibly his finest design, the G class 4-4-0 express locomotive. Intended principally for working between Derby and the North Wales resort of Llandudno, four were built in 1910. In the same year two more six-coupled goods engines were turned out but fitted with Belpaire fireboxes; they were designated class H1.

The first Adams design to incorporate both superheater and piston valves was the K class 4-4-2 tank locomotive, intended for passenger working, with seven built in 1911/12. Former Ashford and Stoke colleague Basil Kingsford Field was by now chief draughtsman at the Brighton works of the LBSCR (after an interim spell in the motor car industry), and it is perhaps no coincidence that the new K class had many features in common with the contemporary Brighton 4-4-2 tank designs!

The K class 4-4-2 passenger tanks were the first locomotives built at Stoke to feature superheaters and piston valves. No. 8 was one of four completed in 1911. (ETH Archive)

A solitary tender version of the class, designated KT, was turned out as a 4-4-0 in October 1912. Numbered 38, it could also claim to be the first NSR locomotive to be fitted with Ross 'pop' safety valves rather than the hitherto standard Ramsbottom style.

John Adams' last design was the C class 0-6-4 tank, a type which totalled eight engines completed in 1914/15. Like the K and KT, they were superheated, but this time with the Robinson type, rather than the Schmidt pattern of their predecessors. All four bogie wheels were braked, and in another unusual NSR feature they had a feedwater heater and pump, along with a single injector.

Seven class K locomotives were completed, but the intended eighth was actually turned out as the solitary class KT 4-4-0 tender locomotive. No. 38 entered service in 1912. (ETH Archive)

1914 saw the introduction of the New C class 0-6-4T design, which was Adams' last. Intended mainly for freight traffic, they featured brakes on the bogie wheels, superheaters and piston valves. No. 31, in common with the rest of the class, only worked for around twenty years until withdrawal. (ETH Archive)

A particular interest of John Adams was the improvement of valve piston packing, which he saw as an imperative to achieving the full benefit from a superheated boiler, and the Proceedings of the Institution of Civil Engineers for 1913-14 contain a contribution by him on the subject. Unlike his father, he was not a member of the ICE, yet they both described themselves as civil engineers at various times during their careers, and indeed the William Adams/Frank Pettigrew paper 'Trials of an Express Locomotive' had been published by the ICE rather than a journal of mechanical engineering.

John Adams was of course also responsible for carriages and wagons, and he not only introduced bogie passenger stock in 1906, but in a period of five years between 1909 and 1914 built 625 new wagons at Stoke works which represented about ten per cent of the total owned by the company.

Sadly, at the age of just fifty-five, John Adams died unexpectedly on 7 November 1915 at his Congleton home. He had a known heart condition, but had been at work, as normal, the previous day. Just four days later, he was buried alongside his father at Putney Vale cemetery, with Stoke Works closed for the day.

Apart from his purely professional life at Stoke, he had, once again like his father, been a strong advocate for education amongst his staff, and was held in high regard. He also upheld the family's reputation for making music and enjoyed singing.

By 1913 he was responsible for a total of 1,615 employees, encompassing the locomotive, carriage and wagon workshops, plus running staff. During his time in office sixty-four new locomotives were constructed for the NSR, of which fifty-five were built in-house at Stoke.

His locomotives, which were all well regarded, lived on, but following the grouping the mighty LMS pursued a ruthless policy of standardisation and the last one in service, M class 0-4-4T No. 41 (which was by then LMS No. 1434), was withdrawn in August 1939. He was succeeded by John Hookham, who built more New L class 0-6-2 tanks, four of which were subsequently sold for industrial service with Manchester Collieries Ltd. Fortunately, one of these, originally NSR No. 2, finally retired in 1965, has survived. It was actually restored to its original NSR livery in 1960 as part of the Stoke-on-Trent Golden Jubilee celebrations and continued to work in that guise for another five years. It eventually became part of the National Collection but was de-accessioned in 2018 and was found a new home at the Foxfield Railway in its native Staffordshire.

William Pettigrew was clearly well regarded by William Adams, and the two men enjoyed a good working relationship in the last decade of the older man's career, as witnessed by their joint 1891 paper 'Trials of an Express Locomotive'. In the months leading towards Adams' retirement, it became increasingly evident that it fell to Pettigrew to keep not only Nine Elms works but the entire department functioning.

He had been born in Glasgow in January 1858, the son of a marine engineer, but by 1871 his family was resident in Southampton. Although his father hailed from Scotland his mother had been born near Cowes in the Isle of Wight, the daughter of a physician, but possibly it was the shipping industry that had brought them together. He was educated at Wolvesey Palace School at Winchester and then continued his studies at Finsbury Technical College and University College, London. Articled to William Adams at Stratford in 1874, he remained there under his successor Massey

Bromley, becoming first a time-served draughtsman. After a spell at Millwall working with hydraulic cranes, followed by a period working with his father in Scotland, he returned to Stratford as Assistant Works Manager under Thomas Worsdell and then James Holden until his move to Nine Elms in 1886.

William Pettigrew's predecessor as Locomotive Superintendent of the Furness Railway, Richard Mason, had held the post for no less than forty-six years, being appointed in 1850. Mason's retirement in 1896 was only one of a number of senior management changes at the company at around that time. The origins of the railway, which was centred around operations in the Furness area of Lancashire, were rooted in wagonways built in the 1840s for the transport of iron ore. The subsequent development of the iron and steel industry led to the significant investment by the company in new docks at Barrow from the 1860s. The new management also sought to increase revenue from passenger traffic, and in this it was remarkably successful, with the more dynamic approach of new officers resulting in a forty per cent increase in traffic receipts during a period of eight years.

One of Pettigrew's first tasks involved the updating of the existing D1 class of six-coupled tender engines, but before long his own designs included larger and more powerful 0-6-0s for both goods and mixed traffic work, classes D3-5, and 4-4-0s for fast passenger trains, both of which types he was very familiar with at Nine Elms, although he adopted inside cylinders for the four-coupled engines. However, another early project in 1898 was the design of an 0-6-2 tank locomotive, his L1 class, intended for banking duties, but also useful for passenger work. Later, in 1913, came his final 4-4-0 design, the K4, followed two years later by a 4-4-2 tank locomotive, the M1 class, intended for branch line service, but also found suitable for workmen's trains in the Barrow area.

It was standard Furness railway practice to contract out the building of new locomotives, and in Pettigrew's time at Barrow the only exception was the construction

Above left: A portrait of William Frank Pettigrew, probably circa 1910-18.

Above right: Like John Henry Adams at the NSR, Pettigrew produced a series of designs for 0-6-2 tank locomotives. The L1 class was intended to replace older engines from the Whitehaven and Cleator Railway. Numbered 112-4, the three locomotives were delivered in 1898. (ETH Archive)

No. 129 was one of four locomotives ordered from Sharp, Stewart in 1901, which were classified K3. (Alon Siton)

Pettigrew produced several variants of a six-coupled goods locomotive, including the D4 class, of which four were built, numbered 3-6, in 1907. (ETH Archive)

Ten more 0-6-2Ts followed between 1904 and 1907, with boiler pressure increased from 150 to 160lb. Nicknamed Cleator Tanks, they were built in two batches by Nasmyth Wilson and North British, numbered 98-107. (ETH Archive)

The larger bunker of the L3 class is clearly demonstrated by No. 110, one of a class of six locomotives built in 1907. (ETH Archive)

In 1905 two steam railmotors were constructed at Barrow, and No. 1 is seen here with four-wheel trailer car No. 123. They were used on branch routes to Lakeside and Coniston. (David Cannings-Bushell)

of two 0-4-0 railmotors to his design in 1905. Remarkably, railmotor trailer car No. 193 has survived, although completely enclosed within a bungalow at Kirkby-in-Furness, yet still retaining many features such as carriage prints depicting local scenes!

Given his experience with the Adams vortex blast pipe and its variants, it is interesting to note that he trialled the Macallan variable blast pipe on two D3 class six-coupled engines, which was found to be of no appreciable benefit and was removed after the trial period.

Towards the end of his career, he also experimented with the Phoenix Superheater, a device which had been patented by S.S. Macaskie in 1909 and required the fitting of an extended smokebox. Trialled on a small selection of locomotives, it was not widely adopted by the Furness Railway, despite showing an appreciable fuel saving of 23 per cent.

It is interesting to compare the design philosophy of Pettigrew and John Adams. Both were keen advocates of standardisation of parts, that belief extending to rebuilding older designs that they each inherited. For express passenger work, inside cylindered 4-4-0s were favoured, rather than their mentor's preference for outside cylinders, whilst the two men each produced heavier 0-6-2 and 4-4-2 tank locomotives, all also with inside cylinders. In a further quirk, the two railways enjoyed a brief flirtation with steam railmotors, albeit with Pettigrew utilising and building his own design whilst the North Staffordshire bought in 'off the shelf'.

The D5 class totalled nineteen locomotives built between 1913 and 1920, four of which were ordered from Kitson, with the remainder, including No. 1 illustrated here, constructed by North British Locomotive Company. (ETH Archive)

The K4 class was a later development for express passenger work, and No.132 was one of four built by North British in 1913/14 which remained in service until 1932/3. (ETH Archive)

Although the FR's M1 class 4-4-2Ts were built as late as 1915/16, they only had fairly short working lives, as, following the grouping, the LMS policy of eliminating non standard designs meant that the six members of the class were withdrawn in 1932/3. Seen here in LMS days, No. 41 still carries its original number. (Cameron Scott)

Apart from his locomotive department, Pettigrew's responsibilities included the Lake Windermere steamers, and the mechanical equipment of the railway-owned Barrow Docks. During his period in office two new vessels were added to the Windermere fleet, SS *Swift*, with a capacity for 781 passengers, followed by the much smaller steam yacht *Britannia*, built in 1907. The latter was scrapped as early as 1919, but *Swift* remained in service until 1981, albeit dieselised in 1956/7. Although built before he took over, cargo steamer *Raven* is preserved as part of the Windermere Steamboat Museum collection.

In 1901, he presented a paper on the early history of Furness Railway locomotives to the Institution of Mechanical Engineers, to which he had been elected in 1897, proposed by James Holden, his last chief at Stratford, and four years later he wrote a report on automatic couplers for the International Railway Congress held in Washington. He was also the author of *A Manual of Locomotive Engineering*, a widely respected textbook which was first published in 1899 and ran to several editions.

During the First World War he was a member of the Committee of Railways in the North West, and in the year that the conflict ended he retired to Redhill in Surrey, where he died aged eighty-four in 1942.

One further Adams apprentice who rose to attain high office was Oliver Robert Hawke Bury, who started his career at Nine Elms at the age of eighteen in 1879. Following a spell at Hunter and English, a steam engine builder based at Bow, he moved to South America to become locomotive superintendent of the Great Western Railway of Brazil in 1885, later becoming its Chief Engineer and Manager. He then went to Argentina, initially to join the Entre Ríos Railway before moving on to the Buenos Aires and Rossario company. On his return to England in 1902, he took up the position of General Manager and later a director of the Great Northern Railway, but continued to maintain business interests in South America. Following the grouping, he served on the board of the London & North Eastern Railway until 1945, the year before his death.

Chapter 10

Legacy and Preservation

Fortunately, five locomotives designed by William Adams have survived into the preservation era, all from his time with the LSWR, and together they represent the final express designs, as well as the importance of the suburban tank locomotives and the humble dock tank/shunting locomotives.

The Stephenson Locomotive Society recognised the importance of preserving an Adams 4-4-0 design as the last examples were withdrawn in the mid-1940s, initially suggesting the idea to Oliver Bulleid, then Locomotive Superintendent of the Southern Railway, and at the time of nationalisation commenced formal negotiations to preserve T3 class No. 571, presenting the argument to Sir Cyril Hurcomb, Chairman of the British Transport Commission, and R.A. Riddles of the Railway Executive, at a meeting held on 19 March 1948.

T3 class No. 571 had been withdrawn in 1943, leaving No. 563 as the last working member of the class. That too was withdrawn following the end of the war in summer 1945. After two years languishing in store at Eastleigh intended for scrap, both were towed in January 1948 to Awbridge Sidings, between Kimbridge Junction and Romsey. However, following an inspection on 4 May, No. 563 was selected to take part in the Waterloo Station centenary celebrations, and a fortnight later taken to Eastleigh for restoration to original condition and LSWR livery. Although essentially intended as a cosmetic restoration, it was retubed which allowed it to work light engine at a reduced boiler pressure of only 60lb, and on 7 June it duly went to Micheldever for official photographs, just a week before the commencement of the celebrations.

After the Waterloo event it was put into store in various locations until the opening of the Clapham Transport Museum in south London in the 1960s which finally presented the opportunity for it to be publicly displayed. Following the closure of the Clapham venue it then moved north to become part of the new National Railway Museum at York. It returned to LSWR home territory to feature in a stage production of E. Nesbit's classic story, *The Railway Children*, held in the former international platforms of Waterloo station, vacated by the Eurostar move to St Pancras in 2007. After two seasons it was taken across the Atlantic in 2011 for a similar production at a specially constructed temporary theatre at Roundhouse Park, Toronto. Following its return to the UK, it was once again used for the role in 2015 at King's Cross, London.

On 30 March 2017, No. 563 was de-accessioned by the NRM and generously gifted to the Swanage Railway Trust. Whilst the locomotive is undoubtedly in very good hands, it is perhaps surprising that the National Collection should choose to dispose of its only Adams locomotive, whilst retaining both an M7 0-4-4 tank and T9 class 4-4-0 by his successor Dugald Drummond. It is not so much the matter of the disposal

> Turbett, Townrow and Painter Foreman Miller and I went to Kimbridge Junction on the 4th May and inspected the row of engines awaiting removal to Dinton for cutting up. There were 4 Adams 4-4-0 engines all with 6'7" driving wheels. Nos. 563, 572 - T/3's, and 658 and 666 - X.6 class, in the siding.
>
> AGREED that 563 should be selected for preservation. The engine will be sent to Eastleigh and alterations made as follows :-
>
> Adams chimney to be fabricated and fitted.
> 2 cast iron Number Plates of Adams style to be made and affixed to cab sides.
> 2 Whistles to be added and pipe work to be replaced.
> Engine need only be complete externally.
>
> I have left the following with Mr.Mills, Chief Draughtsman, who is co-ordinating the work :-
>
> Photograph of engine 661 Railway Magazine coloured plate showing Drummond painting of LSW.395.
> 2 transfer Ellis Coats of Arms to be used on 563 and a photographic card of No.561 showing the condition in which the engine is to be preserved.
>
> Left with Mr.Allen photograph of Tri-compo coach No.633, a similar coach will be preserved and painted in salmon pink and plain chocolate.
>
> A copy of painting details of LSW engine in Drummond style and coach were left with Mr.Mills (Locomotive) and Mr.Hurleigh (Carriage) side.

Left: Notes made by Alastair MacLeod following the visit to Kimbridge Junction to inspect 563 on 4 May 1948. The reference to No.572, which had been withdrawn in 1931, is surely an error, and should be 571. Alastair MacLeod was Chief Stores Superintendent for the Southern Region, and as a member of the Stephenson Locomotive Society had doubtless been instrumental in the approach to Bulleid several years earlier. (Terry Hastings)

Below: 563 being retubed at Eastleigh as part of its 1948 restoration. (Ewan MacLeod)

of such an important and fine locomotive but, it can be argued, more a failure to recognise the story of the man that it represents. The NRM does, however, retain an Adams vortex blast pipe in its collection.

The suburban tank locomotives are represented today by the surviving Radial tank, 415 class No. 488, and O2 class No. 209. The Radial, one of the stalwarts of the Lyme

A few years after its restoration for the Waterloo centenary, T3 class 563 is seen at Eastleigh, with Brighton Atlantic 32424 for company. Curiously, the surviving record card for No. 563 indicates, incorrectly, that ownership had been transferred to the Stephenson Locomotive Society. (Kevin Lane)

After the closure of the Clapham museum, 563 was displayed in the roundhouse of the new National Railway Museum at York. (Neil Harvey)

563 arrives at the Swanage Railway by low loader following transfer of ownership in 2017. (Nathan Au)

Shortly after its arrival at the Swanage Railway, 563 was the subject of an after dark photo charter at Corfe Castle station. With the aid of a smoke generator, the scene was set for a late Victorian/Edwardian station arrival. (Calum Hepplewhite)

Restoration of 563 underway at the Flour Mill workshops in the Dean Forest, late 2021. (Nathan Au)

Regis branch, was withdrawn in 1961 as British Railways No. 30583 and bought by the Bluebell Railway where it has been preserved since.

O2 class No. 209 was withdrawn in March 1967 as W24 *Calbourne*, having worked on the Isle of Wight for the previous forty-two years. Bought from British Railways by the Wight Locomotive Society for £900, it is now the flagship locomotive of the Isle of Wight Steam Railway. In 2012, it returned to the mainland for the first time since 1925 and visited the Bodmin and Wenford, Swanage and Mid Hants railways, and later undertook another ferry crossing for an event at the Bluebell Railway. One or two other attempts were made to secure another O2 for preservation in 1966/7 but foundered largely because of the difficulty in that era of removing a steam locomotive from the island. There was an eleventh hour bid in August 1967 to secure sister locomotive W31 *Chale*, originally LSWR No. 180, after it had been sold for breaking up. The scrap merchant actually halted work in an attempt to secure a deal, but to no avail, and by the end of September only one O2 remained.

However, two B4 class four-coupled tanks are still with us. In 1964, several Butlins holiday centres acquired a number of steam locomotives for display, with one large express locomotive accompanied by a much smaller engine at each site. At three of the four venues, the smaller engine was a Stroudley Terrier class 0-6-0, and there is little doubt that B4 class 102 *Granville* was only selected because there were no more Terriers left for disposal, whilst it was available and a similar size. It was moved by road to Skegness where it joined ex-LMS 6100 *Royal Scot* until 1971 when the Butlins collection was disposed of, and it was sold to the Bressingham Steam Museum at Diss, Norfolk, where it has remained. The second B4 is No. 96 *Normandy*, which

In March 2019, O2 class W24 *Calbourne* visited the Bluebell Railway, which enabled three of the surviving Adams locomotives, all in British Railways livery, to be seen together. Bluebell residents 30096, and Radial tank 30583 joined the O2 and were displayed at Horsted Keynes alongside another LSWR veteran, Beattie well tank No. 30587. (John Faulkner)

as described earlier, was sold to P.D. Fuels at Dibles Wharf, Southampton, where it remained at work, by then named *Corrall Queen*. Finally retired in 1972, it was sold to members of the Bulleid Society and later moved to the Bluebell Railway, where it has proved its worth as a shunter.

Although all the T1 class locomotives were scrapped, one boiler was sold for further industrial use as a stationary steam plant, and was discovered, along with several other types, at a sawmill at Maldon, Essex, in the 1980s. It has now been stored for many years at the Avon Valley Railway, with the possible long-term aim of a new-build locomotive project, a not entirely impossible dream as one of its former Essex stablemates formed the basis of the new-build LBSCR Atlantic H2 class *Beachy Head*, at the Bluebell Railway.

It is unfortunate that William Stanier ordered the destruction of the last NLR 4-4-0 tank which had been set aside in 1929 and stored in the paint shop at Derby works. Although it dated from the H.J. Pryce years, it still essentially represented the Adams No. 1 class design.

A variety of carriages from the Adams years at each of the three railways have survived, but perhaps most importantly from the NLR, which represent the early introduction of the close-coupled block train sets, with a guard's van at each end. Examples of NLR carriages have been restored by the Isle of Wight Steam Railway and Furness Railway Trust, whilst two others operate in a rebuilt form as short bogie carriages at the Pallot Steam Museum, Jersey. The East Anglian Railway Museum has a birdcage brake thought to date from 1872, and other carriages are awaiting restoration elsewhere. The NLR Directors' Saloon is in the care of the National Railway Museum, York, and unlike most of the other preserved examples, which spent many years as grounded bodies prior to rescue, has survived complete with original underframe and running gear.

Restored examples of four-wheel Great Eastern carriages can be found at the East Anglian Railway Museum and the Mid-Suffolk Light Railway. Most of these were

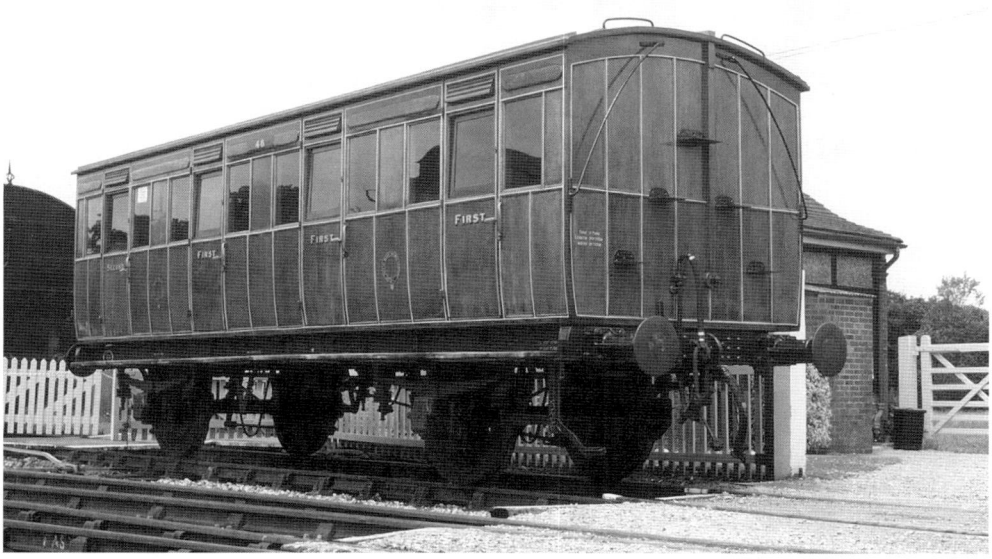

NLR first class No. 46 dating from 1864 is in regular service at the Isle of Wight Steam Railway, where it has been restored on a Southern Railway shortened PMV steel underframe. Sold to the Isle of Wight Railway in 1897, and withdrawn in 1926, it became a chalet on Hayling Island before rescue in 1975. (Iain Whitlam)

The East Anglian Railway Museum is also home to former Great Eastern Railway first class carriage No.19 of 1878. (Roger Jones)

ordered from outside contractors such as Brown Marshall or Birmingham Railway Carriage & Wagon Company, but the body of a former six-wheel family saloon, one of four built at Stratford in 1877, has survived. It was converted for use by Edward 'Prince of Wales' in 1881, a project which cost £350 and involved rebuilding the roof with a modified Great Northern Railway style profile. It relinquished its Royal duties in 1897, reverting to its original use until withdrawn in 1921. It has been preserved as part of the Stephen Middleton Stately Trains collection. The bodies of many carriages were sold for a variety of static uses following withdrawal, and that of 1875 built GER No. 5, a five-compartment Third, has been refurbished with an Orient Express inspired theme, for continued use as a summer house at Brockdish, Norfolk.

Several LSWR carriage bodies serve as holiday lets, including former six-wheel 5-compartment Third, No. 205 dating from 1887 at Longdown near Exeter. Although built in 1896, just after Adams' retirement, the body of a four-wheel passenger luggage van serves a similar purpose, adjacent to the main line station platform at St Germans in Cornwall.

Twelve first-class carriages built in 1893 for transatlantic liner traffic to and from Southampton Docks, and known as Eagle Saloons, were sold to the War Department in 1916 and sent to Palestine, converted for use as ambulance trains. Two of them, originally LSWR Nos. 314 and 316, have survived as part of the collection of the Israel Railway Museum at Haifa, although both are in very poor condition.

However, one other carriage which has received much attention is the former LSWR Royal Saloon No. 17, dating from 1885. Originally constructed as an Open First, it

Former LSWR Royal Saloon No. 17 was one of four carriage restorations featured in a Channel 4 television series in 2018. It is preserved at the Embsay and Bolton Abbey Railway where it forms part of Stephen Middleton's Stately Trains fleet. (Stephen Middleton)

became part of the Royal Train, and modified with clerestory roof, frequently used by Queen Victoria between London and Gosport, whence she would continue across the Solent to Osborne House in the Isle of Wight. It was later relegated to use as a family saloon before withdrawal in 1930. The body then became part of a bungalow at Chiltington, Sussex, until rescued for preservation in 1989. It was later acquired by Stephen Middleton, and in 2017 its restoration was featured in the Channel 4 TV series, *Great Rail Restorations*.

The three railway works at Bow, Stratford and Nine Elms are long gone, but Nine Elms running shed survived to the last days of Southern Region steam in July 1967, and the site was subsequently redeveloped as the New Covent Garden market. A simple Blue Plaque unveiled at Stratford International station in 2012 commemorates the site of the former works and running sheds, whilst a cosmetically restored 0-6-0 saddle tank, named *Robert*, built for industrial use in 1933 by Bristol based Avonside Engine Company, is displayed nearby.

William Adams undoubtedly enjoyed a distinguished career as a locomotive designer, but in the twenty-first century world of specialist professional disciplines and careers, it is easy to forget the wider range of experience and interest of engineers of his generation. Before he took up his position with the NLR, with his years of marine and civil engineering training and practice, he had little or no experience of railway locomotives and their operation, yet within a few years he had produced a series of successful locomotive designs – so successful in fact that they continued to be built with only minor modifications, not only by his immediate successor, but the following holder of the post too.

The patented bogie was widely adopted, as was the vortex blast pipe, but the French engineer André Chapelon, who took locomotive draughting to a more advanced and complex level with his Kylchap blast pipe, considered that British engineers gave up on the concept far too early. As stated earlier, Drummond removed the vortex units from the LSWR engines, but in fairness, this may have been partly to reduce the additional maintenance in keeping them clean. Nonetheless, any savings in maintenance probably did not offset the efficiency advantage of a locomotive with improved draughting. Chapelon also cited the Stirling eight-foot singles and the Adams 4-4-0s as two of the most impressive British locomotive designs of the nineteenth century, and furthermore that Adams was probably the last British steam locomotive engineer to wield any influence abroad. The latter is quite a telling remark considering that the UK was still building main line steam locomotives over half a century after his retirement.

In all, William Adams was responsible for the design of over 700 steam locomotives, which were noted for their robust construction, free steaming capabilities plus efficient well-designed steam passages and valves. The only really unsuccessful design was the Great Eastern Mogul class, withdrawn and scrapped after only a few years of service, but it is impossible to know what Adams would have done to improve the engines had he remained at Stratford, and although he returned to the Mogul arrangement at the end of his career, that design was never built. It is also interesting that he should consider the idea of a single driver express locomotive as late as 1893. He was clearly impressed by those still being built by others such as Johnson and Stirling, yet in many respects, particularly when increasing train weights are taken into account, the concept of a single driven axle was already outmoded by that time.

Adams' locomotives have been described as being the work of an artist as well as an engineer, and his designs so often showed an elegance and certain subtlety of line which many others did not quite achieve. Some would argue that, perhaps, the one aesthetic improvement made to many of the LSWR locomotives during their lifetime was the fitting of the Drummond-pattern chimney with its flared top, rather than the austere stovepipe for so long favoured by Adams.

Born two years before the opening in 1825 of the Stockton and Darlington Railway, the first public railway in the world to use steam locomotives, William was in his mid-teens when the London and Greenwich Railway became the first steam-operated passenger-carrying line in the capital and was just completing his marine engineering apprenticeship when the 'Railway Mania' bubble burst. At the time of his retirement, steam power still reigned supreme, but just three years later the LSWR became responsible for the operation of electric trains on the independently-owned Waterloo and City Railway, the first hint of the electrified system to come. The legacy of his railway career of over four decades encompasses not only locomotive design, but his development and organisation of the works at each of the three railways by which he was employed. A remarkable man, and without doubt one of the finest locomotive engineers of the later Victorian era, whose work is still recognised today, particularly by the custodians of his surviving engines.

Appendix A

Ships built and/or fitted with engines by Miller & Ravenhill 1841-46

Date built	Name	Builder	Type	Tonnage (Grt)	Engine notes	Initial owner
1841	Blackwall	Ditchburn & Mare	Passenger paddle steamer	262	1 cyl, 90hp	London & Blackwall Railway
1841	Satellite	Ditchburn & Mare	Passenger paddle steamer	124	80hp	Gravesend & Milton New Steam Packet Co.
1841	Elberfeld	Miller & Ravenhill	Passenger paddle steamer	Not known	2 cyl 80hp	DGNM (note a)
1842	Trent	William & Henry Pitcher	Passenger/cargo paddle steamer	1,666	Side lever, 2 cyl, 440hp	Royal Mail Steam Packet Co.
1842	Isis	William & Henry Pitcher	Passenger/cargo paddle steamer	1,900	Side lever, 2 cyl, 400hp	Royal Mail Steam Packet Co.
1843	Pink	Miller & Ravenhill	Passenger paddle steamer	59	28hp	London & Westminster Steamboat Co.
1843	Prince of Wales	Miller & Ravenhill	Passenger paddle steamer	246	120hp Engine (note c)	Margate & London Steam Packet Co.
1843	HMS Infernal, renamed Rosamund in 1846	Sir W. Symonds	Paddle steamer	1,058	Direct, 287hp	Admiralty
1844	HMS Amphion	HM Dockyard Woolwich	Screw	1,474	2 cyl horizontal direct acting 300hp	Admiralty
1844	Blue Bell	Ditchburn & Mare	Passenger paddle steamer	65	Side lever	London & Westminster Steamboat Co.
1844	Delta	Miller & Ravenhill	River screw steamer	240	120hp screw	P&O (note b)
1844	Elberfeld (2) (note d)	Miller & Ravenhill	Passenger paddle steamer	Not known	110hp	DGNM

Date built	Name	Builder	Type	Tonnage (Grt)	Engine notes	Initial owner
1844	HMS Gladiator	Sir W. Symonds	Paddle steamer	1,190	430hp oscillating	Admiralty
1844	Meteor	Miller & Ravenhill	Passenger paddle steamer	174	80hp	Gravesend & Milton New Steam Packet Co.
1845	Ondine	Miller & Ravenhill	Passenger paddle steamer	86	Two x 50hp	Bushell, Dover
1845	Madrid	Miller & Ravenhill	Passenger/cargo paddle steamer	479	2 cyl side lever, 160hp	P&O
1845	Concordia	Miller & Ravenhill	Passenger paddle steamer	Not known	100hp	DGNM
1845	Blasco de Garay	Money, Wigram & Co	Paddle steamer	1,396	350hp oscillating	Spanish Navy
1846	HMS Minx	Sir W. Symonds	Screw	303	2 cyl 100hp oscillating	Admiralty
1846	Ripon	Money, Wigram & Co	Passenger/cargo paddle steamer	1,508	2 cyl oscillating, 900hp	P&O
1846	Ranger	Unknown, London	Cargo, screw	259	2 cyl oscillating, 40hp	Malcolmson Brothers, Waterford
1846	Llewellyn	Miller & Ravenhill	Passenger paddle steamer	643	Not known	City of Dublin Steam Packet Co

Notes:
a) Dampfschiffahrtsgesellschaft für den Nieder und Mittelrhein
b) Peninsular & Oriental Steam Navigation Company
c) Engine fitted from PS *Royal George*, built for the Margate & London Steam Packet Co., by Henry Fletcher, Son & Fearnall in 1830
d) *Elberfeld* (I) was lost in the English Channel when being returned to England for engine adjustments in February 1844, with three of the crew drowned

Appendix B

An abridged version of the paper entitled 'Trials of an Express Locomotive' by William Adams and W.F. Pettigrew is reproduced below courtesy Institution of Civil Engineers

Sect. II.—OTHER SELECTED PAPERS.

(*Paper No. 2755.*)

(*Abridged.*)

"Trials of an Express Locomotive."

By William Adams and William Frank Pettigrew, MM. Inst. C.E.

The engine upon which the trials described in the Paper were made is one of twenty built from the designs of the Authors for the London and South Western Railway Company, at the Nine Elms Works, for the heavy main-line express trains between Waterloo, Salisbury, Southampton and Bournemouth. These engines run from Waterloo to Basingstoke, a distance of 48 miles, within an hour, and during the summer months accomplish the journeys to Salisbury and Christchurch, distances of 84 miles and 104 miles respectively, without a stop. They have four wheels coupled, and a four-wheeled bogie. The cylinders, placed outside the frames, are 19 inches in diameter, and have a stroke of 26 inches; with a clearance at each end equivalent at the front to 7·7 per cent., and at the back to 6·6 per cent. of the capacity of the cylinder. The slide-valves have a range of $3\frac{5}{8}$ inches, with 1-inch outside lap and $\frac{1}{8}$-inch lead, in full gear. The coupled driving-wheels are 7 feet 1 inch, and the bogie and tender wheels 3 feet $9\frac{3}{4}$ inches in diameter. The frames are of mild steel 1 inch thick; and the boiler-barrel is 11 feet long and 4 feet 4 inches in outside diameter, the plates being of mild steel $\frac{1}{2}$ inch thick. Between the tube-plates the length is 11 feet 4 inches; and there are two hundred and forty tubes of $1\frac{3}{4}$ inch outside diameter. The height of the centre of the boiler-barrel above the rail-level is 7 feet 9 inches. The fire-box is of copper, and is 5 feet $6\frac{7}{16}$ inches long at the top, and 5 feet $7\frac{7}{8}$ inches at the bottom, the height being 5 feet $9\frac{1}{2}$ inches to the bottom, and 5 feet 7 inches to the top of the foundation-ring, and the width 3 feet 6 inches at the top and 3 feet $2\frac{1}{2}$ inches at the bottom. The plates are $\frac{1}{2}$ inch thick except the tube-plate, which is 1 inch thick. A total heating-surface of 1,358·65 square feet is provided, and the grate-area is 18·14 square feet. The working boiler-pressure is 175 lbs. per square inch. The weight on the driving-wheels is 33,488 lbs., on the trailing-wheels 33,152 lbs., and on the bogie 42,280 lbs.; the weight of the tender full of water and with 2 tons of coal is 74,816 lbs.; the total weight of the engine and tender in working order being 183,736 lbs. The total wheel-base of the engine and tender is 44 feet $3\frac{1}{8}$ inches; the extreme length over the buffers being 53 feet $8\frac{5}{8}$ inches. The length from the front of the buffer to the centre of the bogie is 8 feet $4\frac{3}{4}$ inches, from the centre of the bogie to the centre of the driving-axle 10 feet 9 inches, from the centre of the driving-axle to the centre of the trailing-axle is 8 feet 6 inches, and from the centre of the trailing-axle to the back of the frame is 4 feet 3 inches. Steel castings were used where possible in the construction of these engines, thus dispensing with intricate and difficult forgings. The driving-, trailing-, and bogie-wheels, together with all bogie-castings, pistons, crossheads, motion-plate, horn-blocks, spring-hanger brackets and other smaller parts were made of this material. The engines are fitted with the automatic vacuum- and steam-brakes, and also with the Adams vortex blast-pipe.[1]

Five trials were made while the engine was performing its regular duty under ordinary circumstances. The first was on the 9th July, 1891, with the 5.50 A.M. down train from Waterloo to Bournemouth, a distance of 111 miles, with eleven intermediate stops. The load hauled, exclusive of engine and tender, and with no allowance for the weight of passengers and luggage was, from Waterloo to Woking, $24\frac{3}{4}$ miles, 239 tons 17 cwt. 3 qrs., from Woking to Basingstoke, $23\frac{3}{8}$ miles, 217 tons 6 cwt. 3 qrs., from Basingstoke to Eastleigh, $25\frac{3}{4}$ miles, 166 tons 16 cwt., from Eastleigh to Brockenhurst, 19 miles, 135 tons 15 cwt. 2 qrs., and from Brockenhurst to Bournemouth, $18\frac{1}{2}$ miles, 116 tons 16 cwt. 2 qrs. The mean load throughout the journey was 179 tons 16 cwt. 3 qrs. The profile of the road is shown in *Fig. 1*, the steepest up gradient being 1 in 99 for $1\frac{1}{4}$ mile. The speed, indicated horsepower, actual running-time, boiler-pressure, smoke-box temperature and vacuum curves are also shown. The maximum speed obtained was 68·5 miles per hour, while running on a down gradient of 1 in 251, at the sixty-fifth mile-post. The indicated horse-power, as shown by the diagram taken immediately after, at 68 miles per hour, *Fig. 2*, was 480·2, with steam cut-off at 17 per cent. of the stroke, the number of revolutions being 269 per minute. Particulars of the observations made during

---

[1] For a fuller description of the engine see *The Engineer*, vol. lxxix. 1895, p. 244.

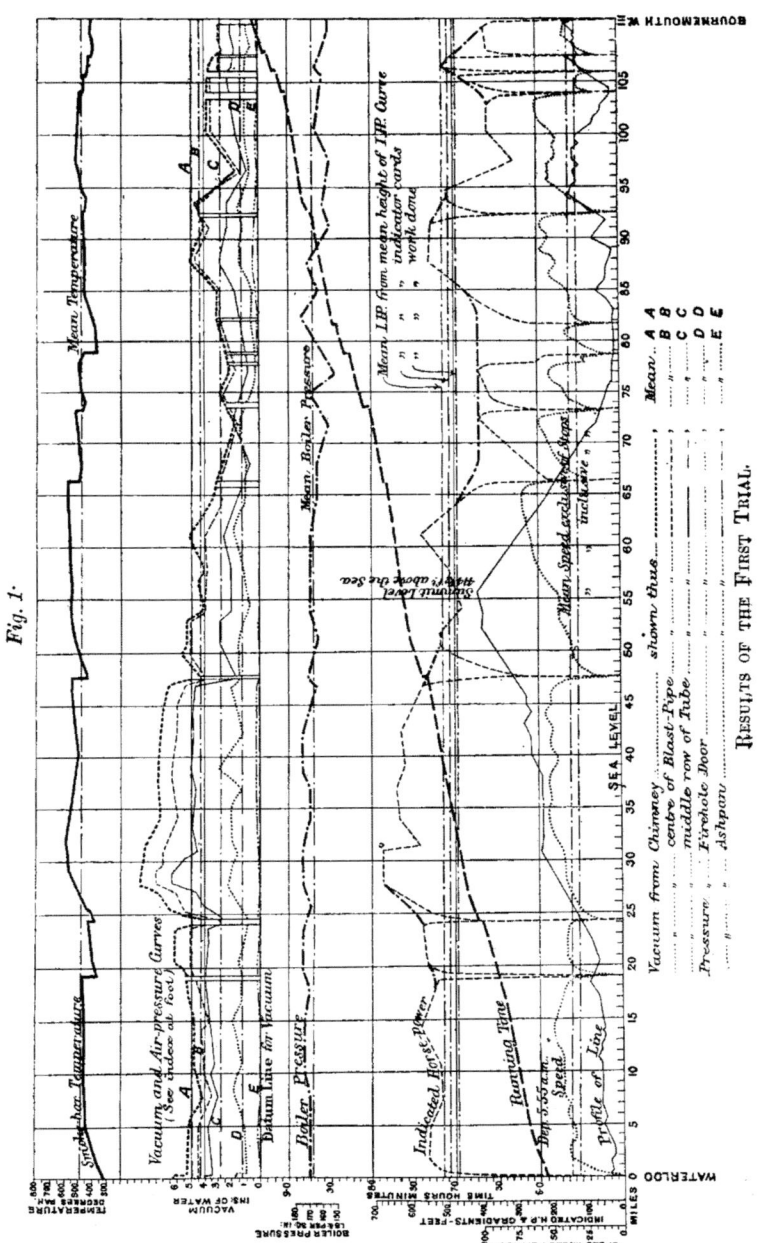

Fig. 1.

Results of the First Trial.

the trials are given in Table I of the Appendix. The maximum indicated horse-power developed was 684·1, *Fig. 3*, with a cut-off of 29·5 per cent. on an up gradient of 1 in 314, at the twenty-eighth mile-post, the speed being 40 miles per hour, and the number of revolutions 157 per minute. With regard to forced draught, special observations were made during each journey of the vacuum obtained, at the base of chimney, in the smoke-box, on a level with the exhaust nozzle, in the centre of the blast-pipe,

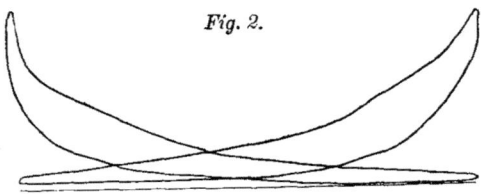

Fig. 2.

Mean effective pressure, 24·37 lbs. per square inch.

in front of the centre of the middle row of tubes, through the fire-hole door, and in the ash-pan. The diameter of gases-pipe of the blast-pipe was 5 inches and its area 19·6 square inches; the area of annular exhaust being 13·9 square inches and its width $\frac{11}{16}$ inch. The temperatures of the gases in the smoke-box was also taken at 1-mile intervals, the maximum being 585° F., and the mean 488·91° F. The weather was fine with a strong head wind.

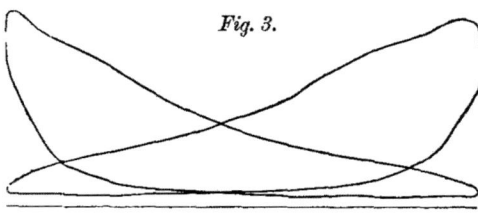

Fig. 3.

Mean effective pressure, 59·88 lbs. per square inch.

The second trial extended over the return journey from Bournemouth to Waterloo on the same day, the time of departing being 1.55 P.M. Three intermediate stops were made in addition to that at Vauxhall. The load hauled, exclusive of the engine and tender, and with no allowance for weight of passengers and luggage, was, from Bournemouth West to Bournemouth East, 3½ miles, 89 tons 11 cwt. 2 qrs.; and from Bournemouth East to Waterloo, 107¾ miles, 137 tons 11 cwt. 2 qrs. The mean load throughout the

286 ADAMS AND PETTIGREW ON AN EXPRESS LOCOMOTIVE. [Selected

journey was thus 136 tons 3 cwt. 2 qrs. Observations, similar to those recorded of the first trial, were taken, the results being shown in Table I of the Appendix. The maximum speed obtained was 67 miles per hour while running on a down gradient of 1 in 386 between the twenty-third and twenty-fourth mile-posts from Waterloo. The I.HP. taken immediately after this observation, at a speed of 66 miles per hour, was 571·6, with a steam cut-off 17 per cent. of the stroke, the number of revolutions per minute being 261. The maximum I.HP., 610·1, was developed with a steam cut-off of 26 per cent.; on an up gradient of 1 in 249, at the sixtieth mile-post, the speed being 43 miles per hour, and the number of revolutions 170 per minute.

The third trial was run on the 10th July, from Waterloo with the 11.0 A.M. down train to Exeter, a distance of $171\frac{1}{2}$ miles, with three intermediate stops; the load hauled, exclusive of engine and tender, and with no allowance for the weight of passengers and luggage, was 168 tons 7 cwt. 2 qrs. The steepest up gradients were 1 in 70 for $\frac{1}{2}$ mile, and 1 in 80 for 4 miles. The maximum speed obtained was 78 miles per hour, while running on a down gradient of 1 in 100 at the 158th mile-post, when the I.HP. was 517·2, with a steam cut-off at 17 per cent. of the stroke, the number of revolutions being 309 per minute. The maximum I.HP., 803·6, was developed with a steam cut-off of 44 per cent., on an up gradient of 1 in 80, at the 152nd mile-post, the speed being 31 miles per hour, and the number of revolutions 123 per minute.

The fourth trial was made during the return journey from Exeter to Waterloo on the following day, the 11th July, with six intermediate stops, departing at 12.54 P.M. (nine minutes late). Owing to many unforeseen stoppages and delays which occurred after leaving Woking, it was impossible to record several of the most important items. The distance from Woking to Waterloo, only $24\frac{3}{8}$ miles, occupied 1 hour $15\frac{1}{2}$ minutes, and the trial was therefore ended at Woking. The load hauled, exclusive of engine and tender, and with no allowance for the weight of passengers and luggage was, from Exeter to Yeovil, 197 tons 9 cwt. 2 qrs., from Yeovil to Templecombe, 244 tons 9 cwt. 2 qrs., and from Templecombe to Waterloo, 195 tons 4 cwt. 2 qrs., the mean load being 198 tons 17 cwt. 3 qrs. The profile of the line and the several curves are shown in *Fig. 4*. The steepest gradient was 1 in 80. The maximum speed obtained was 81 miles per hour, while running on a down gradient of 1 in 80 between the 148th and 149th mile-post from Waterloo. The I.HP. taken just after

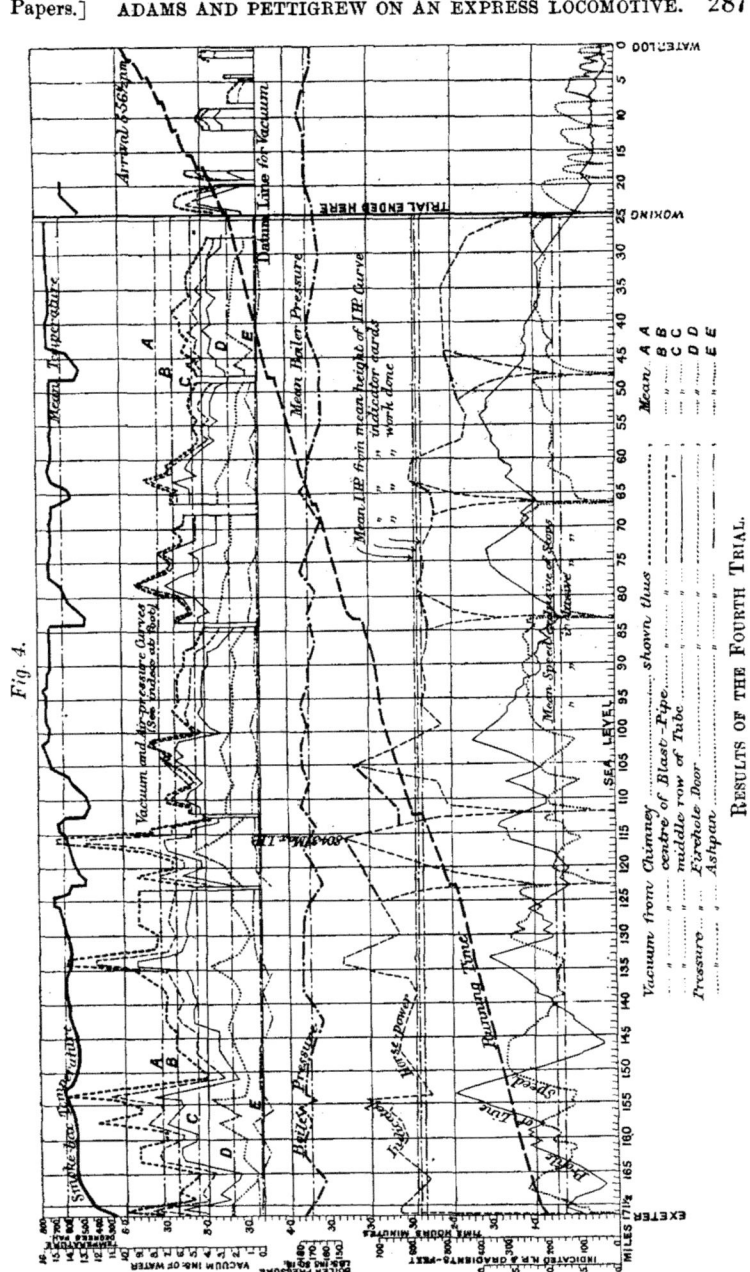

Fig. 4.

RESULTS OF THE FOURTH TRIAL.

this, at 80 miles per hour, was 636·2, *Fig. 5*, with the steam cut-off 17 per cent. of the stroke, the number of revolutions per minute being 316. The maximum I.HP. developed was 804·3, *Fig. 6*, the steam cut-off being 48 per cent. This was obtained on the level, and just leaving an up gradient of 1 in 200 at the 115½ mile-post, the speed being 27½ miles per hour, and the number of revolutions 109 per minute. The weather was fine with a moderate side wind.

The fifth trial was run on the 13th July from Waterloo with

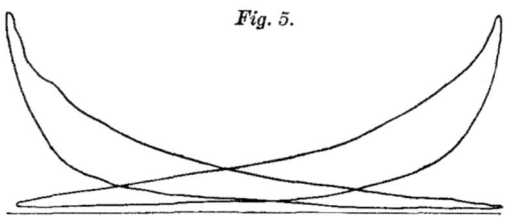

Fig. 5.

Mean effective pressure, 26·75 lbs. per square inch.

the 2.40 P.M. train to Salisbury, a distance of 83⅝ miles, with three intermediate stops. The load hauled, excluding engine and tender, and with no allowance for the weight of passengers and luggage, was 137 tons 10 cwt. 2 qrs. The steepest gradient was 1 in 141. The maximum speed obtained was 75 miles per hour, running on a down gradient of 1 in 178 at the 65th mile-post. The I.HP. taken at the 64½ mile-post, at 72½ miles per hour,

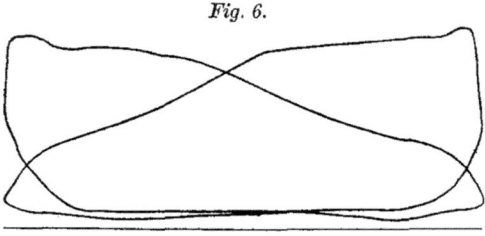

Fig. 6.

Mean effective pressure, 101·75 lbs. per square inch.

amounted to 601·9, with steam cut-off 17 per cent. of the stroke, and the number of revolutions 287 per minute. The maximum I.HP. was 626·1 when the steam was cut-off at 23 per cent. This was obtained on an up gradient of 1 in 264 at the 69th mile-post, the speed being 50 miles per hour, and the number of revolutions 198 per minute. The weather was fine with a head wind.

The speed was taken by a Boyer speed indicator and recorder

driven from the bogie-wheel. This instrument consists essentially of a rotary-pump forcing oil into a cylinder at a pressure dependent on the speed of the train. A pencil is carried by the piston-rod, and is controlled by a spring, the tension of which is the resisting force overcome by the pump. The speed was thus recorded on metallic paper, the divisions agreeing exactly with the mile-posts on the line. The indicator diagrams were taken with Crosby indicators, the springs used having a scale of 100 lbs. per inch of diagram. The instruments were tested before the trials. For the purpose of measuring the feed the tender was first filled and the contents passed out through a Worthington water-meter (previously corrected), a gauge fitted to the tender, being graduated in cubic feet as the water passed out. In calculating the engine efficiencies the amount of steam used by the ejector in connection with the automatic vacuum brake, as also that used by the steam-brake cylinder, has been neglected, consequently the actual engine efficiency would be in excess of that given. The coal was weighed before each trial on to a clean tender, any remaining at the end of the journey being weighed and allowed for.

The Paper is accompanied by eighteen sheets of tracings, from a selection of which the *Figs*. in the text have been prepared. The tracings include copies of the indicator diagrams, taken at frequent intervals during the five trials, which may be inspected at the Institution.

APPENDIX.—TABLE I.—RESULTS OF FIVE TRIALS.

		1st Trial.	2nd Trial.	3rd Trial.	4th Trial.	5th Trial.
Mean boiler-pressure throughout journey	lbs. per sq. in.	167·5	167·2	171·7	169·4	170·8
Total coal used, exclusive of lighting up	lbs.	3,395·0	3,120·0	4,872·0	4,856·0	2,352·0
,, ,, inclusive ,,	,,	3,563·0	3,288·0	5,208·0	5,248·0	2,520·0
Coal burnt per hour running time	,,	1,136·4	1,270·8	1,309·2	1,467·0	1,315·8
,, ,, journey	,,	974·7	1,162·8	1,198·2	1,283·0	1,137·9
,, ,, square foot of grate area per hour of running time	,,	62·54	70·0	72·18	80·89	72·49
,, ,, ,, ,, ,, ,, journey	,,	53·7	64·1	66·05	70·76	62·7
,, ,, I.HP. per hour running time	,,	2·31	2·61	2·34	2·52	2·45
,, ,, ,, ,, journey	,,	1·98	2·39	2·14	2·20	2·12
,, ,, train-mile	,,	30·5	28·1	28·4	32·98	28·16
,, ,, engine-mile	,,	29·5	27·13	27·8	32·21	27·02
Calorific value of 1 lb. of coal	B.T.U.	13,903	13,903	13,583	12,840	13,477
Total water evaporated	lbs.	32,887	27,406	43,104	38,415	21,966
Water evaporated per hour running time	,,	11,000·0	11,167·0	11,559·1	11,600·0	12,288·6
,, ,, ,, journey	,,	9,442·1	10,214·0	10,601·0	10,150·0	10,627·0
,, ,, sq. foot of total heating-surface per hour of running time	,,	8·09	8·22	8·5	8·54	9·04
,, ,, ,, ,, ,, ,, journey	,,	6·95	7·51	7·8	7·47	7·82
,, ,, I.HP. per hour running time	,,	22·4	23·02	20·7	19·94	22·9
,, ,, ,, ,, train-mile	,,	296·28	246·9	251·3	260·9	262·6
,, ,, ,, ,, engine-mile	,,	281·0	234·2	246·2	254·8	252·4
,, ,, lb. of coal, exclusive of lighting up	,,	9·68	8·78	8·84	7·91	9·34
,, ,, ,, ,, inclusive ,,	,,	9·23	8·34	8·27	7·32	8·71
,, ,, ,, ,, from feed temperature	,,	9·68	8·78	8·84	7·91	9·34
,, ,, ,, ,, equivalent from and at 212° F.	,,	11·35	10·30	10·4	9·28	10·96
Maximum I.HP.		684·1	610·1	803·6	804·3	626·1
Mean I.HP. from indicator cards		490·6	485·1	558·1	582·0	536·7
,, ,, work done		477·6	475·9	541·0	565·8	522·0
,, ,, curve of HP. (mean height)		511·5	497·53	540·14	585·473	540·0
Maximum speed	miles per hour	68·5	67·0	78·0	81·0	75·0
Mean speed, exclusive of stops	,,	37·0	45·2	46·1	44·45	46·7
,, ,, inclusive ,,	,,	31·86	41·34	42·1	38·92	40·44
Actual running time	hrs. mins.	2 50¾	2 27¼	3 43¼	3 15¾	1 47¼
,, journey ,,	,,	3 29	2 41	4 4	3 47	2 4

Train-miles		111	111	171½	147¼	83⅝
Engine-miles		115	115	175	150¾	87
Time from lighting up to taking out fire	hours	15	15	8½	8¾	12¾
Temperature of water in boiler at time of lighting up	° F.	205	205	125	165	61
Maximum vacuum at base of chimney	inches of water	8·5	11·0	14·0	15·0	7·0
Mean " " "	" "	4·93	6·43	6·54	7·33	3·83
Maximum vacuum level with the top and in centre of vortex blast-pipe	" "	7·5	7·1	11·0	12·8	6·8
Mean ditto	" "	4·34	4·1	4·21	6·27	4·96
Maximum vacuum at middle of middle row of tubes	" "	6·2	5·8	8·0	9·0	5·4
Mean " ". " "	" "	2·84	3·34	3·83	4·77	3·82
Maximum pressure through firehole door	" "	2·8	2·2	3·6	5·0	2·2
Mean " " "	" "	1·25	1·36	1·63	2·16	0·98
Maximum pressure through ashpan	" "	0·5	0·2	0·6	0·8	0·8
Mean " " "	" "	0·08	0·07	0·12	0·19	0·16
Maximum temperature of smoke-box gases	° F.	585·0	575·0	740·0	780·0	740·0
Mean " " " "	"	488·91	494·76	604·62	627·0	575·1
Efficiency of engine	per cent.	9·8	9·55	10·7	11·02	9·61
" boiler	"	77·5	70·0	71·1	66·6	75·5
" engine and boiler combined	"	7·7	6·68	7·6	7·34	7·25
Maximum gradient		1 in 99 up	1 in 90 up	1 in 70 up	1 in 80 up	1 in 141 up
Coal stated includes that used while standing for	hours	3½	5⅓	3¾	3⅔	3¼
		T. C. Q.	T. C. Q.	T. C. Q.	T. C. Q.	T. C. Q.
Maximum load hauled in tons, exclusive of engine, tender, passengers and luggage		239 17 3	137 11 2	168 7 2	244 9 2	137 10 2
Mean " " " " " " "		179 16 3	136 3 2	168 7 2	198 17 3	137 10 2
Maximum number of carriages hauled		21·0	11·0	11·0	16·0	9·0
Mean " " "		15·0	10·86	11·0	13·2	9·0
Maximum number of carriage journals		112·0	66·0	74·0	106·0	62·0
Mean " " "		81·4	65·2	74·0	87·4	62·0
Mean load per mile per carriage journal	lbs.	4,948·8	4,680·0	5,096·7	5,091·5	4,968·6
Back pressure at maximum I.HP.	lbs. per sq. in.	10·07	6·63	15·63	13·94	7·63
" " " speed	" "	5·38	5·69	6·07	5·88	7·69
Heat carried away by the products of combustion	B.T.U.	2,394	2,427	3,052	3,179	2,884
" expended in evaporating the water	"	10,774	9,737	9,655	8,544	10,173
" lost by radiation, imperfect combustion and evaporative moisture in coal	"	735	1,739	876	1,117	420
" converted into work per minute		20,970	20,730	23,850	24,880	22,950
" taken up by the feed-water per minute		213,835	217,209	224,816	225,734	238,817

TABLE II.—BALANCE

Total heat of steam at 167·5 lbs. pressure per square inch . . = 1,228 B.T.U.
Deduct feed-temperature . . . .   61°
                                                              ———
Thermal units taken up per lb. of steam   1,167

Lbs. of water evaporated per lb. of coal . . . . = 9·232
Therefore 1,167 × 9·232 = 10,774 B.T.U. expended per lb. of coal in evaporating the water.
Assuming that the specific heat of air . . . . = 0·237
  and that the quantity of air required per lb. of coal . . . = 24 lbs.
Let T = mean temperature of smoke-box gases . . . . . = 488·91° F.
and t = mean temperature of air . . . . = 68° F.
Then the heat carried away by smoke-box gases

$$= 24\,(T-t)\,0·237$$
$$= 24\,(488·91-68)\,0·237 = 2{,}394 \text{ B.T.U.}$$

Heat units per lb. of coal . . . . = 13,903
Loss in smoke-box . . . . = 2,394 B.T.U. per lb. of coal.
                                          ———
Available heat 11,509   ,,   ,,   ,,

Then $\dfrac{11{,}509}{1{,}167} = 9·86$ lbs. of water that should have been evaporated as against 9·23 lbs. evaporated.
Therefore the heat lost by radiation and imperfect combustion &c. = 735 B.T.U. per lb. of coal.

Heat evolved per lb. of Coal.		Heat expended per lb. of Coal.	
	B.T.U.		B.T.U.
Calorific value of 1 lb. of coal used	13,903	Heat expended in evaporating the water	10,774
		Heat carried away by the products of combustion, lost by radiation and imperfect combustion, &c.	3,129
	13,903		13,903

SHEET, TRIAL No. I.

Heat expended in evaporating the water . . . . = 10,774 B.T.U.
Mean I.HP. . . . . = 490·6
Water evaporated per I.HP. per hour (running time) . . . 22·4 lbs.
" " " minute (running time) . . 0·373 "
Water actually evaporated per lb. of coal, inclusive of lighting up . . . . } = 9·23 "

Then the heat taken up by the feed-water per minute

$$= \frac{10{,}774 \times 0\cdot 373 \times 490\cdot 6}{9\cdot 23} = 213{,}835 \text{ B.T.U.}$$

Joule's equivalent . . . . = 772

The units of heat per HP. $= \frac{33\cdot 000}{772} = 42\cdot 75$

Then the heat turned into work per minute

= the mean I.HP. × 42·75 = 490·6 × 42·75 = 20,970 B.T.U.

Efficiency of the engine

$$= 100 \times \frac{20{,}970}{213{,}835} = 9\cdot 8 \text{ per cent.,}$$

" " boiler $= 100 \times \frac{10{,}774}{13{,}903} = 77\cdot 5$ per cent.,

" " engine and boiler combined

$$= \frac{77\cdot 5 \times 9\cdot 8}{100} = 7\cdot 7 \text{ per cent.}$$

Heat evolved per lb. of Coal.		Heat expended per lb. of Coal.	
	Per Cent.		Per Cent.
Calorific value of 1 lb. of coal used	100·00	Heat expended in evaporating the water	77·50
		Heat carried away by the products of combustion, lost by radiation and imperfect combustion, &c.	22·50
	100·00		100·00

TABLE III.—BALANCE

Total heat of steam at 169·4 lbs. pressure per square inch . = 1,228·2 units.
Deduct feed-temperature . . . . 61·0°

Thermal units taken up per lb. of steam . . . . . . 1,167·2

Lbs. of water evaporated per lb. of coal . . . . . . = 7·32
Therefore $1{,}167 \cdot 2 \times 7 \cdot 32 = 8{,}544$ B.T.U. expended per lb. of coal in evaporating the water.
Assuming that the specific heat of air . . . . = 0·237
and that the quantity of air required per lb. of coal . . = 24 lbs.
Let T = mean temperature of smoke-box gases . . . . = 627·0° F.
and t = mean temperature of air . . . . = 68° F.
Then the heat carried away by smoke-box gases

$$= 24 (T - t) \, 0 \cdot 237$$
$$= 24 \, (627 \cdot 0 - 68) = 0 \cdot 237 = 3{,}179 \text{ B.T.U.}$$

Heat units per lb. of coal . . . . . . = 12,840
Loss in smoke-box . . . . = 3,179 B.T.U. per lb. of coal.

Available heat . . . . 9,661 ,, ,, ,,

Then $\dfrac{9{,}661}{1{,}167 \cdot 2} = 8 \cdot 27$ lbs. of water that should have been evaporated as against 7·32 lbs. evaporated.
Therefore the heat lost by radiation, imperfect combustion, &c. = 1,117 B.T.U. per lb. of coal.

Heat evolved per lb. of Coal.		Heat expended per lb. of Coal.	
	B.T.U.		B.T.U.
Calorific value of 1 lb. of coal used	12,840	Heat expended in evaporating the water	8,544
		Heat carried away by the products of combustion, lost by radiation and imperfect combustion, &c.	4,296
	12,840		12,840

SHEET, TRIAL No. IV.

Heat expended in evaporating the water . . . . =8,544 B.T.U.
Mean I.HP. . . . . = 582
Water evaporated per I.HP. per hour (running time) . . . 19·94 lbs.
„ „ „ minute (running time) . . 0·3323 „
Water actually evaporated per lb. of coal, inclusive of lighting up } = 7·32 „
Then the heat taken up by the feed-water per minute

$$= \frac{8{,}544 \times 0{\cdot}3323 \times 582{\cdot}0}{7{\cdot}32} = 225{,}734 \text{ B.T.U.}$$

Joule's equivalent . . . . = 772

The units of heat per HP. $\frac{33{,}000}{772} = 42{\cdot}75$

Then the heat turned into work per minute

= the mean I.HP. × 42·75 = 582·0 × 42·75 = 24,880 B.T.U.

Efficiency of the engine

$$= 100 \; \frac{24{,}880}{225{,}734} = 11{\cdot}02 \text{ per cent.,}$$

„   „   boiler $= 100 \times \frac{8{,}544}{12{,}840} = 66{\cdot}54$ per cent.

„   „   engine and boiler combined

$$= \frac{66{\cdot}54 \times 11{\cdot}02}{100} = 7{\cdot}34 \text{ per cent.}$$

Heat evolved per lb. of Coal.		Heat expended per lb. of Coal.	
	Per Cent.		Per Cent.
Calorific value of 1 lb. of coal used	100·00	Heat expended in evaporating the water	66·54
		Heat carried away by the products of combustion, lost by radiation and imperfect combustion, &c.	33·46
	100·00		100·00

Appendix C

Summary of William Adams' Locomotive Designs and Principal Dimensions

North London Railway
Classes built at Bow Works

Class	43	51	1
Date built	1863 - 5	1865 – 9	1868 – 1874 (note a)
Wheel arrangement	4-4-0T	4-4-0T	4-4-0T
Cylinders	16 x 24in	17 x 24in	17 x 24in
Bogie wheels	3ft 2in	3ft 0in	2ft 9in
Coupled wheels	5ft 3in	5ft 9in	5ft 4in
Wheelbase	19ft 4½in	22ft 2in	23ft 7¾in
Boiler diameter	4ft 1in	4ft 1in	4ft 1in
Boiler length	10ft 1in	11ft 8in	10ft 1in
Firebox length	4ft 0in	5ft 2in	4ft 5½ in (note b)
Grate area	14.20sq ft	16.72sq ft	16¾sq ft
Total heating surface	977.80sq ft	960sq ft	996sq ft
Boiler pressure	160lb	160lb	160lb
Water capacity	844gallons	1200gallons	844gallons
Coal capacity	25cwt	25cwt	25cwt
Weight in working order	44 tons 3cwt	45 tons	43 tons 12cwt

Notes:
a) Refers to locomotives built to the original Adams design
b) Later 4ft 8½ in

Great Eastern Railway

Class	61	K9	265	527
Date built	1875-8	1877-8	1876-7	1878-9
Wheel arrangement	0-4-4T	0-4-2T	4-4-0	2-6-0
Cylinders	17 x 24in	15 x 22in	18 x 26in	19 x 26 in
Bogie wheels	2ft 10in	3ft 8in	3ft 1in	2ft 10in
Coupled wheels	4ft 10in	4ft 10in	6ft 1in	4ft 10in
Wheelbase	21ft 7in	14ft 0in	23ft 0in	23ft 2in
Boiler diameter	4ft 2in	4ft 2in	4ft 4in	4ft 6⅛in
Boiler length	10ft 0in	9ft 1in	11ft 5in	11ft 5in

Class	61	K9	265	527
Firebox length	4ft 8in	3ft 9in	5ft 5¾in	5ft 3in
Grate area	15.30sq ft	12.3sq ft	17.3sq ft	17.80sq ft
Total heating surface	1,084sq ft	950.3sq ft	1,109sq ft	1,393sq ft
Boiler pressure	140lb	140lb	140lb	140lb
Water capacity	1,000gallons	850gallons	2,300gallons	2,620gallons
Weight in working order	46 tons 17cwt	38 tons 11cwt	45 tons 1½cwt Engine only 76 tons 1½cwt with tender	46 tons 12cwt Engine only 74 tons 13cwt with tender

London and South Western Railway
Classes 46 and 415

Class	46 (as built)	46 (rebuilt)	415
Date built	1879	1883-6 (rebuild dates)	1883-5
Wheel arrangement	4-4-0T	4-4-2T	4-4-2T
Cylinders	18 x 24in	18 x 24in	17½ x 24in
Coupled wheels	5ft 7in	5ft 7in	5ft 7in
Bogie wheels	2ft 6in	2ft 6in	3ft 0in
Trailing wheels	Not applicable	3ft 0in	3ft 0in
Wheelbase	21ft 8½in	28ft 5½in	29ft 5in
Boiler diameter	4ft 2in	4ft 2in	4ft 2in
Boiler length	10ft 0¾in	10ft 0¾in	10ft 0in
Firebox length	6ft 6in	6ft 6in	6ft 2in
Grate area	16sq ft	16sq ft	18¼sq ft
Total heating surface	983¾sq ft	983¾sq ft	1,053sq ft
Boiler pressure	160lb	160lb	160lb
Water capacity	1,000gallons	1,650gallons	1,000gallons
Coal capacity	1¼ tons	3 tons	2 tons
Weight in working order	52 tons 16cwt (note a) 50 tons 15cwt (note b)	58 tons 19cwt	54 tons 17cwt

Notes:
a) Quoted by builder
b) Quoted by LSWR

The 380, 135, 445 and 460 classes

Class	380	135	445	460
Date built	1879	1880-81	1883	1884
Wheel arrangement	4-4-0	4-4-0	4-4-0	4-4-0
Cylinders	18 x 24in	18 x 24in	18 x 24in	18 x 24in
Bogie wheels	2ft 6in	3ft 4in	3ft 7in	3ft 4in

Class	380	135	445	460
Coupled wheels	5ft 7in	6ft 7in	7ft 1in	6ft 7in
Wheelbase	21ft 8½in	21ft 11½in	21ft 11½in	21ft 11½in
Boiler diameter	4ft 6in	4ft 6in	4ft 4in	4ft 4in
Boiler length	10ft 0¾in	10ft 0¾in	10ft 2½in	10ft 2½in
Firebox length	6ft 0in	6ft 0in	6ft 0in	6ft 0in
Grate area	17sq ft	17.80sq ft	17.75sq ft	17.75sq ft
Total heating surface	1,126sq ft	1,216sq ft	1,162sq ft	1,162sq ft
Boiler pressure	160lb	160lb	160lb	160lb
Weight in working order Engine and tender	74 tons 17cwt	76 tons 0cwt	74 tons 11cwt	76 tons 13cwt (note a) 75 tons 14cwt (note b)

Notes:
a) Locomotives built by Neilson
b) Locomotives built by Robert Stephenson

Class T1 and O2 0-4-4T, class G6 0-6-0T

Class	T1	O2	G6
Date built	1888-90	1889-95	1894 – 1900 (note e)
Wheel arrangement	0-4-4T	0-4-4T	0-6-0T
Cylinders	18 x 26in	17 x 24in (note a) 17 ½ x 24in (note b)	17½ x 26in
Coupled wheels	5ft 7in	4ft 10in	4ft 10in
Bogie wheels	3ft 0in	3ft 0in	Not applicable
Wheelbase	23ft 0in	20ft 4in	14ft 3in
Boiler diameter	4ft 4in	4ft 2in	4ft 2in
Boiler length	11ft 0in	9ft 5in	9ft 5in
Firebox length	6ft 0in	5ft 0in	5ft 0in
Grate area	17sq ft	13.80sq ft	13.80sq ft
Total heating surface	1,231sq ft	987sq ft	987sq ft
Boiler pressure	160lb	160lb	160lb
Water capacity	1,200gallons	800gallons	1,000gallons
Coal capacity	2 tons	2 tons	2 tons
Weight in working order	53 tons 0cwt	44 tons 11cwt (note c) 44 tons 15cwt (note d)	45 tons 4 cwt

Notes:
a) Locomotives Nos. 177 - 96
b) Locomotives Nos. 197 – 236
c) Locomotives Nos. 178 – 226
d) Locomotives Nos. 227 – 236
e) Dimensions are given for the original Adams design. Locomotives built under Drummond were fitted with various spare boilers, with minor variations.

Class 395 0-6-0

Class	395
Date built	1881-6
Wheel arrangement	0-6-0
Cylinders	17½ x 24in
Coupled wheels	5ft 1in
Bogie wheels	Not applicable
Trailing wheels	Not applicable
Wheelbase	16ft 6in
Boiler diameter	4ft 4in
Boiler length	10ft 6in
Firebox length	5ft 10in
Grate area	17¾sq ft
Total heating surface	1,177sq ft
Boiler pressure	140lb
Water capacity	2,500gallons
Coal capacity	4 tons
Weight in working order	69 tons 11cwt (note a) 70 tons 7cwt (note b)

Notes:
a) Engine and tender, short frame, built 1881-4
b) Engine and tender, long frame, built 1885-6

Class A12 0-4-2

Class	A12
Date built	1887 - 95
Wheel arrangement	0-4-2
Cylinders	18 x 26in
Coupled wheels	6ft 1in
Trailing wheels	4ft 0in
Wheelbase	16ft 10in
Boiler diameter	4ft 4in
Boiler length	11ft 0in
Firebox length	6ft 0in
Grate area	17sq ft
Total heating surface	1,233-1,248sq ft
Boiler pressure	160lb
Weight in working order (engine only)	42 tons 7cwt – 43 tons 8cwt

Various tenders attached to this class, with water capacities ranging from 1,950 to 3,300 gallons

The X2, T3, T6 and X6 classes 4-4-0

Class	X2	T3	T6	X6
Date built	1890 – 2	1893	1885	1885
Cylinders	19 x 26in	19 x 26in	19 x 26in	19 x 26in
Bogie wheels	3ft 9¾in	3ft 7in	3ft 9¾in	3ft 7in
Coupled wheels	7ft 1in	6ft 7in	7ft 1in	6ft 7in
Wheelbase	23ft 0in	23ft 6in	23ft 9in	23ft 9in
Boiler diameter	4ft 4in	4ft 4in	4ft 4in	4ft 4in
Boiler length	11ft 0in	11ft 0in	11ft 0in	11ft 0in
Firebox length	6ft 4in	6ft 10in	6ft 10in	6ft 10in
Grate area	18sq ft	19.75sq ft	19.75sq ft	19.75sq ft
Total heating surface	1,367sq ft	1,320sq ft	1,320sq ft	1,320sq ft
Boiler pressure	175lb	175lb	175lb	175lb
Weight in working order With tender	81 tons 7cwt (note a) 84 tons 10cwt (note b)	84 tons 8cwt	85 tons 19cwt	85 tons 10cwt

Notes:
a) Locomotives Nos. 577 – 82
b) Locomotives Nos. 583 - 96

Class B4 0-4-0T

Class	B4
Date built	1891-3 / 1908
Wheel arrangement	0-4-0T
Cylinders	16 x 22in
Coupled wheels	3ft 9¾in
Wheelbase	7ft 0in
Boiler diameter	3ft 8in
Boiler length	10ft 8in
Firebox length	3ft 9in
Grate area	10¾sq ft
Total heating surface	823sq ft
Boiler pressure	140lb
Water capacity	600gallons
Coal capacity	½ ton
Weight in working order	33 tons 9cwt

Variations for 0-4-2 crane tank:
Trailing wheels 3ft 0in diameter
Wheelbase 14ft 2in
Lifting capacity 6 tons maximum
Total weight in working order 41 tons 0cwt

London, Tilbury and Southend Railway

Class	1
Date built	1880 – 92
Wheel arrangement	4-4-2T
Cylinders	17 x 26in
Coupled wheels	6ft 0in
Bogie wheels	3ft 1in
Trailing wheels	3ft 1in
Wheelbase	29ft 4in
Boiler diameter	4ft 1in
Boiler length	10ft $10^{5}/_{16}$in
Firebox length	6ft 2in
Grate area	17.25sq ft
Total heating surface	1,020sq ft
Boiler pressure	160lb
Water capacity	1,320gallons
Coal capacity	2 tons
Weight in working order	59 tons 11cwt

Lynn and Fakenham Railway (included for comparative purposes)

Class	Peacocks
Date built	1882 – 8
Wheel arrangement	4-4-0
Cylinders	17 x 24in
Coupled wheels	6ft 0in
Bogie wheels	3ft 0in
Tender wheels	3ft 7½in
Wheelbase	21ft 5in
Boiler diameter	4ft 1in
Boiler length	10ft 3½in
Firebox length	6ft
Grate area	17.70sq ft
Total heating surface	1,083sq ft
Boiler pressure	140lb
Water capacity	2,000gallons
Coal capacity	3 tons
Weight in working order	41 tons 3cwt engine only 77 tons 12cwt with tender

Appendix D

Summary of locomotives built by William Adams
North London Railway

Class 21, 4-4-0T
Total number built: 5

Engine no	Date built	Builder	Withdrawal
21-25	1855	Robert Stephenson & Co.	1868-71

Class 30, 4-4-0T
Total number built: 8

Engine no	Date built	Builder	Withdrawal
30-37	1861	Slaughter, Grüning & Co.	1876-1882

Class 43, 4-4-0T
Total number built: 8

Engine no	Date built	Builder	Withdrawal
43-50	1863-5	NLR, Bow	1887-1915

Class 51, 4-4-0T
Total number built: 24

Engine no	Date built	Builder	Withdrawal
11-18, 51-66	1865-9	NLR, Bow	1888-1925

Class 1, 4-4-0T
Total number built whilst William Adams was in office: 28
However, most locomotives were replaced with new locomotives to the same design, incorporating later modifications such as enclosed cab, but using the number of the original. Furthermore, additional engines were constructed, essentially to the same design, by Adams' successors until 1907, with the last withdrawn in 1929.

Engine no	Date built	Builder	Withdrawal and replacement by new
1-10, 19-29, 34/5, 38-42	1868-74	NLR, Bow Works	1890-1905

Specialist and experimental conversions
0-4-0ST, converted to 0-4-2CT crane locomotive in 1872

NLR Engine No.	Builder	Works No.	Date built	Withdrawal
37, later 29	Sharp, Stewart & Co	1039	1858	1951

0-4-2ST, Total number built: 5

NLR Engine No.	Builder	Works No.	Date built	Withdrawal
38-42	Beyer, Peacock	186-90	1860	1874

Nos.38 and 41 converted to 0-4-4ST wheel arrangement in 1861

Great Eastern Railway
Class K9 0-4-2T
Total number built: 10

Engine No.	Builder	Date built	Withdrawal
7, 9, 20, 21	GER, Stratford	1877	1903-07
8, 10, 22-25	GER, Stratford	1878	1903-07

Class 61, 0-4-4T
Total number built: 50

Engine No.	Builder	Works No.	Date built	Withdrawal
211-220	Neilson & Co	2013-2022	1875	1906-13
61-75	Neilson & Co	2023-2037	1875	1906-13
76-78	Robert Stephenson & Co	2211-2213	1876	1906-13
79, 80	Robert Stephenson & Co	2214, 2215	1877	1906-13
221-225	Robert Stephenson & Co	2216-2220	1877	1906-13
170-184	Kitson & Co	2201-2215	1878	1906-13

Class 265, 4-4-0, Ironclads
Total number built: 20

Engine No.	Builder	Works No.	Date built	Withdrawal
265-274	Dübs & Co	893-902	1876	1894-97
255-264	R. & W. Hawthorn & Co	1705-1714	1877	1894-97

Class 527, 2-6-0, Moguls
Total number built: 15

Engine No.	Builder	Works No.	Date built	Withdrawal
527-531	Neilson & Co	2393-2397	1878	1885-87
532-541	Neilson & Co	2398-2407	1879	1885-87
512 (Belgian State Railways)	Neilson & Co	2739	1881	1906

Class C8, 4-4-0
Total number built: 2

This was essentially an S. W. Johnson design, but built by Adams after he took office, and incorporating his revisions, for example improved cab design.

Engine No.	Builder	Date built	Withdrawal
301/2, 305/6 from 1878	GER, Stratford	1874	1897/8

London, Tilbury & Southend Railway
Class 1, 4-4-2T, *Tilbury Tanks*
Total number built: 36

Engine No.	Builder	Works No.	Date built	Withdrawal
1-12	Sharp, Stewart & Co	2880-2891	1880	1930-35
13-18	Sharp, Stewart & Co	2969-71, 3018-20	1881	1930-35
19-21	Sharp, Stewart & Co	3217-19	1884	1932-35
22-30	Sharp, Stewart & Co	3220-28	1885	1930-35
31-36	Nasmyth, Wilson & Co	425-30	1892	1930-35

London & South Western Railway

The following tables generally denote original locomotive numbers as built. Engines which continued in service after their numbers were allocated to replacements were usually renumbered in the duplicate series by the simple expedient of adding the prefix '0' to their existing identity. The Southern Railway era did not result in a widespread renumbering, but to avoid confusion with numbering systems from other constituent companies, a prefix letter was added where necessary. Those locomotives which survived into British Railways ownership were renumbered in accordance with the Southern Region policy, into a new 30xxx series. Engines transferred by the SR to the Isle of Wight were numbered in a separate series.

For a more detailed study the reader is referred to *Locomotives, The Adams Classes*, by the late D.L. Bradley.

Class 46, 4-4-0T, later all rebuilt as 4-4-2T, Ironclads
Total number built: 12

Engine No.	Builder	Works No.	Date built	Date rebuilt	Withdrawal
46, 123/4/30/32, 374-379	Beyer, Peacock & Co	1832-43	1879	1883-36	1914-25

Class 415, 4-4-2T, Radial Tanks
Total number built: 71

Engine No.	Builder	Works No.	Date built	Withdrawal
415-26	Beyer, Peacock & Co	2167-2178	1882	1916-25
45, 47-57, 427-32	Robert Stephenson & Co	2501-18	1883	1921-27
169-71, 173, 490-5	Dübs & Co	2000-9	1884	1921-26

Engine No.	Builder	Works No.	Date built	Withdrawal
479-89	Neilson & Co	3200-10	1885	1917-28 (note a)
496-505	Kitson & Co	Order cancelled	Order cancelled	n/a
516-25	Dübs & Co	2105-14	1885	1921-28, No. 520 1961
68, 77/8, 82, 104, 106/7, 125/6, 129	Robert Stephenson & Co	2601-10	1885	1921-27, No. 125 1961

Note:

a) No. 488 sold 1917, repurchased from East Kent Railway by Southern Railway in 1946 and finally withdrawn by British Railways July 1961. Preserved at Bluebell Railway

Class 380, 4-4-0, Steamrollers
Total number built: 12

Engine No.	Builder	Works No.	Date built	Withdrawal
380-97	Beyer, Peacock & Co	1854-65	1879	1913-25

Class 135, 4-4-0
Total number built: 12

Engine No.	Builder	Works No.	Date built	Withdrawal
135-46	Beyer, Peacock & Co	1948-59	1880	1913-24

Class 445, 4-4-0
Total number built: 12

Engine No.	Builder	Works No.	Date built	Withdrawal
445-56	Robert Stephenson & Co	2535-46	1883	1923-25

Note: 446 trialled as a compound locomotive 1886-91

Class 460, 4-4-0
Total number built: 12

Engine No.	Builder	Works No.	Date built	Withdrawal
460-69	Neilson & Co	3190-99	1884	1926-29
147, 470-8	Robert Stephenson & Co	2561-70	1884	1926-29
526	Robert Stephenson & Co	2650	1887	1928

Note: 526 built by Robert Stephenson & Co for display at the 1887 Newcastle Jubilee Exhibition

Class 395, 0-6-0, Jumbos
Total number built: 70

Engine No.	Builder	Works No.	Date built	Withdrawal
395-406	Neilson & Co	2747-58	1881/2	1916-57
153-9 163-7	Neilson & Co	2939-50	1883	1916-56

Engine No.	Builder	Works No.	Date built	Withdrawal
433-44	Neilson & Co	2956-57	1883	1916-58
496-515	Neilson & Co	3376-95	1885/6	1916-57
27-30, 67, 71, 101, 105, 134, 148, 168, 172, 174/5	Neilson & Co	3453-66	1885/6	1916-59

Note: 67 and 71 renumbered 83 and 84 in 1889

Fifty locomotives were withdrawn in the period 1916-18 and sold to the British government for service in the Middle East

Class A12, 0-4-2, Jubilees
Total number built: 90

Engine No.	Builder	Order ref.	Date built	Withdrawal
527-536	LSWR, Nine Elms	A12	1887	1928-31
537-546	LSWR, Nine Elms	E1	1888	1928–31
547–556	LSWR, Nine Elms	M2	1889	1928–44
597-606	LSWR, Nine Elms	O4	1893/4	1933–47
607-646	Neilson & Co	4506–45 (Neilson works nos.)	1892/3	1932–48
647-656	LSWR, Nine Elms	K6	1894/5	1932-47

Class T1, 0-4-4T
Total number built: 50

Engine No.	Builder	Order ref.	Date built	Withdrawal
61-70	LSWR, Nine Elms	T1	1888–89	1931-34
71-80	LSWR, Nine Elms	D2	1889–90	1932-36
1-10	LSWR, Nine Elms	F6	1894	1948-51
11-20	LSWR, Nine Elms	S6	1895	1933-51
358-367	LSWR, Nine Elms	A7	1896	1938-49
368-77	Order cancelled by Drummond			

Class O2 0-4-4T
Total number built: 60

Engine No.	Builder	Order ref.	Date built	Withdrawal
177-186	LSWR, Nine Elms	O2	1889–90	1940-67
187-196	LSWR, Nine Elms	B3	1890–91	1937-62
197-206	LSWR, Nine Elms	K3	1891	1953-66
207-226	LSWR, Nine Elms	D4	1891–92	1933-67
227-236	LSWR, Nine Elms	R6	1894–5	1933-61

Twenty-three O2 class locomotives were transferred to the Isle of Wight between 1923 and 1949, renumbered and named as follows:

IW number	Name	LSWR No.	Date transferred	Withdrawal
W14	*Fishbourne*	178	1936	1967
W15	*Cowes*	195	1936	1956
W16	*Ventnor*	217	1936	1967
W17	*Seaview*	208	1930	1967
W18	*Ningwood*	220	1930	1965
W19	*Osborne*	206	1923	1955
W20	*Shanklin*	211	1923	1967
W21	*Sandown*	205	1924	1966
W22	*Brading*	215	1924	1967
W23	*Totland*	188	1925	1955
W24	*Calbourne*	209	1925	1967
W25	*Godshill*	190	1925	1962
W26	*Whitwell*	216	1925	1966
W27	*Merstone*	184	1926	1967
W28	*Ashey*	186	1926	1967
W29	*Alverstone*	202	1926	1966
W30	*Shorwell*	219	1926	1965
W31	*Chale*	180	1927	1967
W32	*Bonchurch*	226	1928	1964
W33	*Bembridge*	218	1936	1967
W34	*Newport*	201	1947	1955
W35	*Freshwater*	181	1949	1966
W36	*Carisbrooke*	198	1949	1964

Note: No.209, later W24 *Calbourne*, is preserved at the Isle of Wight Steam Railway

Class X2, 4-4-0
Total number built: 20

Engine No.	Builder	Order ref.	Date built	Withdrawal
577-86	LSWR, Nine Elms	X2	1890–91	1931–42
587-96	LSWR, Nine Elms	F3	1891–92	1930-37

Note: Locomotive No. 582 was used for the 1891 trials

Class T3, 4-4-0
Total number built: 20

Engine No.	Builder	Order ref.	Date built	Withdrawal
557-66	LSWR, Nine Elms	T3	1892/3	1930–45
567-76	LSWR, Nine Elms	S5	1893	1931-43

Note: No.563 preserved

Class T6, 4-4-0
Total number built: 10

Engine No.	Builder	Order ref.	Date built	Withdrawal
677-686	LSWR, Nine Elms	T6	1895/6	1933–43

Class X6, 4-4-0
Total number built: 10

Engine No.	Builder	Order ref.	Date built	Withdrawal
657–666	LSWR, Nine Elms	X6	1895/6	1933–46

Class B4, 0-4-0T
Total number built: 20

Engine No.	Builder	Order ref.	Date built	Withdrawal
85-94	LSWR, Nine Elms	B4	1891/2	1949-63
81,95–100/2/3/76	LSWR, Nine Elms	D6	1893	1949-63

Notes:
An order for three 0-4-2 crane locomotives, with maximum 6 ton lifting capacity, based on the B4 design, was placed in 1894 but subsequently cancelled.

In 1908 Drummond built five more, designated class K14 and numbered 82 – 84, 746/7.

No.84 was the last locomotive constructed at Nine Elms works.

Twelve Adams and two Drummond K14 locomotives were transferred to the Southampton Docks Department between 1893 and 1908.

Two examples are preserved, 96 at the Bluebell Railway, and 102 at Bressingham, Norfolk.

Class G6, 0-6-0T
Total number built: 34

Engine No.	Builder	Order ref.	Date built	Withdrawal
257-66	LSWR, Nine Elms	G6	1894	1949-61
267-70	LSWR, Nine Elms	C7	1896	1949–59
271-5	LSWR, Nine Elms	X7	1897/8	1948-60
237–40, 279	LSWR, Nine Elms	D9	1898	1948-62
160/2,276-8	LSWR, Nine Elms	M9	1900	1949-61
348/9, 351/3/4	LSWR, Nine Elms	R9	1900	1948-61

Note: All orders after the original G6 batch were placed after Adams' retirement and built using spare or second-hand boilers

Lynn and Fakenham Railway (Adams influenced design)
4-4-0, Total number built: 15

Engine No.	Builder	Works No.	Date built	Withdrawal
21-24	Beyer, Peacock & Co.	2105-8	1882	1933-37
25–28	Beyer, Peacock & Co.	2338-41	1883	1933-41
29-35	Beyer, Peacock & Co.	2939-42	1888	1933-36

The first two orders were placed by the Lynn & Fakenham Railway, but the remainder were ordered after takeover by the Eastern & Midlands Railway, which itself became part of the Midland & Great Northern Joint Railway in 1893.

The M&GN designated the locomotives class A, popularly known as Peacocks.

Bibliography

Ahrons, E.L., *The British Steam Railway Locomotive 1825 – 1925*, Locomotive Publishing Co. 1927
Bloomfield, Peter, *The North London Railway Source Book*, 2017, www.nlr.org.uk
Bloomfield, Peter, Hanson, David, *The Senior Officers of the North London Railway*, 2015, www.nlr.org.uk
Bradley, D.L., *LSWR Locomotives, The Adams Classes*, Wild Swan Publications, 1985
Bradley, D.L., *LSWR Locomotives, The early Engines and the Beattie Classes*, Wild Swan Publications, 1989
Chacksfield, J.E., *The Drummond Brothers, A Scottish Duo*, The Oakwood Press, 2005
Curl, Barry, *The LSWR at Nine Elms*, KRB Publications, 2004
Fell, M., *Journal No. 23*, North Staffordshire Railway Study Group, 2008
Hamilton Ellis, C., *Twenty Locomotive Men,* Ian Allan, 1958
Hamilton Ellis, C., *Dandy Hart,* Victor Gollancz, 1947
Leech, Kenneth H., *Loco Profile 27, Tilbury Tanks*, Profile Publications, 1972
Lovett, Dennis, *The North London Railway, 1846 – 2001*, Irwell Press, 2001
Main, Thomas, and Brown, Thomas, *The Marine Steam Engine*, Herbert, 1849
National Railway Museum, *North London Railway, A Pictorial Record,* HMSO, 1979
Pettigrew, William Frank, *A Manual of Locomotive Engineering, with an Historical Introduction*, Charles Griffin, 1899
Robbins, Michael, *The North London Railway,* Oakwood Press, 1937
Turner, David, *Managing the 'Royal Road': The LSWR 1870 – 1911*, PhD Thesis, University of York, 2013
Wilson, E.H., *William Adams 1823 – 1904*, Transactions of the Newcomen Society, Volume 57, 1988

Other sources

British-history.ac.uk
Grace's Guide to British Industrial History, www.gracesguide.co.uk
Shippingandshipbuilding.uk
National Archives:
Miller and Ravenhill,
The Brodie Papers RAIL 1057/3497, 1057/3500, 1057/3502
North London Railway
RAIL 529/115 William Adams Miscellaneous Books and Records

RAIL 529/132/1 Staff records, appointment of William Adams
RAIL 529/202 Contract for eight locomotives with Edward Slaughter and Henry Stothert 1860
RAIL 529/205 Licence to use William Bridges Adams' patents
RAIL 529/206 Licence to use William Adams' patent bogie
RAIL 529/127 Bow works, etc photographic Album
Locomotive and stores committee minutes
RAIL 529/42 - 46
Great Eastern Railway
Locomotive Committee Minutes
RAIL 227/113 - 118
London & South Western Railway
Locomotive Committee Minutes
RAIL 411/182
RAIL 411/184
RAIL 411/188
RAIL 411/201 - 205
London, Tilbury & Southend Railway
RAIL 437/40 Specification for four wheels coupled bogie and pony truck tank engine....with notes by William Adams

The North London Railway Historical Society Journal, Volumes 28, 71-73, 81
The Engineer, various
The Locomotive Magazine, various
Herapath's Railway Journal, various
The Jubilee Chronicle, Newcastle Daily Chronicle, 1887
The Society of Engineers, Proceedings of, various

Index

A
Association of Railway Locomotive Engineers, 144
Avonside Engine Co., 72, 173

B
Baldwin Locomotive Company, 107
Baltimore & Ohio Railroad, 78
Barker's Hydraulic Brake, 48, 85
Barnes & Miller, 22
Belgian State Railway, 80–81
Beyer, Peacock & Co., 46, 50, 53, 61, 83, 89, 93, 95, 97, 99, 101, 103, 110, 135, 155–6
Bishopstoke, 118
Blackwall, 11, 21–8, 31, 38, 68, 73
Blackwall Frigate, 20
Bow & Bromley Institute, 63, 65
Bow Creek, 20, 21
Bow works, 45–72
Brunswick Dock, 11
Bushell, Messrs., 25

C
Christie & Seager, 23
City Canal, 11, 13
Commercial Railway, 38
Compound locomotive, 112, 141, 151
Crane, 61, 62, 117, 119, 130, 136, 160

D
Dalkey Atmospheric Railway, 19
Devons Road, 48, 62, 71
Ditchburn & Mare, 21
Donna Thereza Christina Railway, 152
Dübs & Co., 62, 77–8, 83, 103–4

E
East India Company, 9, 13, 20
East India Docks, 11, 15, 16, 17, 18, 25, 38
East & West India Dock Company, 17
East & West India Docks & Birmingham Junction Railway, 38–40
East Kent Railway, 104
Eastern Counties Railway, 39, 52, 55, 72, 81, 83, 112
Eastleigh, 118–9, 123, 131, 136, 151, 165
Everitt & Adams, 66–7
Export Dock, 11, 13

F
Fairfield Locomotive Works, 52, 63
Fawcett, Preston and Co., 31
Forrestt & Sons, 17, 41
Furness Railway, 151–2, 160–4, 170

G
General Steam Navigation Co., 23
Grand Junction Railway, 38–9
Great Eastern Railway, 7, 66, 72–87, 102, 144, 146, 171, 173
Great North of Scotland Railway, 47
Great Northern Railway, 83, 100, 115, 145, 164, 172
Great Western Railway, 37, 88, 127, 164

H
Hack & Co., 47, 48
Hawthorn, R. & W., 76–7, 147

I
Import Dock, 11, 13
Institution of Civil Engineers, 17, 63, 102, 140, 159

Institution of Mechanical Engineers,
  63–4, 87, 150, 151, 153
International Congress on Railways,
  141, 164
Iraq State Railway, 108
Isle of Wight, 42, 47, 56, 113, 127–131,
  142, 159, 169, 170, 173

K
Kitson & Co., 74, 76, 81, 83, 163

L
La Foce, Genoa, 31
Limehouse Basin, 9, 11, 16
Livery, locomotive, 48, 50, 69, 76, 119,
  147, 151, 154, 159, 165
Locomotives:
  Furness Railway:
    D1 class, 160
    D3-5 classes, 160–3
    K4 class, 160, 163
    L1 class, 160
    M1 class, 160, 164
    Railmotor, 162–3
  Great Eastern Railway:
    61 class, 73–76, 126
    230, 81
    265 class, 76–7
    527 Mogul class, 78–83, 173
    C8 class, 73, 77
    K9 class, 81–2
    T7 class, 73
    Y class, 72, 76
    Y5 class, 73
    Z class, 76
  London & South Western Railway:
    2-6-0 proposed, 146
    46 class, 94–7
    135 class, 99–100, 102, 119
    298 class, 89–92
    348 class, 89–91
    380 class, 97–9, 102
    395 class, 107–9, 115, 123
    415 class, 103–107, 144
    445 class, 110–2, 115, 136
    460 class, 113–4

    A12 class, 120–3
    B4 class, 135–7, 151
    Crane tank, 136
    Canute class, 88
    Centaur class, 89
    Double-framed Goods, 92–4, 123–4
    G6 class, 131, 133–4, 151
    Ilfracombe Goods, 93
    Metropolitan A class, 88, 93–6
    O2 class, 92, 124, 126–133, 151
    Single-framed Goods, 89, 93
    Single-proposed, 144–6
    T1 class, 123–6, 144
    T3 class, 141–3
    T6 class, 143
    Vesuvius class, 89, 91
    X2 class, 136, 138, 140–1, 143
    X6 class, 143–4
  London Brighton & South Coast
    Railway Gladstone class, 120
  London Tilbury & Southend
    Railway No. 1 class Tilbury Tanks,
    84–5
  Lynn & Fakenham Railway Peacock
    4-4-0 class, 99–102
  National Rifle Association
    Merryweather steam tram, 146–7
  North London Railway:
    43 class, 49–51, 56, 71
    51 class, 56–7, 69, 71
    Beyer Peacock, 0-4-2ST, 46, 53, 61
    Crane tank, 61–3
    No. 1 class, 57–9, 69, 71, 95–6
    Sharp Stewart, 0-4-0ST, 61–3
    Slaughter Grüning, 4-4-0T, 46, 49
    Stephenson, Robert, 4-4-0T, 46
    Stothert & Slaughter, 2-4-0T, 46
  North Staffordshire Railway:
    C class, 158
    DX class, 154
    G class, 157
    H class, 156
    H1 class, 157
    K class, 157
    KT class, 158
    L class, 155–7

M class, 155, 159
New L class, 156, 159
Railmotor, 155–6
Novelty, 25
St Helens Railway *White Raven*, 52–3, 56
London & Birmingham Railway, 38–9, 46
London & Blackwall Railway, 17, 38–9
London & Croydon Railway, 18
London & North Western Railway, 39, 40, 42, 48, 52–3, 56, 62, 69–71, 85, 88, 112, 151
London & South Western Railway, 7, 37, 87–151, 165, 169, 170, 172–4
London & Suburban Railway Officials' Association, 95
London & Westminster Steamboat Co., 23
London Brighton & South Coast Railway, 61, 86, 120, 127, 156–7, 170
London Chatham & Dover Railway, 108, 153
London Tilbury & Southend Railway, 84–5, 103
Longmoor Military Railway, 123
Lynn & Fakenham Railway, 99, 101

M
Margate & London Steam Packet Company, 23
Maignen's Patent Water Softening process, 117
Malcolmson Brothers, 25
Manchester Sheffield & Lincoln Railway, 115
Maudslay, Sons & Field, 22, 32
Melbourne Military Railway, 123
Melbourne, Mount Alexander & Murray River Railway, 44
Midland Railway, 72, 89, 99, 145–6
Midland Counties Railway, 18
Mill Place, Limehouse, 9, 10
Miller & Ravenhill, 20–9, 32–3, 66
Money, Wigram & Co., 25

N
National Rifle Association, 146–7
Neilson & Co., 72–4, 76, 78, 80–1, 103–4, 107–8, 113, 123
New South Wales Government Railways, 83, 101
Nine Elms, 87–8, 98, 101–2, 111–5, 117–124, 129, 136, 141–4, 146–8, 151–3, 159, 160, 164, 173
North London Junction Railway, 38
North London Railway, 7, 38–72, 77, 84–7, 95–6, 170–1, 173
North Metropolitan Junction Railway, 38
North & South West Junction Railway, 40
Northumberland & Durham Coal Co., 42, 46, 48

O
Orchard Place, Blackwall, 21, 23, 66

P
Palestine Military Railway, 107–109
Patent blast pipe, 8, 115–6, 151, 162, 167, 173
Patent bogie, 7, 54–6, 61, 73, 94, 129, 155, 173
Patent radial axle, 52–4, 56, 61
Peninsular & Oriental Steam Navigation Co., 23, 32
Pennsylvania Railroad, 79
Personalities:
 Adams, Alfred, 47
 Adams, Alice (aunt), 13
 Adams, Alice (sister), 9
 Adams, Amy, 101
 Adams, Catherine Alice, 43, 47
 Adams, Charles, 47, 86
 Adams, George Spencer, 57, 66
 Adams, Henry (nephew), 7, 63
 Adams, Herbert, 57
 Adams, Isabella (wife), 36, 43–4, 57, 68–9
 Adams, Isabella (daughter), 47
 Adams, Jane, 9

Adams, John Henry (brother), 9, 39, 43, 63
Adams, John Henry (son), 47, 83, 152–9, 163
Adams, John Samuel, 9, 13, 17, 18, 43
Adams, Robert, 9, 44
Adams, Rosetta, 13
Adams, Sidney, 66
Adams, Thomas, 56
Adams, William Bridges, 52–4, 56, 63, 84
Adams, William John, 42, 47, 66, 101, 149
Ansoldo, Giovanni, 37
Archbould, Ralph, 102
Armand, Armadec, 28
Attock, Frederick, 85
Baldwin, Edward, 25
Barnes, John, 21
Batchelor, John, 42
Beattie, Joseph, 87–92, 102, 115, 120, 126–7, 133
Beattie, William George, 89, 93, 110–11, 118–9
Beattie, William, 102
Braithwaite, John, 25
Bromley, Massey, 78, 85–6, 117, 160
Brunel, Marc, 28
Bury, Oliver, 164
Chapelon, André, 8, 173
Clark, Daniel Kinnear, 47
Clark, John, 48, 53, 111
Colburn, Zerah, 56, 64
Coutts, John H.S., 23
Craven, John Chester, 61
Cross, James, 52
Cudworth, James, 61
Cuthill, James, 13
Docteur, M., 80–81
Drummond, Dugald, 8, 92, 124, 133–4, 136, 143–4, 146, 151, 153, 165, 173–4
Ericcson, John, 25
Everitt, Percival, 66–7
Fernihough, William, 55
Frankland, Edward, 117

Garrett, Gilbert Henry, 102, 152
Hall, Samuel, 21
Holden, James, 75, 117, 160, 164
Jacomb, William, 111, 148
Jameson, James, 37
Jessup, William, 11
Johnson, Samuel Waite, 72–78, 80, 85–6, 144–6, 153, 173
Lewis, Charles, 13
MacLeod, A.B., 127, 166
Maitland, Dudley, 95
Maitland, Isabella (nee Adams), 95
Martin, Henry Daniel, 13, 17, 38, 42, 45, 47
Maudslay, Henry, 22
Miller, Joseph, 21
Milligan, Robert, 9
Murdoch, William, 21
Neale, Deodatus Hillin, 78
Panter, William, 115, 118
Park, Charles, 36–7, 57
Park, Isabella, 36–7
Park, John Carter, 36, 59, 68–9, 71
Pascoe, Edward, 25
Pettigrew, William Frank, 117–9, 140, 148–9, 151–3, 155, 157, 159–164
Penn, John, 22
Pettit Smith, Francis, 22
Pintsch, Julius, 85
Pitcher, Henry, 25
Pitcher, Thomas, 31
Pitcher, William, 25
Pitt, William, 9
Prandi, Fortunato, 28–9, 37
Pryce, H.J., 60, 71, 170
Ravenhill, Richard, 22, 25
Rennie, Sir John, 18, 38
Scott, Archibald, 87–8, 115
Scotter, Charles, 115, 149
Shadrake, Thomas, 17
Sinclair, Robert, 72–3, 76–8, 82, 144
Spencer, George, 54–8
Stephenson, Robert, 38
Sterne, Lewis, 63, 102
Stride, Arthur Lewis, 84
Stroudley, William, 120, 151, 169

Taylor, Phillip, 28–30, 36, 37
Telford, Thomas, 15
Urie, Robert, 151
Vignoles, Charles, 18, 42
Walker, Jane, 9
Walker, James, 15, 18
Walker, Ralph, 11, 13, 15
Walker, Robert, 21
Watt, James, 21
Webb, Francis, 48, 73, 79, 103, 112, 151
Whitehead, Robert, 28
Whitelegg, Thomas, 84
Worsdell, Thomas, 117, 160
Pintsch, Pischen & Co., 85
Putney Club, 63

R
Railway Rifles, 65
Railway Operating Division, 107
Rainhill Trials, 8, 25
Regent's Canal Dock, 9, 11
Rennie, J. & G., 22
Rothwell & Co., 37, 46, 69
Royal Dockyard, 8, 20
Royal Mail Steam Packet Co., 25
Royal Road, 113
Royal Sardinian Navy, 7, 29–37, 69

S
St. Olave's church, 9, 43
St. Helens Railway, 52–3
Saltwater Bridge, 44
San Pier d'Arena, 28
Schneider et cie, 76
Seaward & Capel, 22
Sharp, Stewart & Co., 61, 69, 84–5, 89, 161
Ships:
  Ambuscade, HMS, 25
  Amphion, HMS, 25
  Archimedes, SS, 22, 25
  Authion, PS, 31
  Blazer, HMS, 22
  Cape Breton, SS, 21
  Constituzione, PS, 32
  Delta, SS, 23

Elberfeld, PS, 25
Ganges, PS, 32
Governolo, PS, 32–3
Great Britain, SS, 28
Gulnara, PS, 31
Ichnusa, PS, 31
Infernal, HMS, 25
Isis, PS, 25
Lady St. John, 21
Llewellyn, PS, 25
Madrid, PS, 25, 33
Malfatano, PS, 31
Meteor, PS, 23
Mongibello, PS, 31
Monzambo PS, 32
Ondine, PS, 25
Pink, PS, 23
Pioneer, PS, 21
Pollux, PS, 32
Prince Albert, PS, 23
Prince of Wales, PS, 23
Ripon, PS, 25
Rosamund, HMS, 25
Royal George, PS, 23
Sophia Jane, PS, 22
Trent, PS, 25
Tripoli, PS, 31
Undine, PS, 25
Victoria, PS, 23
Slaughter Grüning & Co., 46
Society of Engineers, 56, 63, 79
Soho Foundry, 21
South Eastern Railway, 18
Star Steam Packet Co., 22
Stephenson, Robert, & Co., 46, 55
Stothert & Slaughter, 45–6
Stratford, 28, 72–89, 102, 117, 126, 144, 146, 152, 159, 160, 164, 172–3
Sydney, 22, 66

T
Tannett Walker & Co., 66, 152
Taradale Viaduct, 44
Taylor & Prandi, 37
Thames Ironworks & Shipbuilding Company, 21

Trials of an Express Locomotive, 140, 159
Two Sicilies Steam Navigation Co., 32

V
Vacuum brake, 66, 85, 111
Victoria Railways Board, 45
Vortex blast pipe, 8, 115–7, 123, 151, 162, 167, 173

W
West Bute Docks, 42
West India Docks, 9, 13, 15–7, 25, 38, 40
Westinghouse brake, 49, 85, 111, 123
Wigram & Green, 20